# Practical Horse and Pony Nutrition

# PRACTICAL HORSE AND PONY NUTRITION

## GILLIAN McCARTHY BSc, MBIAC

J. A. ALLEN
London

British Library Cataloguing-in-Publication Data.
A catalogue record for this book is available from
the British Library.

ISBN   0.85131.697.2

Published in Great Britain in 1998 by
J.A. Allen & Company Limited,
1 Lower Grosvenor Place, Buckingham Palace Road,
London, SW1W OEL.

Typeset by Setrite Typesetters Ltd., Hong Kong
Printed By Dah Hua Printing Press Co. Ltd., Hong Kong

Illustration by Maggie Raynor

# Contents

# Dedication

This book is dedicated to the late Anne Leighton-Hardman who, in the early 1970s, made the first serious attempt in decades to apply a modicum of science to the art of horse feeding for the ordinary horse owner. I beg to differ with many of her conclusions and reasoning but applaud her attempt to pick a way through the minefield of myth and magic, science and pseudo-science in horse nutrition.

... And also to Flash, whose love of ice cream and ham and salad sandwiches made me realise that there was more to horse and pony feeding than I'd learnt for my Pony Club B test!

# Foreword

I hope you will learn something useful from this book but I know you will learn a lot more from observation. Take notice of what the horses that you handle can teach you and use what you learn from books to assist your deductions, not to supply them.

What I hear I forget,
What I see I remember,
What I *do* I know.

Gillian McCarthy

# Introduction

In order to understand horse and pony nutrition and to be able to apply it to formulating practical feeding programmes for the horses and ponies in our care, it is important that we have an understanding of the process of the digestion of feeds and how this may be influenced by the nature and quality of feedstuffs. We must also consider the specific nutrient requirements of the horse and how these requirements may be influenced by environment, handling and type of work, as well as the age, breed or type and sex of the individual horse.

'Traditional' feeding may be perfectly adequate but in some situations, given different conditions and the varying properties of feedstuffs which may well have evolved since traditional routines were first developed, a more specific regime may be more appropriate, particularly when feeding the high-performance horse.

The horse has evolved through the millennia as a free-ranging herbage eater, although a somewhat inefficient one when compared with the ruminant (e.g. cow, sheep, goat, deer, camel).

The comparatively recent practice, in evolutionary terms, of keeping a horse at grass and in captivity cannot be reasonably described as a 'natural' system, although it may be convenient and desirable. The nearest we have to a 'natural' system is keeping ponies in range conditions, such as on Exmoor in England or on the Welsh mountains. However, we should not look at natural management through rose-coloured spectacles. Mountain and moorland ponies frequently die of starvation and/or exposure and are infertile for years at a time or else abort, miscarry or die at birth. Only the toughest, or luckiest, survive while we, of course, strive for a 100 per cent survival and performance rate in our domesticated horses and ponies.

If we are going to impose our own system of management on horses in captivity, we must also take on the responsibility of controlling the horse's environment with the object of maintaining health and well-being. In order to do that, we need a combination of stockmanship ('horse sense' or the art of horse management) plus technical knowhow (the science). Horse nutrition should no longer be described as an 'art which defies arithmetic'. Much can now be quantified scientifically. Much more can be achieved by thinking things through and using a logical approach based on both scientific knowledge and an appreciation of the practical application of this knowledge. Without this, a piecemeal approach, developed on a hit-and-miss basis, is likely to occur, with equally hit-and-miss results.

# Part 1
# Feedstuffs for Horses

# 1 The Digestive System and Digestive Processes in the Horse

Basically, the horse's digestive system consists of a long tube, varying in diameter, which runs from mouth to anus. Food passes along this and is acted on physically (by churning and squeezing), chemically (by the action of acids and enzymes) and microbially (through fermentation caused by bacteria and protozoa in the hind gut). These processes release the nutrients contained in the food and enable them to be absorbed into the bloodstream for distribution to the various organs and tissues. The nutrients thus acquired are used to provide energy, growth, repair in the body and in reproduction.

## Influences on the Digestive System

### Teeth

Feed will not be broken down efficiently if it is inadequately chewed, so the horse's teeth require regular attention by your vet or equine dentist every six to twelve months or whenever problems are suspected. Donkeys should be checked every two years, particularly after the age of fourteen years. Specific indications of problems with teeth may include quidding (dropping food from the mouth while chewing), head tossing and shyness about the mouth and head.

### Parasites

Feed will be wasted: (a) if parasites are consuming a share of it; and (b) if

3

parasites damage the gut walls or cause blockages in the gut and prevent the maximum uptake of nutrients from the feed. Regular and frequent treatment with some form of anthelmintic (wormer) or natural vermifuge is considered vital, even for stabled horses. Be guided by your vet and remember that not all of the wormers that you can buy without prescription, e.g. from a tack shop, are active against all parasites, particularly in the immature larval stages which can cause the most damage (e.g. by blocking blood vessels supplying the gut). It has been suggested that as many as 90 per cent of all colic cases can be related to parasite damage, particularly that caused by migrating red worm larvae, either as a direct cause or as a contributory factor.

## Digestive Micro-organisms

The relationship between the horse and the resident population of billions of intestinal micro-organisms in its hind gut is of the utmost importance to its health and well-being. It is almost a case of 'look after the bugs and the horse will look after itself'! These micro-organisms include minute plant-related organisms called bacteria, single-celled animals called protozoans and yeast-like organisms (fungal organisms related to moulds and mushrooms).

The factors which alter the balance of the populations of these micro-organisms and control gut motility (movement) and acidity (pH) are frequently management-orientated and, therefore, controlled by us. A disruption or imbalance may have a devastating effect on the harmony that exists between the micro-organisms and the horse, with consequent health problems ranging from the obvious and acute (e.g. laminitis) to less obvious problems to do with temperament or reduced disease resistance.

The micro-organisms are important because they help to break down the fibrous walls of plant cells which contain nutrients. When the plant cells of forage and the walls (bran) of cereal grains are broken down during the digestive process, they make these nutrients available to the horse. The horse does not have any other means of breaking down the fibres so, without the help of these micro-organisms, useful feedstuffs would pass through its system virtually undigested.

### The main characteristics of micro-organisms

Individually, these 'bugs' may live for only a few hours; other types for much longer. That is one reason why we feed little and often. Another reason is the small size of the horse's stomach, which should not be overloaded with concentrate feed. Do not give more than 2 kg ($4\frac{1}{2}$ lb) of concentrates at one feed and, ideally, use chaff to keep the ration 'open'. (This amount is suitable for a 450 kg/1,000 lb horse.) The horse is a natural 'trickle feeder'. If we try to imitate this system in the way that we feed it, we will be working in accordance with its natural ability to digest food and should encounter fewer problems.

Different bugs digest different feedstuffs. Simplistically put, it is almost as if there are oat-eating bugs, sugar-beet-eating bugs, hay-eating bugs, etc. This is why we should feed a little of each feedstuff in each feed in order to keep all of the different bugs ticking over and working at maximum efficiency, rather than giving, say, oats for breakfast, bran and sugar beet for lunch and cubes for supper.

Some bugs can manage, but will not thrive, on feeds (substrates) that are less than ideal but they will then produce different by-products which may upset the horse. Alternatively, they may die off and another, less friendly group of bugs may take their place, like *E.coli* bacteria or *Candida* fungi. In a balanced population and in comparatively small numbers, these unwelcome bugs cause no trouble but if they proliferate, serious illness can result.

Because different bugs tend to digest different grains and forages, it takes at least two weeks for the microbial population to adjust if there is a change from a high-cereal or concentrate diet to a high-forage ration (or vice versa). For this reason there should be *no* sudden changes in feeding, and transitions from one type of feed to the next (including going out to grass and bringing up again) should be done gradually over seven to 21 days.

This also applies to changing from one type of hay to another, especially from an old crop to a new crop, or one batch of, say, oats or brand of nuts to another. It is especially important for high-performance horses, pregnant and lactating broodmares and rapidly growing youngstock.

At the very least, upsetting the microbial population can mean reduced efficiency in the utilisation of feed, through to scouring (diarrhoea), constipation, colic and even laminitis. The reason why some horses will get acute laminitis after breaking into a feed store is that the sudden flood of available carbohydrate (not, as is often erroneously stated, protein) upsets the digestive bugs and causes them to produce endotoxins which, ultimately, cause 'fever in the feet'.

Other endotoxins produced by an unsuitable diet may cause the horse to be bad tempered or unpredictable and are increasingly thought to affect the ability of the immune system to resist disease, including viruses and cancer.

### Feed Quality – Cleanliness, Freshness and Nutritional Value

Feed should be of the best physical as well as 'chemical' quality. Dust can cause coughing due to irritation of the mucous membranes, and moulds can cause allergic responses, such as COPD (chronic obstructive pulmonary disease or broken wind/heaves) and breeding problems.

If mycotoxins and aflotoxins (microbially produced toxins from moulds and fungi) are present, they can cause severe ill-health which may result in death, abortion in pregnant mares, infertility or, at the very least, loss of performance. It is possible that mycotoxins on grass and clovers are responsible for, or involved in, grass sickness and other, related syndromes.

Feedstuffs do not have to be visibly mouldy to the naked eye to contain moulds or mycotoxins.

It should be remembered that once cereals are rolled or crushed, they start to deteriorate and decay. Plant a whole oat and it will grow because it is a viable seed – it is alive; plant a rolled one and it will rot because it is dead. Apart from this, the vitamins contained in the whole oat are destroyed when air is allowed in during rolling. Feedstuffs should only be rolled or crushed if absolutely necessary and only as much as can be used in two weeks (winter) or one week (summer) should be rolled at one time. If ready-rolled or crushed grain is purchased, you should check with the merchant or mill that it has been freshly prepared. (We shall look at the use of preservatives later.)

## The Digestive Process

Briefly, the digestive process, by means of which nutrients are released from the various feedstuffs for use by the horse's body, is as follows:

### Step 1

Food is gathered into the mouth by the lips and then bitten off and chewed by the teeth. The fibrous feed is broken up by chewing and physically exposed to the chemical action of saliva while still in the mouth.

It should be noted that the whiskers are sensory organs used to detect food, especially in the dark, and therefore should not be cut or singed off, particularly in horses kept outdoors or with defective eyesight.

Elderly horses may, for various reasons, lose some or all of their teeth, or may have to have them removed and it is quite possible to prepare suitable meals for horses in this state.

### Step 2

The bolus of food, plus enzymes from the saliva, is pushed down the oesophagus (or gullet) to the stomach, by waves of muscular contraction called peristalsis.

### Step 3

In the stomach (which holds only 8–15 litres/14–27 pt of material), the food is flooded with gastric juices, which consist of water, mineral salts, mucus, hydrochloric acid (HCl) and pepsinogen, and is churned around by the muscular stomach walls. The food may stay in the stomach for as little as twenty minutes.

### Step 4

From the stomach, the food passes through a one-way sphincter, which prevents the backflow of digesta, into the small intestine. This is a long, convoluted tube which is subdivided into three sections according to its diameter and the nature and properties of the sections of wall. These are called the duodenum, jejenum and ileum. Over all, the small intestine holds 40–50 litres (70–88 pt) of material and is some 20–30 m (60–90 ft) long (i.e. the width of a dressage arena!). Here, bile and pancreatic juices are secreted from the walls into the lumen, or hollow, of the tube, where they are mixed with the now semi-liquid digesta for further breakdown of the non-fibrous part.

Proteins and glucose that are released are absorbed through the gut wall into the bloodstream and can now truly be said to have entered the body, where they become available for use, storage or later excretion.


### Step 5

The semi-digested food, mixed with digestive juices, then passes into the hind gut or large intestine which comprises the caecum, colon and rectum.

This is where the fibre in the diet will be broken down by the gut micro-organisms to produce volatile fatty acids (VFAs) which are absorbed by the horse and used as an energy source.

This process of fermentation occurs in the caecum and colon, effectively a large 'fermentation vat'. The fact that this process occurs *after* the food has passed through the stomach and small intestine is a major flaw in the design of the equine digestive system as far as its efficiency of utilisation by a large herbivore goes, although it may have the advantage for humans of increasing the horse's potential for speedy movement! The horse is therefore classed as a 'posterior (after the stomach) fermenter'.

In ruminants (four-stomached herbivores, including cow, goat, sheep, deer and camel), fermentation occurs in the rumen (a giant fermentation vat) before the food passes into the true stomach (also called the abomasum) and on into the small intestine. This allows for the maximum utilisation of the nutrients in the feed as the 'exposed' or pre-digested (fermented) nutrients have the full length of the rest of the digestive tract in which to be further digested and absorbed. Ruminants are thus 'anterior (before the stomach) fermenters'. They are better at utilising forage efficiently but generally less able to do fast work as a result of this difference in digestive process.

It is undeniable that the horse benefits from the fermentation process, even although it occurs near the end of the gastro-intestinal tract. Without it, the horse would not benefit from eating grass, hay or bran-coated cereals and, as has been mentioned before, its relationship with its millions of gut micro-organisms, many of them in the caecum, is vital to health in other respects.

The products of microbial digestion include high-energy-value volatile fatty acids (VFAs), water and electrolytes (tissue salts), as well as B vitamins, vitamin K and protein.

The colon is also rather badly designed from the domestic horse's

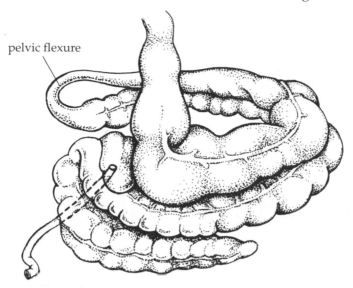

pelvic flexure

*The large colon showing the narrow pelvic flexure which can get blocked*

point of view in that it has a very narrow right-angled bend, the pelvic flexure, which can become blocked, leading to impacted colic. This risk can be avoided by supplying adequate water, feeding regular small feeds and paying attention to both parasite control and to fibre levels in the diet.

Food may remain in the large intestine or hind gut for a considerable period, usually two to four days. The more fibrous it is, the longer it remains to be worked on by the digestive micro-organisms. Horses and ponies fed on stemmy, poor-quality hay, straw or pasture develop a 'hay belly' as the caecum becomes distended because of the slow transit time that becomes necessary as the digestive system tries to extract some goodness from the meagre feed, especially if the poor forage is not balanced with other, more nutritious, feed sources.

Any remaining undigested or partly digested feed is passed into the rectum after surplus water has been resorbed and is then expelled via the anus as faeces (droppings). All experienced horse keepers will be well aware of the importance of the consistency, colour, quantity and smell of the droppings in evaluating the health of the horse.

# 2  The Nutrient Requirements of Horses and Ponies

The nutrients provided by feed and drink are classified chemically into the following groups:

- water
- carbohydrates (including fibre, see below)
- fats and oils (including essential fatty acids – EFAs)
- proteins (including certain specific protein constituents known as amino acids)
- vitamins (and vitamin-like substances)
- minerals (which may be subdivided into macro-minerals and micro- or trace minerals or trace elements)

There is also a physical requirement for fibre to 'exercise' the gut, nourish the horse's symbiotic population of digestive micro-organisms and to provide bulk to keep the ration 'open'. (Fibre is technically a complex carbohydrate, see above.)

The proportions in which these nutrients are required are dependent on the age and condition of the animal, the amount of work it is doing, whether it is pregnant or lactating, the environmental conditions prevailing (including whether or not it is clipped, kept in or out and if wearing rugs or bandages), whether it has a high exposure to environmental pollutants (xenobiotics) (e.g. from main roads, industry or industrial agriculture) and the prevailing weather conditions.

A number of specific health problems will increase or decrease the requirements for certain nutrients, as will the use of specific drugs. The presence of a deficiency or excess of one nutrient will affect the levels required of others, while the physical and chemical form in which the nutrients are supplied will both affect the total levels required in the final diet.

The overall requirements for carbohydrates, protein and fats and oils are now fairly well quantified, although there is still much scientific debate on specific requirements, particularly for young, growing animals and high-performance horses. Macro-mineral levels are also fairly well established but there is still much work to be done on the micro-nutrients, trace minerals and vitamins and on the most desirable forms and sources of these nutrients in high-performance training.

When looking at requirements, it is important to remember that while it is relatively easy to establish the requirements for specific nutrients to maintain life, the requirements to maintain optimum health and maximum performance may vary considerably from these values. As these optimum levels are difficult and expensive to establish, particularly in the performance horse (because the amount of work it is doing is difficult to measure scientifically), there are literally thousands of products on the market worldwide, all purporting to 'supply optimum nutritional requirements'. These may differ radically in their make up and cost and leave the horse owner bewildered and confused.

Some horse keepers shy away completely from the whole question, as do many vets, because they are overwhelmed by the many different claims that are made and the difficulty of differentiating between the very good and cost-effective products on the market and the useless, harmful or uneconomic ones. It is a true minefield for the uninitiated. However, in the right circumstances, the right product can make all the difference, particularly at stud and for the high-performance or convalescent horse. It makes sense to keep yourself as well informed as possible to enable you to make a reasoned decision, see through what might be spurious claims and maximise the performance of the horses in your care until such time as more accurate data may become available.

Precise nutrition is complicated by the complex biochemical interactions that take place between different nutrients, both in the feed and within the horse. In turn, these interactions are influenced by an almost infinite number of factors which can never be reproduced satisfactorily in acceptable scientific trials. It is likely, therefore, that the fine tuning of the equine diet will always remain to some extent an 'art that defies arithmetic'. However, that is absolutely no reason why we should not attempt to ascertain the principles necessary to establish a diet which is in overall balance. We can then make informed decisions about the fine tuning of the individual diet of individual horses in the light of the most up-to-date knowledge available about the nutritional make up of specific feedstuffs, the effects of processing on those nutrients, their digestibility and absorbability and how they are utilised by the horse.

This is, and always will be, a grey area, although it is an exciting and expanding subject and students who are trying to get a grip of the basic concept should endeavour to consolidate their theoretical knowledge. This will enable them constantly to refine their techniques as their practical knowledge increases.

The most highly trained nutritionists and the most successful horse managers in the world are only too well aware that they are constantly learning, revising and adapting their techniques. The biggest enemy to maximising the performance of the horse is the closed mind and fixed ideas of the horse keeper. Do not be too ready to dismiss old ideas out of hand, provided you are quite sure about the basis on which those ideas were developed and how well they really work (or not as the case may be), nor to shy away from (or even overenthusiastically embrace) newer techniques.

## Water

Water ($H_2O$) may be regarded as the most important 'nutrient'. Over 50 per cent of the horse's bodyweight (70–80 per cent in foals) is made up of water contained in body fluids and tissues.

The loss of 20 per cent of body water can rapidly cause death. In a 500 kg (1,100 lb) horse, that may mean only 50 litres (88 pt), an amount which can easily be lost by a horse that travels badly for a number of hours in its trailer. (Excessive sweat loss while travelling could lead to the loss of 5–7 litres (9–12 pt) of body water per hour.)

Water is needed to maintain the integrity, or shape and form, of every cell and every tissue and is present in every body fluid.

It is a carrier of substances both into and out of the body, e.g. saliva (in), urine, sweat and exhaled moisture (out) and is vital for many digestive processes and the correct working of the metabolism, i.e. the entire functioning of the body, from the tiny microscopic cells which make it up, to the whole organism.

Water plays an essential role in regulating body temperature which is created by the ambient temperature and also by heat produced in muscles during work and by the digestive process. The hotter the horse, the more it sweats, the more water it requires, and vice versa. In inactivity, the horse requires less water.

Water is also a lubricant in joints, eyes and throughout the body. It transports sounds or vibrations and carries nutrients and other materials around the body (such as blood and lymph), in which cells are bathed.

A horse may become dehydrated (i.e. deficient in water) through excessive sweating and/or inadequate water supply, blood loss due to injury or excessive urination due to illness. As it becomes dehydrated the horse can overheat and its blood supply to the muscles may be restricted (peripheral circulation) as the dehydrated blood becomes too thick to permeate the tissues, so that waste products, such as lactic acid, are not efficiently removed from the muscles, leading to fatigue or cramps.

This is the principal reason why it is bad practice to deprive the high-performance horse of water at competitions. A horse will not drink to excess before competitive work, provided it has not been deprived of water for a long period beforehand and has had access to a continuous supply. This is especially important in horses that have been travelled long distances to a hunt meet, sale or competition, especially as they may lose considerable amounts of water as sweat during the journey (although they may arrive looking quite dry if the box or trailer is well ventilated). Be sure to arrive at your destination with ample time for the horse to drink its fill before the competition (*at least* one hour's recovery period for every hour in transit). Stop to water on long journeys and take your own water or add a little molasses to local water, if necessary, to encourage the horse to drink. Stop and even unload on long journeys, to encourage staling, especially for stallions and geldings who need to feel themselves on stable ground to straddle for urination.

*Do not* deprive the horse of water for more then half an hour before exertion and allow it to drink its fill whenever possible during endurance events or hunting.

Between the phases of a one-day horse trial, the horse should be offered water at frequent intervals and allowed to drink as much as it wants. Research for the three-day event at the Atlanta Olympic Games showed that giving water in the ten-minute box after the roads and tracks and steeplechase was helpful in avoiding heatstroke and dehydration.

Reduction of performance and delay of recovery afterwards are likely to be far greater if the horse is dehydrated than if it drinks a reasonable amount (up to 2 litres or 4 pt) before fast work. Ask your vet to show you how to do the pinch or skin-fold test for dehydration, which will give you a very rough idea of the horse's condition.

Colic after a competition or journey is more likely in a dehydrated horse, as excess water may be resorbed from the hind gut, causing impaction as the digested food becomes too dry to keep moving along the gut. In severe cases, the blood supplying the gut may become too thick and sluggish to circulate properly, especially if there is a considerable parasite burden or a history of parasite damage.

Dehydration is also relatively common in grass-kept ponies in winter if the ice on their water troughs is not regularly broken and this may, again, cause colic and other problems, especially in ponies with a larval red-worm infestation.

Broodmares require extra water when lactating, although many owners fail to consider this. A Thoroughbred broodmare may produce up to 18 kg (39.6 lb) of milk daily, containing about 90 per cent water. This effectively doubles her water requirement.

Safe water troughs should also be readily accessible to growing foals at foot to enable them to supplement their fluid intake. A dehydrated mare can result in a dehydrated foal. If the milk is too rich (which can be due, in part, to lack of water) this may further compound the problem by causing the foal to scour.

A typical 450-kg (1,000 lb) bodyweight stabled horse requires 20–40 litres (5–10 gal) of fresh water per day. This figure may vary slightly in individual horses without cause for concern. The important thing is to know your own horse's normal water intake so that any deviation from this will be noted and can be acted upon if necessary.

## Water Supplies

Change the water in stables frequently and scrub out buckets regularly. If you merely top up stable buckets, the water absorbs ammonia from the atmosphere (from urine) and becomes stale, 'flat' and unpalatable so that even a thirsty horse may not drink its fill. Some horses are very sensitive to water pollution and this should be checked in known problem areas, if the horse's water intake suddenly causes concern or in cases of ill-defined chronic illness. It may be necessary to fit a water filter in some cases. This may sound rather over the top but dramatic improvements in health and temperament have been noted in some cases when horses have been given filtered water.

If you are giving an electrolyte drink (see page 136), always offer plain water at the same time. If the horse doesn't need the electrolytes but *does* need the water, it may go thirsty rather than drink the electrolyte drink. Human athletes say that electrolyte drinks taste like nectar when you need them and like 'canned sweat' when you don't! This opinion probably prevails among horses too. Be very careful about using paste-type electrolytes or about adding electrolytes to the feed, as 'force feeding' these materials in this way can, in fact, lead to dehydration by raising the horse's water requirements unnaturally – the very thing you are trying to avoid.

Field troughs should be kept clean and functioning properly. They must be checked regularly to ensure that they are working and do not contain dead leaves, animal corpses or excessive algae. Ice should be broken twice daily in winter. A handful of barley straw in an old stocking (protect it from consumption by the horses by wrapping it in chicken wire) can help to keep down algae. (Make sure the cut edges of the wire are folded in safely!)

Natural water sources should be checked for pollution from upstream in flowing water and algae, especially poisonous blue-green algae, in sluggish streams or ponds. It is safest to fence off stagnant ponds. A safe access, with good footing and wide enough to provide an escape route, is vital. An unpolluted running stream with a pebble bottom is ideal. Sandy bottoms can lead to the ingestion of sand which can collect in the gut and cause sand colic. If in doubt, fence it off and be constantly aware of any new sources of pollution upstream, tracing the water course to its source if possible. This includes industrial as well as agricultural pollution.

Water deprivation has been suggested by some authors as a means of training difficult horses. In my opinion, this is one of the cruellest and most potentially damaging practices I have encountered and should not be contemplated by right-thinking horse keepers. Frankly, any horse keeper who feels the need to practise this is not fit to manage the horses in their care.

## Carbohydrates (Made Up of Carbon, Hydrogen and Oxygen in the Proportions $CH_2O$)

The horse eats carbohydrates in two main forms: simple carbohydrates, such as sugars and starches, and complex carbohydrates in the form of fibre or cellulose. Carbohydrates are major sources of energy. They are mainly obtained from herbage, cereals and by-products such as sugar beet. Once absorbed, they may be used immediately or stored in the form of glycogen in the muscles and liver. (Glycogen is the storage carbohydrate of the animal kingdom. Starch is the main storage carbohydrate of the plant kingdom.)

The sugars include dextrose (a form of glucose), sucrose, maltose, fructose (fruit sugar) and lactose (milk sugar).

In recent years, a number of short-chain carbohydrate polymers have been developed for use by human athletes. (These are artificially produced 'strings' of sugar molecules, usually with five or seven sugars in a chain or string, whereas starch is made up of chains of hundreds of sugar molecules.) Some of these products have been adapted for equestrian use. They are not sugars as such but have similar nutritional qualities, although they are absorbed differently, which makes them especially suitable for athletes.

## Fats and Oils

These are also made up of carbon, hydrogen and oxygen. They are also called lipids or lipins and may be referred to in a feed analysis as components of the 'ether extract' or 'EE per cent', which represents the amount of oil or fat which can be detected in a feed by a specific technique of analysis.

By weight, fats and oils are 2.25 times as rich a source of energy as carbohydrates. They also function as sources of, and a means of feeding, fat-soluble vitamins (A, D, E and K) and essential fatty acids (EFAs). They are present in most feeds at low levels but may be added as fish or vegetable oil or animal fats (e.g. tallow). The use of high-fat diets is discussed below.

When referring to the fat or oil content of a diet, the terms are usually interchangeable but there is now increasing interest in the *type* of fat or oil present and its effect on health. Most people have heard of saturated fats (animal fats such as lard and tallow, and plant-derived ones such as palm oil and coconut oil), monounsaturated fats (like olive oil), polyunsaturates (like sunflower, sesame and soya oil) and mixed types like rice oil which contains one third of each. All may be used in horse feed but we do not yet know what, if any, the optimum proportions should be, so a mixture that leans towards the mono- and polyunsaturates that a horse would find in the wild is currently the safest bet.

## Energy

Energy is mainly obtained from carbohydrates, fats and oils, as well as (although expensively) from excess protein.

It is important to note that the terms protein and energy are not interchangeable. Protein *can* be used as an energy source if excessive levels are fed, but energy can never be used as protein, although it is needed for protein synthesis. Muscular activity is fuelled by energy, not by protein. Energy is used up by muscles; protein is not. Protein is part of the body structure not its fuel. As performance levels increase, so do energy requirements. Once a horse is mature it does not need significant extra protein for extra work. However, the quality of the protein it does receive is likely to become more important in hard work (see page 20).

Energy is required for virtually all life processes and is probably the most important factor, from a practical feeding point of view, in the diet, although it is not a nutrient in its own right.

Energy is required to fuel the action of the heart, the maintenance of blood pressure, the transmission of nerve impulses, muscle tone and activity, growth, the maintenance of body temperature, gut movements, the secretion of milk, and protein and fat synthesis and their transport across membranes. It is the horse's fuel and, without it, the horse cannot function. It even needs energy to blink, swish its tail and chew its food.

Every horse requires a certain level of energy or, more specifically, digestible energy (DE) measured in joules (which are metric calories – 1 calorie = 4.184 joules) for the maintenance of the status quo. You can measure whether your horse is receiving adequate energy for maintenance by monitoring its bodyweight. Assuming that the horse is not working, if it is neither gaining nor losing weight it is receiving adequate energy for maintenance. Measurement of bodyweight and the calculation of digestible energy requirements are discussed on page 86 under 'Rationing'.

The reason why the concept of digestible energy is applied to horses rather than metabolisable energy (ME) (more commonly applied to ruminants) is that, effectively, energy in the diet is 'partitioned' as shown in the diagram on page 18.

So, **GE (gross energy)** is the total number of joules or calories of energy obtained when a feedstuff is burned in a machine called a bomb calorimeter; i.e. it is the total energy that the feed contains. It does not differ greatly between feeds, except for those high in fat, so GE does little to describe

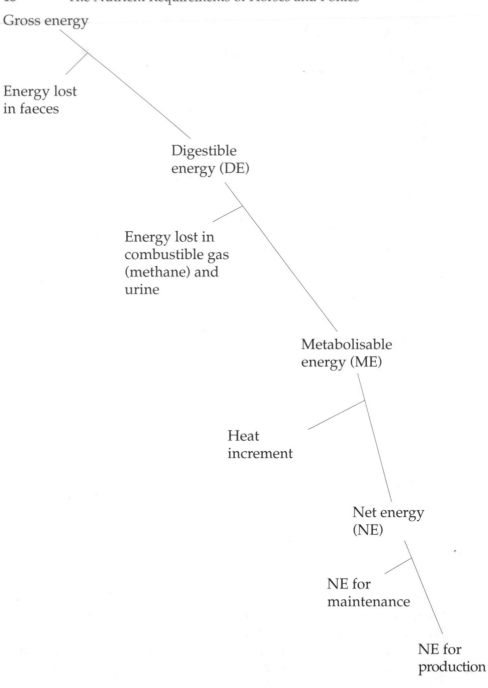

Gross energy

Energy lost
in faeces

Digestible
energy (DE)

Energy lost in
combustible gas
(methane) and
urine

Metabolisable
energy (ME)

Heat
increment

Net energy
(NE)

NE for
maintenance

NE for
production

the useful energy in feeds. Not all of the GE in a feedstuff is available to the animal for work, maintenance and production anyway, as some will be indigestible or unabsorbable.

**DE (digestible energy)** is simply the energy in the feed minus the energy lost to the animal in faeces, i.e. the indigestible part of the feed. This is the measure most usually applied to horses and is similar to the old TDN (total digestible nutrients) system in application, although DE gives more accurate results.

**ME (metabolisable energy)** is DE minus the energy lost in urine and gases, which, for the ruminant, may be considerable. Methane gas production in horses, especially those on high-fibre diets, is not negligible but, as it would be very difficult to measure, it is not generally used when calculating horse feed requirements and DE is generally considered near enough for practical purposes.

**NE (net energy)** is ME minus heat increment, or heat lost by the animal in processing the feed (and, incidentally, in keeping the animal warm), giving the NE or net energy available for use by the animal.

Obviously, the NE content of a feed would be the most useful information to have but it would be prohibitively expensive to evaluate this for practical rationing purposes. DE is, therefore, the energy measure of choice for horses because it is relatively easy to evaluate and takes into account the monogastric (single-stomached) nature of the horse's digestive system. DE is probably more accurate for horses on high-cereal diets than for those on more fibrous diets, who will be producing more combustible gases as a by-product of digestion in the hind gut, but, as the latter are less likely to be in hard or fast work, the fine tuning of their diets is less crucial anyway.

DE may be expressed as kilojoules (kJ) or megajoules (mJ) per kilogram.

**TDN (total digestible nutrients)** is no longer used because it tends to be rather less accurate than DE as a means of estimating the horse's dietary requirements for energy production.

## Protein and Amino Acids

These are made up of carbon, hydrogen, oxygen and nitrogen, plus, in some cases, sulphur.

Proteins are found in all living cells where they are intimately involved in all the activities which sustain the life of the cell. Each tissue, organ or organism is made up of cells and has its own particular types of protein.

For instance, the principal proteins in the liver are different from those in the heart, or, say, in soya milk, oats, eggs or grass.

Protein is used to build up new tissue in the young, growing animal and the pregnant mare, and for replacing worn-out tissue, particularly in elderly and severely debilitated horses.

Proteins are made up of amino acids which may be likened to the pieces of a jigsaw puzzle or, more accurately, an intricately patterned, unfastened necklace. Each type of amino acid has a distinct shape and fits in a particular place in the necklace but may be used to make up different types of necklace. There are 25 amino acids known in nature, 22 of which are known to be required by the horse. These 22 are subdivided into two types. Twelve are called **non-essential amino acids**. These can be synthesised by the horse itself and need not be present in the diet as such as the horse can manufacture them as its body functions demand. They are essential to the horse but, as their name stresses, are *non*-essential in the diet, provided the overall protein (specifically nitrogen and, where necessary, sulphur) and energy content of the diet is adequate to provide the necessary raw materials.

The other ten amino acids are described as **essential amino acids** (EAAs) as they must be provided in the diet because they cannot be synthesised by the horse. For optimum health and performance, adequate levels of these ten amino acids must be supplied in the horse's feed.

In practice, it is fairly difficult to underfeed seven of these essential amino acids to a mature horse being given reasonable quality feedstuffs but three, methionine, tryptophan and, in particular, lysine, are deficient or marginal in many diets, especially those based on cereals or cereal by-products (oats, barley, maize, wheat bran, etc.). These three amino acids are often referred to as **limiting amino acids** or LAAs.

A deficiency in these three amino acids may not be crucial for the mature horse in light work but they are increasingly necessary for performance horses, growing youngsters and broodmares. Lysine deficiency may reduce performance, the efficient take up of feed and growth; methionine deficiency may manifest itself in hoof and coat problems; tryptophan deficiency as hyper-excitability.

Amino acids also play a role in the absorption and utilisation of many other nutrients and in specific health problems.

It is not, therefore, just the quantity of protein in the diet which is important, but also the quality of that protein, i.e. the proportions and amounts of EAAs it contains, as well as the digestibility of the feed containing it and its subsequent absorption by the horse.

Recently, attention has been paid to another amino acid, glycine (dimethyl glycine or DMG), as an energy source for high-performance horses but, unfortunately, the misuse of this amino acid can cause more problems than it solves.

The protein level given on the feed-sack label is the crude protein (CP) content which is not, in fact, a good measure of the usefulness of that protein to the horse. Old leather boots have a relatively high crude protein content but are not renowned for their digestibility by horses! We should also interest ourselves in the digestible crude protein (DCP or digestible protein) in the feed. It may be more economical and better for the horse to feed a ration of 10 per cent crude protein which is 80 per cent digestible, than 14 per cent crude protein which is only 40 per cent digestible, particularly when feeding high-performance horses.

In fact, CP and DCP are a measure of the nitrogen-containing compounds in the feed and you may also see the term true protein which refers to actual protein content.

The desirable lysine content of the overall diet is 0.7 per cent for foals and weanlings, 0.6 per cent for yearlings, 0.5 per cent for two year olds and 0.25–0.4 per cent for mature horses, depending on the level of performance. Elderly horses would probably benefit from a little more, say, 0.6 per cent, plus a good supply of methionine for coat and hoof condition. (Elderly horses do not *have* to look moth eaten and scruffy!)

Mature horses and ponies require 8.5–10 per cent crude protein in the *total* diet. This is as fed, not on a dry matter basis, and refers to the level in the forage plus concentrates, not just concentrates alone. So, in a poor year for hay the concentrates will obviously need to be higher in protein to maintain the required levels and vice versa, or you may feed less forage and more concentrate but this is physically less desirable.

For the average mature horse doing medium work, no supplement containing a high level of crude protein (e.g. soya, linseed, meat and bone meal, fishmeal, skimmed milk) is necessary, although additional lysine may well be beneficial, especially in harder work. Linseed is a particularly poor source of lysine among high-protein feeds.

In fact, excess crude protein levels may be counter-productive. The body's efforts to deaminate (break down) and get rid of the excess may lead to increased sweating and urinating, cause breaking out into a sweat after work,

*Crude Protein Requirements of Horses (as fed)*

|  | % in total diet |
|---|---|
| Pregnant mares (last 90 days of gestation) | 11.0 |
| Lactating mares (first 3 months) | 14.0 |
| Lactating mares (third month–weaning) | 12.0 |
| Foal creep feed 18.0 | |
| Foal (3 months of age) | 18.0 |
| Weanling (6 months of age) | 16.0 |
| Yearling (12 months of age) | 13.3 |
| Long yearling (18 months of age) | 11.0 |
| Two year old | 10.0 |
| Mature horse   – resting | 8.5 |
| – light work | 8.5 |
| – moderate work | 8.5 |
| – hard work | 8.5 |
| Elderly horse (16 years plus) | 12–14 (probably) |
| (Levels assume that the lysine levels discussed above are met.) | |

higher pulse and respiration rates (particularly undesirable for endurance horses and possibly impairing other competition performance), unnecessary stress and, in the long term, possible kidney damage. Horses with foamy, sticky sweat are quite likely to be receiving grossly excessive levels of protein in their diets. The foam may, in fact, be caused by nitrogenous compounds (from protein) in the sweat.

There is still much disagreement among nutritionists about the desirable protein levels for high-performance horses of different types. However, it is simple common sense that an excess of any nutrient has got to be disposed of, and that tying up the metabolic processes in deaminating and redeploying excesses of protein or, indeed, any other nutrient, could very well reduce performance when it counts and make a difference to results. There is evidence of a reduction in speed on a high-protein diet and it is more sensible to err on the safe side. High-protein feeds tend to be expensive and it is foolish to overfeed them. Work out the necessary energy levels first, then the protein, but do make sure you give adequate essential amino acids.

# Vitamins and Vitamin-like Substances

Vitamins (the name is derived from vital amines) are vital substances concerned in many metabolic or life processes. They are micro-nutrients that are required in minute amounts but are vitally important to the health and welfare of the horse.

There are two types: fat-soluble vitamins and water-soluble vitamins.

## *Fat-soluble Vitamins*

The fat-soluble vitamins are A, D, E and K. A precursor of vitamin A, beta-carotene is also thought to be necessary in its own right, especially for unimpaired fertility of breeding stock and protection against certain diseased states by supporting the immune system. Fresh or dried grass, alfalfa (lucerne) and carrots are all rich in beta-carotene (also written as β-carotene).

The fat-soluble vitamins can be stored in the fat depots of the body and a grass-kept horse or pony on good pasture should store enough to see it through from spring until Christmas in the UK. Supplementation may be

*Vitamin requirements for horses*

| Vitamin | Total requirement |
| --- | --- |
| Vitamin A | up to 50,000 iu (international units) |
| Vitamin $D_3$ | up to 60,000 iu |
| Vitamin E | from 600 to 1,800 iu |
| Vitamin K | up to 20 mg (intestinal synthesis) |
| Vitamin $B_1$ (thiamine) | 50–100 mg |
| Vitamin $B_2$ (riboflavin) | up to 50 mg |
| Vitamin $B_3$ (niacin) | up to 400 mg |
| Pantothenic acid | up to 100 mg |
| Folic acid | up to 15 mg |
| Choline | up to 600 mg |
| Pyridoxine | 25–50 mg |
| Vitamin $B_{12}$ | up to 200 μg (micrograms) |
| Biotin | up to 15 μg |
| Vitamin C | intestinal synthesis |

*Role, sources and deficiency signs of vitamins in horses*

| Vitamin | Required for | Source | Deficiency signs |
|---|---|---|---|
| **Water-soluble vitamins** | | | |
| Vitamin B$_1$ (thiamine) | carbohydrate and fat metabolism | yeast, alfalfa, green leafy crops, peas, beans and cereal germ synthesised by bacteria in the hind gut | lack of energy, muscle weakness incoordination, diarrhoea, caused by bracken poisoning |
| Vitamin B$_2$ (riboflavin or lactoflavin) | protein and carbohydrate metabolism | green forage, milk and milk products | poor feed utilisation, reduced growth rate, periodic opthalmia (moon blindness) |
| Vitamin B$_3$ (niacin) | metabolism of carbohydrates, fats and proteins | lucerne, oil seeds and animal by-products; deficiency unlikely | loss of appetite, reduced growth and diarrhoea |
| Vitamin B$_5$ (pantothenic acid) | carbohydrate, fat and protein metabolism; formation of anti-bodies | synthesis in the gut peas, molasses, yeast, cereal grains | weight loss, growth failure, dermatitis and skin disorders |
| Vitamin B$_6$ (pyridoxine) | protein and carbohydrate metabolism | forages, grains and pulses | poor growth, dermatitis; nerve degeneration |

*Role, sources and deficiency signs of vitamins in horses (continued)*

| Vitamin | Required for | Source | Deficiency signs |
|---|---|---|---|
| Vitamin B$_{12}$ (cyanocobalamin) | fat, protein and carbohydrate metabolism | synthesised exclusively by micro-organisms in horse's gut | loss of appetite, poor growth rates and anaemia |
| Folic acid | red blood cell production | grass; made in hind gut; linked to vitamin B$_{12}$, B$_2$ and C | anaemia and poor growth |
| Biotin | fat, protein and carbohydrate metabolism | maize, yeast, soya grass | skin changes, poor hoof horn and faulty keratinisation |
| Choline | fat metabolism and nerve transmission | green leafy forages, yeast and cereals | slow growth and increased fat deposition in the liver |
| Vitamin C (ascorbic acid) | immune system antioxidant; structure of skin and connective tissue | horse can synthesise its own vitamin C; green leafy forage | bleeding ulcerated gums internal bleeding |

*Role, sources and deficiency signs of vitamins in horses (continued)*

| Vitamin | Required for | Source | Deficiency signs |
|---|---|---|---|
| **Fat-soluble vitamins** | | | |
| Vitamin A (retinol) | vision, the health of mucous membranes, growth, reproduction and resistance to disease | green, leafy forages and carrots | reduced sight and eye damage resulting in night blindness; uneven, poor hoof growth; slow growth; reproductive failure and susceptibility to disease |
| Vitamin D (calciferol) | absorption, uptake and transport of calcium and phosphorus | occurs as two provitamins which need the ultraviolet portion of sunlight acting on the skin to be converted to the vitamin; these precursors are found in most forages | swollen joints, skeletal abnormalities, lameness |
| Vitamin K | blood clotting | made by the bacteria of the gut; green leafy material | deficiency is rare |
| Vitamin E (tocopherol) | biological anti-oxidant; fat metabolism reproduction | alfalfa, green fodder and cereal grains | pale areas of skeletal and heart muscle, red blood cell fragility and infertility |

desirable after this time until the next flush of spring grass appears. Stabled horses are likely to benefit from some source of supplementation throughout the year, especially when in hard work.

Although there is as yet no scientific support for such a claim, some horse owners have found additional mega-doses of vitamin E to be beneficial for nervous horses and up to 7,000 iu (international unit) per day of vitamin E may be given for five to seven days before an important competition, provided that adequate selenium levels are present in the rest of the diet.

The benefits of routine, additional vitamin E for breeding stock have not, in my opinion, been satisfactorily proven but an additional 1,000–2,000 iu/day is fed by some stud owners around covering time, as a precaution.

Because of their greater susceptibility to melanoma (a form of skin cancer), older grey horses may benefit especially from adequate maintenance of the levels of antioxidant nutrients, vitamins A (and beta-carotene), E, magnesium, zinc and selenium. (An antioxidant helps to prevent decay.)

Horses on high-fat diets (over 3 per cent oil in the total diet), such as endurance horses, require an additional 5 mg vitamin E per kilogram of feed for each 1 per cent above 3 per cent. Thus, on a 7 per cent oil diet, 7 minus 3 per cent = 4 percentage points over 3 per cent. This gives $4 \times 5$ mg = 20 mg of *extra* vitamin E per kg ($2\frac{1}{4}$ lb) of total feed (forage and concentrates). While the exact amounts of additional vitamin have not yet been established, it should be noted that this is the minimum of vitamin E required.

Horses being fed proprionic acid-treated cereals, hay or silage should be receiving at least 1,000 iu/day of vitamin E. A number of other feed preservatives will also increase the vitamin E requirements – an important consideration when choosing manufactured feeds which are not always fully compensated for this fact.

## *Water-soluble Vitamins*

The other, larger, group of vitamins contains the water-soluble ones, which cannot be stored long term by the horse and which it requires anew on a daily basis. Many of these vitamins (particularly in a high-fibre diet) are probably adequately synthesised in the gut by the gut micro-organisms but if these micro-organisms are upset (e.g. by antibiotics or steroids or a sudden change in the diet), or if the horse is on a lower-fibre diet or extremely poor grazing, or has higher requirements than normal (e.g. the high-performance, chronically sick, elderly or very young horse), additional levels may be required. However, there is little to be gained from feeding excessive levels as these vitamins cannot be stored and the horse must waste metabolic effort in disposing of them, which may be crucial in a high-performance situation.

The possible exceptions are folic acid, of which some horses seem to require high levels, biotin, again apparently underutilised or improperly absorbed by some horses and therefore needed at higher levels to maintain the integrity of hoof and coat (usually increased for three to nine months, then a drop to normal levels can be introduced), and, possibly, vitamin C in some disease situations. These higher requirements may well be due to malabsorption or poor utilisation rather than a dietary deficiency *per se*.

In my experience, horses which respond to these mega-doses have often been subjected to prolonged courses of antibiotics or steroids or are suffering from metabolic dysfunction for some other reason, particularly in the case of biotin which may be in short supply if there is an overgrowth of yeasts in the gut as these have a voracious appetite for biotin. The use of appropriate probiotics can help to resolve these problems. (Probiotics help to restore a healthy micro-organism population in the gut.) Having said this, some horses do seem to have a reduced ability to absorb or utilise specific nutrients, including vitamins, and if the reason cannot be found and corrected, megadosing may be the only way round this problem. However, great care must be taken to ensure that overdoses of one nutrient are not preventing the uptake of other nutrients in the diet. Specialist advice should always be obtained on this matter.

The water-soluble vitamins are the B vitamins – thiamine ($B_1$), riboflavin ($B_2$), niacin (nicotinamide – $B_3$), pantothenic acid (pantothenate – $B_5$), folic acid (folate), pyridoxine ($B_6$) and cobalamin ($B_{12}$).

Biotin, choline, inositol and vitamin C are the other water-soluble vitamins and vitamin K is also manufactured in a water-soluble form.

A number of other vitamins and vitamin-like substances have also been identified, including bioflavinoids, and it is possible that this list will be added to in the future.

Vitamins are destroyed by heating and cooking and exposure to air, light, damp and moulds. You should always add vitamin supplements after hot or cooked feeds have cooled, always reseal supplement containers and store them in a cool, dry place and never roll or otherwise process more feed at a time than you have to.

*Role, sources and deficiency signs of minerals in horses*

| Mineral | Required for | Source | Deficiency signs |
|---|---|---|---|
| **Major minerals** | | | |
| Calcium (Ca) | bone growth, maintenance and development, blood coagulation, lactation, nerve and muscle function | green leafy foods, especially legumes e.g. alfalfa; cereals and bran are poor sources; horses on high cereal diets need additional calcium | developmental orthopaedic disease (DOD); azoturia (equine rhabdomyolysis) |
| Phosphorus (P) | bones and teeth; energy metabolism | cereal grains e.g. oats, bran, barley | bone abnormalities and subnormal growth in young horses |
| Magnesium (Mg) | associated with calcium and phosphorus metabolism; enzyme systems | alfalfa. clover, bran and linseed | mental apprehensiveness, excitement and muscular spasm and twitching |
| Potassium (K) Sodium (Na) Chlorine (Cl) | body fluid regulation, acid-base balance, nerve and muscle function | grass and conserved forages e.g. hay | dehydration, weakness, exhaustion, depraved appetite |

*Role, sources and deficiency signs of minerals in horses (continued)*

| Mineral | Required for | Source | Deficiency signs |
|---|---|---|---|
| **Trace elements** | | | |
| Copper (Cu) | haemoglobin synthesis; cartilage and elastin production; bone development | depends on soil content from which feed is grown; interacts with sulphur and molybdenum | anaemia, poor growth, hair depigmentation and weight loss, DOD |
| Zinc (Zn) | normal cell metabolism; enzyme activator; bone growth | yeast, bran and cereal germ | skin lesions and reduce appetite and growth |
| Manganese (Mn) | cartilage formation | bran – content in grass and thus hay varies widely | abnormal skeletal development and reproductive failure |
| Iron (Fe) | haemoglobin production; enzyme activation | most feeds | anaemia weakness and fatigue |
| Iodine (I) | synthesis of the hormone thyroxine | most feeds, especially of marine origin e.g. seaweed | infertility, goitre |
| Selenium (Se) | closely related to vitamin E as a cell membrane stabiliser and protector | pasture, but soils may be selenium-deficient; excess selenium is toxic | muscle disease, tying up |
| Cobalt (Co) | synthesis of vitamin $B_{12}$ | trace levels present in most feeds | anaemia, loss of weight and reduced growth |

A factor which may also affect vitamin (and mineral) requirements and could lead to revised recommendations in the future is increasing levels of pollution as many vitamins and minerals play an important role in the detoxification of a number of pollutants and toxins. This is worth bearing in mind for horses pastured near industrial complexes, next to main roads or in intensive arable-farming areas.

## Minerals

Minerals are another essential part of a balanced ration for horses. They form the major constituent of bones and teeth, as well as being present throughout tissues and fluids and playing a vital role in biochemical reactions. The total mineral content of a feed roughly equals the 'ash' content given on feed bag labels, although much of this may consist of silica.

| Minerals required by horses | per kg of diet | per day for 16hh, 500-kg horse |
| --- | --- | --- |
| Sodium (g) | 3.5 | 44 |
| Potassium (g) | 4.0 | 50 |
| Magnesium (g) | 0.9 | 11 |
| Sulphur (g) | 1.5 | 19 |
| Iron (mg) | 150 | 1,900 |
| Zinc (mg) | 60 | 750 |
| Manganese (mg) | 50 | 625 |
| Copper (mg) | 20 | 250 |
| Iodine (mg) | 0.15 | 1.9 |
| Cobalt (mg) | 0.2 | 2.5 |
| Selenium (mg) | 0.2 | 2.5 |

Again, recommendations may be revised in the future in the light of increasing knowledge about the role of minerals in the detoxification of pollutants as pollution levels increase and as horses, particularly those kept in urban areas, are increasingly showing signs of the effects of atmospheric and ground-water pollution, as well as reacting to unnatural substances and xenobiotics sprayed on to, or added into, feedstuffs for whatever reason.

Minerals, particularly a number of trace elements, play a vital role in the detoxification system in the body, a little-understood body system, which is just as important as the well-known functional systems (cardiovascular, respiratory and so forth).

The minerals are usually subdivided into major and macro-minerals – required in minute traces but no less important than other nutrients.

## Major Minerals

The major minerals are:

- calcium (Ca)
- phosphorus (P)
- sodium (Na)
- potassium (K)
- chlorine (Cl)
- sulphur (S)
- magnesium (Mg)

Given a diet containing reasonable levels of forage (which is rich in potassium), the only major minerals you may have to consider adding to most horses' diets are calcium, phosphorus, sodium and chlorine (the latter two usually in the form of sodium chloride [salt]). Very few diets are adequate in these minerals for working horses and although proprietary cubes and mixes may contain adequate levels, vitamin/mineral supplements rarely do as it would be virtually impossible for the manufacturers to get the levels right for all horses in all situations.

Lack of calcium or phosphorus, or an imbalance between them, can manifest itself as brittle bones (e.g. sore shins or star fractures of the cannon bones), poor bone growth in youngstock (e.g. epiphysitis, caused by lack of minerals, *not* by high protein levels unless protein is excessive). In severe cases, rickets or osteomalacia may occur as well as loss of teeth. Muscle function may also be impaired. High-performance horses, especially endurance horses and eventers, that are deficient in calcium (and possibly potassium) may suffer from 'the thumps' (synchronous diaphragmatic flutter). This can be avoided by ensuring balanced nutrition and practising conditioning techniques.

Apart from the actual amounts present, the ratio of calcium to phosphorus is important. For mature horses, it should be between 1.1:1 and 1.6:1, *never* less than 1.1:1 and preferably no more than 2.1:1. This means between 1.1 g and 1.6 g calcium for every 1 g phosphorus in the diet of adult horses. Desirable ratios of up to 6.0:1 g are sometimes quoted but these are probably excessive in the long run.

Diets containing a lot of cereal products, especially wheat bran, are likely to have an especially unbalanced calcium to phosphorus ratio and they also contain a substance called phytin (phytate, phytic acid), which 'locks-up' calcium from the rest of the diet and renders it indigestible to the horse.

This problem can be alleviated by:

- feeding up to 50 g (2 oz) limestone flour per kilogram ($2\frac{1}{4}$ lb) of wheat bran (for mature horses, less if sugar beet pulp or alfalfa is fed as these are rich in available calcium)
- using chaff or chop instead of wheat bran
- always feeding sugar beet or lucerne/alfalfa nuts or meal when large amounts of cereals, particularly wheat bran, are being fed, as these non-cereals help to counteract the various deficiencies most commonly found in cereal feeds
- a combination of the above three points, as appropriate
- other, more sophisticated (and expensive) calcium sources may be used for high-performance or convalescent horses if necessary, e.g. calcium gluconate and proteinate.

### Vitamin D

Adequate vitamin D levels are also important in the utilisation of calcium and phosphorus. If the horse is not fed on fresh grass or regularly exposed to sunlight, it should be fed supplementary vitamin D. Animals at risk include those kept out but who wear a New Zealand rug in winter (and therefore are shielded from the action of sunlight on the skin) and stabled horses, especially those exercised in an exercise sheet or in the early morning before the sun is out or if the sky is clouded over. Show ponies that are kept rugged and who wear neck guards to encourage early shedding of their winter coat are especially at risk.

There is relatively little vitamin D in feeds stored for more than six months and body reserves of this vitamin, even those built up by grazing horses, are likely to be exhausted by mid-winter (Christmas in UK).

### Calcium

You can easily add calcium, e.g. as a feed-grade limestone flour, or as calcium and phosphorus (for youngstock, e.g. as dicalcium phosphate), although more efficiently absorbable sources might prove more suitable for high-performance animals. Ground Cornish calcified seaweed (in fact a type of coral) also provides useful amounts of trace elements. Bone meal can carry a risk of salmonella infection, so only reputable brands should be used. It is not a product I would choose to use. Other, more expensive but better utilised calcium sources can also be fed.

### Salt

Salt is quite simple. It is a source of both sodium and chlorine. I consider a salt lick to be sufficient for supplementing most non-working (and non-lactating) horses in field or stable but not for lactating broodmares, nor for horses in hard work, when it may be necessary to add 25–100 g (approx. 1–4 tablespoons) of salt per day to the ration, plus keeping a salt lick or loose salt box available 'for insurance'. The rule of thumb is that salt fed should be 0.5–1 per cent of the total diet by weight. Be guided also by the degree of hard work, ambient temperature and humidity. Salt-deficient horses may become dehydrated and will, at the very least, suffer from reduced performance (see also electrolytes below). Sea salt is fine but dishwasher salt is not suitable and neither is table salt with added chemical flowing agents.

### Chlorine

Chlorine is supplied with the salt (which is sodium chloride – use iodised table salt).

### Magnesium

If muscular stiffness is a problem, the possibility of magnesium deficiency should be considered when trying to identify the cause. Magnesium deficiency is not likely to be a problem in most practical situations, as most horses obtain sufficient levels in their normal diet and horses are considered to be less sensitive to magnesium levels in the diet than, say, lactating dairy cows. However, long-term chronic magnesium insufficiency may be suspected in horses with stiffness, muscle tremors and shifting multi-focal lameness and these conditions often respond to magnesium and potassium supplementation in addition to normal balanced supplements.

## Trace Minerals

The important trace minerals are copper (Cu), cobalt (Co), iron (Fe), zinc (Zn), molybdenum (Mo), selenium (Se), iodine (I) and manganese (Mg). These will generally be adequate for grazing horses and those in light–medium work if a trace-mineralised salt lick is made available, although some horses benefit from additional zinc (especially in terms of improved hoof, skin and hair condition) and added selenium may be of value in some areas of the UK (e.g. Devon/Cornwall, Welsh mountains, Scottish Highlands, etc. – all areas where selenium is known to be lacking in the soil), or if high levels of vitamin E are being fed. Care should be taken not to overfeed selenium, however, as it can be toxic if overdosed.

Further levels of trace minerals may be required for stabled horses in hard work and those exposed to high levels of pollution. (See vitamin/ mineral supplements, below.)

A number of other trace elements occur naturally in feed, e.g. chromium (Cr), boron (B) and germanium (Ge). Recent work on chromium indicates an increased requirement in stressed and high-performance animals. Chromium supplements are available for horses and are said to reduce anxiety during training and to maximise energy utilisation as well as aiding recovery after exercise. While boron and germanium may have specific therapeutic benefits, their requirement as an additive in horse feeds has not yet been specifically researched.

## Electrolytes

Electrolytes or tissue salts are minerals and trace minerals in their salt form, which is how they are present in the body. (Also called blood salts.)

### Electrolyte drinks

These are a mixture of tissue salts and usually glucose or another high-energy carrier, which can be mixed with drinking water and given to a dehydrated horse which has lost mineral salts through sweating during exertion and some types of illness. They can be useful after, or even during, a competition (e.g. eventing, endurance riding) or as a pick-me-up after a hard day's hunting and are far more beneficial than oatmeal gruel or hay tea, itself a primitive potassium-rich electrolyte drink. They can also be given after a long journey, especially in hot weather. Many people do not realise that a horse in a trailer may sweat profusely but still appear dry on arrival because the air movement in the trailer will dry the coat rapidly.

There is nothing to be gained from force feeding electrolytes *before* a competition provided the daily diet contains adequate mineral and trace element levels. Unless the horse is already seriously dehydrated, it will know if it needs them. Always offer plain water at the same time as the horse will know whether it requires salts, water or both and should not be forced to drink electrolytes it does not need through sheer thirst.

I prefer not to use electrolyte drinks containing glucose or dextrose for endurance horses or eventers as this prevents them from mobilising their own energy resources and can lead to rebound hypoglycaemia (when the system floods with insulin to 'mop up' unnatural levels of blood-sugar and may, in fact, cause a temporary drop in blood-sugar levels, which manifests itself as fatigue. If your horse is on a well-balanced diet, is fit and is not deprived of feed for more than four hours before strenuous performance, glucose is more likely to hinder than help it.

## Proprietary Vitamin/Mineral Supplements

Vitamins and minerals cannot be considered individually, in isolation. Complicated interactions take place among them and among other nutrients, many of which are not yet clearly understood or identified, although the interactions between vitamin D, calcium and phosphorus, and between vitamin E and selenium are well known.

The perceived wisdom on supplementation is continuously changing and developing. In addition, no one can state which commercial vitamin/ mineral supplement is the 'best one' without knowing exactly what it is to be fed with or what type of horse is being fed.

To supplement or not to supplement is a vexed question. Some people flatly refuse to use commercial supplements at all; some use several different ones at the same time (somewhat ill-advisedly); some pick the cheapest, the one with the longest list of ingredients, the prettiest packaging, the funniest advertisement or the best looking or most persistent sales rep!

Use the following rules of thumb when deciding whether or not to use a supplement and when selecting the brand. However, given that the requirement for supplementation of each individual nutrient is unlikely to be scientifically proven in the near future, if ever (however strong the anecdotal evidence may be) and given the complicated interactions of vitamins and minerals and the practical difficulties of analysing a horse's true requirements and the levels of vitamins and minerals already existing in each sample of feed, it really is a matter of personal judgement.

1   Horses at grass in temperate regions are likely to be lacking in fat-soluble vitamins (stored up in the summer) by midwinter or even before that in a year when grass quality has been poor and sunshine limited (e.g. 1985 and 1992 in the UK). The simplest way to correct this in home-mixed feeds if other micronutrient levels are satisfactory is to feed stabilised cod liver oil until the spring flush of grass. *Do not* overfeed cod liver oil as it is a highly concentrated nutrient source. Follow the instructions on the pack.

2   Be aware of any specific mineral deficiencies in your area – e.g. selenium, iodine, magnesium – and choose a supplement or enhanced salt lick accordingly. You can obtain such information from local farmers, your vet, a local agricultural merchant or your nearest agricultural advisory service.

3   For the grass-kept animal at rest or in light work, a trace-mineralised salt lick should provide adequate mineral nutrition provided the horse is not averse to using one (rare but it does happen). However, if the land is poor or, say, very chalky (the chalk locks up the trace elements) and you are not giving supplementary feed, consider using feed blocks (range blocks) to provide extra protein, energy, vitamins and minerals.

Alternatively, you could feed a vitamin/mineral-rich biscuit which can be fed by hand when you catch the horse up to check it over.

Do not forget the benefits of nutrient-rich pasture herbs or dried herb mixes as a back-up.

Vitamin injections are discussed below.

4 For the stabled animal whose feed intake is being controlled by you, you should consider:

- Which of the horse's nutrient needs may be missing or low in the feed you are giving. For example, is it low in vitamin D? (Six months after harvest, most of the vitamin D is gone from stored hay.) Calcium may be low in a grass, hay and cereals diet; the amino acid lysine in most diets; or phosphorus in an alfalfa/lucerne-based diet.
- Are any nutrients affected by the treatment of the feed? For example, cooking destroys vitamins and proprionic acid treatment, while preserving some nutrients, also increases the vitamin E requirement.
- Does the type of diet reduce the horse's capacity to synthesise its own B vitamins? For example, a high-performance horse on a low-forage/high-carbohydrate diet may not be producing adequate supplies.
- Are the horse's requirements increased, or even reduced, by its level of performance, acute or chronic illness, loss of appetite, or by the use of nutrient-blocking or -draining prescription drugs?
- The requirement for salt increases with work levels (and lactation) and I would expect the high-performance horse to have a salt lick for insurance, *plus* 25–100 g (1–4 oz) salt added to its diet. In compound feeds salt is usually fairly well supplied (because it is a cheap ingredient and feed manufacturers do recognise the need for it) but if you dilute the compound feed (unless it is a cereal balancer) with, say, oats, you will need to add more salt and perhaps a vitamin/mineral supplement. In any case, a horse with a high salt requirement may need, say, 25–50 g (1–2 oz) added daily. (For easy reckoning, 28 g or 1 oz salt is approximately one *level* tablespoon.)
- It also seems likely that the high-performance horse will have an increased requirement for B vitamins, especially on a carbohydrate-rich diet, and possibly also for some trace elements and minerals.

I generally give a carefully selected supplement to all high-performance horses, especially on high-cereal (carbohydrate) home-mixed diets. They will probably be given salt and calcium (unless the diet contains significant amounts of sugar beet or dried alfalfa (lucerne) cubes or alfalfa chaff, which are all rich in calcium). Amino acid supplementation may also need to be considered.

The broad spectrum vitamin/mineral/amino acid product chosen would not necessarily be the one containing the longest list of ingredients or the largest quantities of individual ingredients. I want a balanced product with no gimmicks at an economic price. A few pence a day is not much of an 'insurance' premium when feeding a high-performance horse in which a great deal of time, effort and money may already have been invested.

Without supplementation, a performance horse may seem healthy and may perform apparently quite well but may not thrive or perform at peak levels. On the other hand, a horse on a generally well-balanced diet, with good forage levels and a mix of cereals and non-cereals in the concentrates but no proprietary supplement, will be on a 'better' diet than the horse on, say, oats, bran and grass hay plus an arbitrarily chosen proprietary supplement 'to balance the ration' (which it probably will not).

The weight of evidence in favour of the theoretical benefits of enhancing micro-nutrient levels for high-performance horses, from a nutritional bio-chemical and physiological point of view is, in my opinion, too great to await specific scientific trials (once safe limits have been established). On horses, such trials are rarely satisfactory, so relying on them before choosing to use supplementation even as a safeguard is to adopt a head in the sand approach. Obviously, of course, any trial work is likely to enhance our understanding of the most suitable ingredients to use to maximise the benefits and fine tune our specific supplementation and would be welcomed.

In the meantime, we have to be practical and realistic in our reliance on, and appliance of, science. In days gone by, hay, bran and oats were not subjected to scientific trials before being generally accepted as suitable feeds for horses. None of these is a 'natural' horse feed and the last two are relatively new introductions. So do not be blinded by science but do be guided by it. Do not confuse commercial 'scientific evidence' with real science and practical know-how.

5 For the stabled horse in light to medium work, a less-complex supplement may be required. Alternatively, a trace-mineralised salt lick, calcium or sugar beet/dried alfalfa and possibly cod liver oil may be all that is needed. If the diet is composed of a balanced selection of feedstuffs and especially if cereals are balanced with

non-cereals such as sugar beet feed or dried alfalfa, plus a salt lick, no further supplement should be required unless specific health problems occur.

6 Broodmares and youngstock will almost certainly require salt, calcium and phosphorus and will benefit from a good broad-spectrum vitamin/mineral supplement and a good quality amino acid source if feeds are home-mixed or stud cubes or mixes are diluted with other ingredients. Again, sugar beet and dried alfalfa are useful vitamin and mineral sources. Note that some herbs should not be fed to pregnant mares, so check the labelling on a proprietary herb blend carefully.

7 If one scoop of supplement is good, two scoops are not necessarily twice as good. Follow the feeding instructions and, if possible, feed by bodyweight. *Do not* feed more than one broad-spectrum supplement at a time.

Also be wary of feeding a proprietary supplement with compound cubes or coarse mix which has already had a 'premix' added, although, in some cases, additional supplementation may be beneficial under *qualified* expert guidance.

Giving more than the recommended rate of a specific nutrient can be counter-productive. For example, many people are obsessed by feeding high iron levels to 'raise the blood count' but you cannot raise the blood count above the normal level for a horse by giving extra iron. You are more likely to make the horse dull and lethargic. Manipulation of vitamin and mineral levels in the diet should only be done under expert professional guidance in specific circumstances (i.e. on the advice of a nutritionally sophisticated vet or qualified animal nutritionist). When compound feeds are fed, particular note should be taken that while they may be adequately supplemented for most purposes, occasional addition-al supplementation can be beneficial. It is important, however, that there is no overdosing or incompatibility, hence the need for expert advice.

8 Heat, air, light and moisture can all damage feed supplements by destroying vitamins, so store the feed supplement in a cool, dry place and always reseal the container. If you have a large container, or one that is difficult to open and close, decant some into a clean, dry, properly labelled and dated ice-cream tub for

daily use, to reduce exposure of the bulk to air and moisture. Avoid buying supplements that have been stored in a shop window or next to hot lights or radiators. Also check that they are not past their sell-by date. If you are cooking a feed such as mash, add the supplement after it has cooled. Do not buy more than you can use in three months at the most as the product will deteriorate. If you have supplement left over from the previous year, the minerals will still be there but the vitamins will have deteriorated and the product may be rancid – put it on the roses!

Many minerals, especially salt, have an antagonistic effect on other minerals and vitamins. A number of attempts have been made to market supplements with the minerals and vitamins packaged separately but as this leaves a lot of scope for incorrect feeding by horse owners, adds packaging and transport costs and also discourages purchasers who wish to keep things simple, many manufacturers have shied away from this concept and, sadly, it has never really taken off. Although it would certainly be the ideal way to do things, very many horse owners simply cannot be bothered to take the time and trouble to use products properly, so it is important that you always match the product to the practical organisation of your yard. It is better to use a slightly less than perfect product properly than an expensive, superbly tuned and balanced product incorrectly or inappropriately.

9  Except in veterinary emergencies, or in the case of broodmares turned away on to mountain and moorland and unhandled for months on end, the use of injections as a means of supplying vitamins is quite nonsensical. A vitamin $B_{12}$ shot before an event will not raise the blood count unless the animal is deficient in $B_{12}$ and if it is, it is not fit to compete anyway.

Flooding the system with a nutrient it is not geared up to metabolise is more likely to reduce performance than enhance it. Steer well clear of vets and trainers who habitually give vitamin shots – there is something seriously wrong with their stable management and feeding if these are necessary and if they are not they are simply a source of unnecessary expense for you and unnecessary stress for the horse. There have been repeated cases of horses, including extremely valuable racehorses, dying after the application of inappropriate vitamin shots, often 'falling dead off the end of the needle' due to an extreme allergic (anaphylactic) reaction, almost always to the preservatives in the injection rather than the active ingredients (vitamins).

Obviously, in extreme veterinary emergencies or for horses with chronic malabsorption problems (usually correctable), it may very well become necessary to inject vitamins intramuscularly or give them as intravenous drips. However, we are concerned here with the routine injection of nutrients that are normally available in feedstuffs as a short cut for horse keepers who are too lazy or ill-informed to feed their horses a balanced diet. If, for some reason, it does become unavoidable to give your horse nutrient injections, it is to be hoped that the vet providing these will also advise on suitable dietary measures to restore the situation to normal and prevent the need to repeat the treatment. Your vet might also recommend that you seek the help of a qualified nutritionist.

# 3   Feedstuffs

In order to be able to make judgements about feed-related influences on health and performance in the equine, it is a good idea to familiarise oneself with the attributes of particular feedstuffs.

Before looking at the specifics of feed formulation and feed-related health problems in the performance horse, it is therefore worthwhile discussing the characteristics, advantages and disadvantages of particular feedstuffs. Various considerations must be taken into account when using different feeds, including the effects of different methods of processing and preparation, and their interaction with other feedstuffs.

## Assessing the Nutritional Value and Quality of Feedstuffs

Unless you are buying compound feeds with a known feed value, the only way to ascertain the nutrient content of a feedstuff is to have it chemically analysed. For the performance horse this is most certainly money well spent. Some idea of whether feedstuffs are as good as you expect them to be may be obtained from monitoring your horse's bodyweight, condition and performance but this is necessarily a historical method, as you will not know that something is wrong until after it has happened. You may then waste valuable training and competing time in bringing the horse back to peak condition.

However, you can make an informed guess about certain aspects of feed quality and you can certainly judge by its physical appearance and smell whether a foodstuff is clean and in a generally suitable condition to feed.

1 The nutrient content (i.e. a chemical analysis of the nutrients present) of any feedstuff will be affected by:

   • the soil in which it is grown

- the type and quantity of fertiliser applied, previous fertiliser, cropping management of the field, control of pests and diseases in the growing crop and plant varieties used
- the standard of farming
- weather conditions during the growing season and when the crop is harvested
- the method of preservation, e.g. drying, ensiling, chemical treatment, vacuum packing, etc.
- storage conditions and length of storage
- the method of processing
- storage, packaging and handling during distribution
- storage and handling in the yard
- the method of individual feed preparation in the yard.

2 To a great extent, physical quality can be judged by eye, nose and feel. Poor quality feed should never be bought and feed which has deteriorated in store should not be used. However, microscopic moulds and fungi are invisible to the naked eye and are endemic on foodstuffs.

   Various hay-cleaners and so forth are available now. While these can be useful in the extra cleaning of forage for high-performance horses, they should not be used as an excuse for purchasing inferior forage because even if these contaminants are removed, forage which has become mouldy and dusty is also likely to be nutritionally damaged. No amount of cleaning will correct this and the supplementation of micro-nutrients would, at best, be based on guesswork.

Both forages and grain are now often treated with preservatives, a number of which are perfectly acceptable for use on horse feed. Several of these products are based on natural materials which are found in the digestive system of the horse (e.g. proprionic acid, acetic acid), unlike many of the non-natural preservatives used in feedstuffs for humans. The object of these preservatives is to prevent the formation of undesirable moulds and bacteria and to reduce the deterioration and rancidity of nutrients (including vitamins and fats) due to oxidation. Feedstuffs treated with such materials as proprionic acid will have a decreased vitamin E content but the overall feed value will be well preserved. When using such treated feedstuffs, additional vitamin E, an anti-oxidant nutrient, may be advisable in the diet and this slight disadvantage is nothing when compared to the loss of all vitamins and soluble nutrients in a badly preserved and stored feed sample.

That said, preservatives should not be accepted as a means of feeding overprocessed or inferior quality feeds, nor for the sole convenience of feed distributers. It is likely that preservatives increase the requirement for certain micro-nutrients and their long-term effects, especially when combined with other materials, have simply not been researched for the horse. There may or may not be a risk, but if you try to stay well informed, any risk may at least be a calculated one.

> 3  Feeding value will also depend on such factors as palatability, ease of eating (e.g. is it dusty, too hard or too soft?), digestibility and the health, age and history of the horse, even its breed or type. A nutrient-rich feed such as alfalfa may be of excellent feeding value for a Thoroughbred broodmare but of such high nutrient value that it could be dangerous (if used at the same levels) and have limited actual feeding value for a native pony, for example.

There has been a widely publicised resurgence of interest in the use of organically produced (i.e. pesticide-free and artificial fertiliser-free) feedstuffs. There are many reasons why this practice should be encouraged but at the time of writing the availability of such feedstuffs would not be adequate to feed the entire horse population if more horse feeders were to seek it. However, as agricultural policy alters on an international basis, both from the viewpoint of reducing gluts in the northern hemisphere and also of restricting potential environmental and health hazards, it seems quite possible that organically produced feedstuffs will become more widely available in the UK or, at least, the next best thing, which is 'Conservation Grade' feedstuffs. These are produced with a minimal inclusion of chemicals or may come from farms currently converting to organic methods, especially if viable, extensive, low-input agricultural techniques are encouraged instead of the current iniquitous set-aside system.

The possible benefits of using organic produce should be weighed against the disadvantages of potentially increased levels of diseased materials. It should be noted, however, that once farms have converted and the biological population of pests and friendly organisms in fields have stabilised, pest levels should, in some cases, be less than those in highly fertilised and sprayed crops, while diseases (including moulds) may be reduced as the crop should be healthier and will contain more trace elements to protect it.

It should be remembered that the majority of modern crops are grown from plant varieties specifically produced for growing in conjunction with chemicals. These plants are increasingly falling prey to severe pest and disease problems which, in turn, are increasingly resistant to control by agrochemical sprays. I suspect and hope that, in future years, when more and more research is being directed towards producing high-yielding, disease-resistant crops for growing by organic production methods, this picture will change considerably. There is, however, the danger that, in creating plants with an aggressive resistance to disease, we may also breed in potential allergens, so this whole situation is not as simple as is sometimes suggested.

There is little doubt that the use of pesticides and fertilisers has brought comparatively short-term benefits during the twentieth century. Unfortunately, these methods of waging war on nature, instead of working with it, may not be quite the 'goose that laid the golden egg' that we have been led to believe. An increasing number of problems are now coming home to roost and I believe we are seeing evidence of these in various groups of horses. Certainly, fatalities have been reported which are attributed to nitrate poisoning caused by high levels of nitrate fertilisers, particularly when combined with high levels of nitrates in the drinking water. Some considerable problems have arisen for horse owners in arable areas where massive levels of nitrates were released when ancient grassland was ploughed up for food production during the Second World War. Some of this is only now percolating down into the water table and is causing massive build ups in some areas.

It is salutary to note that a recent study of carrots, produced for human consumption with the aid of pesticides which were used carefully and correctly by the farmers according to the manufacturers' and government-accepted guidelines, showed that 26 per cent of those properly treated carrots contained more than the permitted levels of pesticides at harvest. If consumer demand for organic and Conservation Grade foods and animal feedstuffs grows, then increasing numbers of farmers will consider producing them so that, eventually, the government will have to take this into consideration when forming agricultural policy. You, the horse keeper, are an important consumer when you make decisions about your horse's feed.

In the meantime, it is certainly a good idea to consider attempting to obtain organic or Conservation Grade feedstuffs, certainly when feeding sick, convalescent and elderly horses, pregnant and lactating broodmares, breeding stallions and high-performance horses, and particularly if they have had health problems in the past, both to reduce their intake of xenobiotics (foreign chemicals) and because organic feeds tend to have higher dry matter and trace element contents.

In the last few years of the twentieth century, this is a continually and rapidly evolving situation and horse owners should be aware that the quality and treatment of feedstuffs and even the nutritional value of different varieties of feedstuffs are constantly changing matters, so be very wary about becoming too fixed in your ideas about how to feed the horses in your care.

Feedstuffs are generally classified as forages and concentrates. The concentrates may be home-mixed using 'straights', compounded by a manufacturer (nuts/cubes/pencils/pellets/coarse mixes [sweetfeeds]) or a home-mixed blend of the two. The straights may be divided into cereal concentrates and non-cereal concentrates and, ideally, to achieve a balanced ration, a mixture of materials from the two groups is necessary.

## Forages

The term forage refers specifically to the fresh or conserved leaves and stems of fodder plants. Forage includes bulky feeds such as fresh grazed herbage, hay, feed-grade straw, silage, tower hayage, wilted forage that has been compressed and packed in heat-sealed, semi-permeable plastic – either fermented (e.g. HorseHage, Propack) or non-fermented (Hygrass) and silage (pickled grass!). Chaff or chop may also be considered part of the forage ration, as can treated straw cubes (e.g. Viton), dried grass and dried alfalfa (lucerne), although the latter two are more usually considered with concentrates when calculating ration feed values because of their high nutrient density of nutrients per kilogram of feed.

Hay is dried herbage, usually grasses and legumes, cut when the plants are at a relatively mature stage so that although the yield (i.e. tonnage per hectare) may be high, the maturity of the plant means that much of the nutrient content is unavailable to the horse as it is trapped by the indigestible woody fibre (lignin). This is in comparison to fresh cut or fresh herbage and the intermediate grazed grass, silage and hayage which are cut at a much less mature stage, and also grass meal and cubes and alfalfa (lucerne) meal and cubes which are also cut at a highly nutritious, immature stage but differ from fresh herbage and silage in that they are then dried down until they are as dry as, if not drier than, hay. This has the effect of concentrating the nutrients considerably.

During the twentieth century the types and feeding values of forages and the way they are harvested and stored have been continually evolving and these changes have accelerated noticeably during the late 1970s and 1980s.

Traditionally, hay was cut and cured in the field, stacked in sheaves or stooks and later transferred to the farmyard where it was placed in ricks that were expertly thatched to keep out the worst of the weather. This thatching was later replaced or supplemented by tarpaulins.

Towards the end of the nineteenth century, horse-drawn and, later, tractor-drawn or mounted mechanical means of cutting and collecting the hay were developed. Eventually, baling became common, initially in small round bales which were, in fact, highly convenient for feeding to horses. Small round bales were still being prepared by horse hay specialists in isolated areas into the mid-1970s and were by far the easiest means of filling haynets!

On the whole, mechanisation probably led to an improvement in the quality of hay as the process of harvesting was speeded up, thus reducing the farmer's dependence on the vagaries of the weather. The development of square bales carried some advantages, although, in very leafy hays, which are of a higher nutritional value, considerable loss of valuable material could be incurred during drying as the leaves have a greater tendency to shatter and be lost during baling than the slower drying stems.

As the specific requirements for feeding horses became less important to farmers, who were no longer using horses as a source of locomotive power on the farm, nor supplying the big carriers and transporters who used thousands of tonnes of forage to provide fuel for horse power in the cities, the convenience of feeding forage to horses became less of a priority. The requirements of cattle rose to the fore and the production of silage (in effect 'pickled' grass) became more and more important. Silage production has been known since Roman times but larger and larger proportions of the UK forage crop have been turned to silage in the latter part of the twentieth century.

Initially, most silage was put into clamps or large pits where air was excluded to ensure rapid preservation and the production of a quality product. Increasingly, a drier material, which is more of a cross between silage and hay and would most accurately be called hayage, has become popular, particularly since the advent of the big, round-bale-producing machinery and the development of large plastic bags which can be used to exclude air. While this material can be fed to horses, the increase in its popularity in the UK has meant that good quality hay, which is harder to make from the farmer's point of view, has become less and less readily available, although a number of farmers have gone back to specialising in the production of horse hay and also organically produced hay as a specialist product (often at a premium price). This is actually a response to the introduction of milk quotas and a consequent reduction in the size of the national dairy herd so, in a very small way, things have turned full circle in some areas!

Throughout the twentieth century, the way in which herbage grown for dried forage has been treated has also changed with the increased use of inorganic chemical fertilisers and a dramatic reduction in the use of farmyard manure as a fertiliser. Latterly, the increasing application of pesticides on forage crops has become the trend. Unfortunately, inorganic chemical fertilisers tend to be highly concentrated combinations of single nutrients and are almost totally deficient in trace elements, whereas organic fertilisers, including farmyard manure, are very rich in these vital micro-nutrients. Even where animal manures are used, these may be contaminated by the drugs and additives that are being fed to the animals, supposedly to boost production and efficiency. All of these factors may have benefits and disadvantages as far as the horse is concerned.

At the same time, plant breeding has developed to the extent that the manipulation of genetic material to produce new types of herbage has become a very exact (if slow) science, so that, in many cases, the herbage now used to produce hay bears little resemblance to the old-fashioned permanent pastures of our great grandfathers' day. Again, there are advantages and disadvantages here as this sophisticated plant breeding is aimed at the production of grass for high-yielding dairy cows and high levels of inorganic fertiliser utilisation and is not in any way specifically geared to the needs of horses.

Other developments have included tower hayage, which is another means of preserving forage, although, with the advent of big bales, this has become less and less popular. Conversely, the availability of new varieties and methods has led to the increasing use in the UK of home-grown dehydrated (dried) grass and alfalfa (lucerne) meal and cubes which can be incorporated in both the forage and in concentrate portions of the ration. The pros and cons of all of these different feedstuffs will be considered below.

While I have no intention of criticising traditional feeding methods, it is important that horse owners realise that although they may wish to adhere to traditional methods, they may very well find it difficult to obtain traditional feedstuffs equivalent to those used when the original methods were first developed. It may, therefore, be necessary to modify feeding regimes to take into account the changes in feed value incurred during modern feed production and in the production of new herbage (and, indeed, other feed crop) varieties now being grown. To a very small extent so far, things are turning full circle with the current upsurge of interest in organic and Conservation Grade farming techniques. However, even when developed further, these will still not be directly comparable with methods in days gone by as improved varieties of herbage seed and other crops are developed to improve yields, thus facilitating the use of less chemically dependent methods of cultivation and production. The important point is that horse keepers should be aware of these changes and avoid becoming fixed in their ideas about feeding. If the feeds that are available are changing, techniques for their use need to change with them.

## Selection of Forages

Whatever the methods of production used, your selection of suitable forages should be based on the following guidelines.

### Hay

Hay should be sweet-smelling, crisp to the touch and a good colour. There should be no visible patches of mould or dust. It is essential to check the centre of the bale for such signs.

To obtain the best results, hay should be cut before the grass is in full flower. This is, unfortunately, dependent on the weather unless the crop is to be barn-dried (see below).

Hay which has been mow-burnt (rained on after cutting or mowing and then dried again before baling) will also be sweet-smelling and a varying shade of brown. This may also occur if the hay is baled before the sap in the grass has dried, leading to overheating of the bales, sometimes to the extent that the stack will catch fire. Horses will often relish slightly mow-burnt hay for its sweet taste but its nutritional value has, to a greater or lesser extent, been spoilt.

Baling the hay after it has rained and before it has been thoroughly dried will result in a white, mouldy centre to the bale. The outer surface may often smell and feel of good quality. Rain-washed hay will tend to lose its colour and soluble nutrients (sugars, minerals) may be leached out.

Colour and nutrients (vitamins) can also be bleached out by too much sun, the resultant hay usually being very pale yellow.

**Barn-dried hay** is usually of superior feeding quality as its production is less dependent on weather conditions than field-cured hay and this should, of course, be taken into account when balancing the ration. In fact, in most years, particularly in the UK, barn-dried hay is probably the product of choice for performance horses as there is rarely a sufficient quantity of traditionally cured hay on the market which is of the best feed value. However, barn-dried hay can be rather dusty and some loss of leaf material may occur as it is dried. Barn-dried hay can also be rather a nuisance to handle, because, as moisture is lost, the forage shrinks, which means that the bales are often loose and break up easily, so that they have to be handled with care.

When choosing hay, it is worth remembering that the majority of the available nutrients are found in the leaf material, not the stems which basically provide roughage and a substrate for digestive micro-organisms to act upon. Although this roughage is essential, if one has a horse with a limited appetite it makes sense to use hay of the highest possible nutritional value.

**Legume hays**, which are generally of a very high nutrient value, actually tend to contain too much protein for mature performance horses. They are also difficult to cure without mouldiness occurring because the stems are so thick, which means that the stems and the leaves dry at very different rates. This is also a problem with mixed grass and legume hays.

For performance horses, a 'ley' or seed hay of ryegrasses or Timothy, or a good quality meadow hay are generally the preferred products. Meadow hays may also include beneficial herbs but particular care should be taken to ensure that no potentially poisonous plants are present.

Two-year-old hay is often sold as 'horse hay'. It is, however, likely to be worthless in terms of vitamin content and to contain massive quantities of moulds, which may be invisible to the naked eye, and a high level of dust. It is generally preferable to choose one of the other forages mentioned below rather than accept 'old' hay.

Although dust can cause coughing, the greater problem is caused by the presence of mould spores which can actually cause allergy problems, either on their own or as an aftermath to other respiratory problems such as colds and influenza or parasite damage. Such problems, including chronic obstructive pulmonary disease (COPD), are discussed below but it is obviously not a good idea to subject a valuable high-performance horse to an unnecessary respiratory challenge when the health and action of its lungs are of such vital importance to its performance.

Soaking hay for 30 minutes to four hours will cause the mould spores to swell to such a size that they cannot reach the site in the lungs where they cause the allergic reaction. This makes the hay safer for both horses and humans but it should not be used as an excuse to feed inferior hay.

If this method is practised, it is important that the soaking water is changed regularly and that the hay is fed while still wet, otherwise the spores may eventually shrink again. More will certainly form rapidly on the damp forage. It should also be noted that there is almost certainly a loss of soluble nutrients, including vitamins, minerals and sugars, from the hay, which must be compensated for in the rest of the diet, although the actual amount of this loss has not been ascertained. However, the better the quality of the hay in the first place, the greater the loss of nutrient value that is likely to occur in soaking it.

In recent years mechanical hay cleaners have come on to the market. If you can afford one, there may well be justification in using it to remove dust and spores from a normal sample of hay but it should not be used as a means of feeding inferior quality hay because even with the dust and moulds removed, the nutritional value of this material is likely to be seriously compromised. For a large stable, however, it may be worth looking into the possibility of using this type of equipment for even the cleanest hay.

New-crop hay should, ideally, not be fed until it is a few weeks old as the hay is still alive and various life processes are still occurring as it cures. If a wait is not possible, spread the hay out in an empty stable or barn to 'crisp' for about twelve hours before feeding and *always* mix a new crop with old material which the horse is used to for a few days so that you make no sudden changes in feeding. If necessary, feed a probiotic to help with this transition, or get the horse used to eating straw before the transition and mix some of that with the new hay.

### Hay-feeding equipment

It is essential that you feed hay using safe equipment in field and stable.

### Stable hay feeders

From the horse's point of view, eating from the ground is the method for which it is best adapted but, unfortunately, both in the stable and outside, this can lead to valuable hay being unnecessarily trampled and wasted.

In the stable a number of 'hay-corners' have been developed which can form a useful compromise provided they can be easily cleaned out and have a means to prevent the horse simply dragging all the hay out on to the floor which leaves you back where you started.

Old-fashioned hay racks tend to be dusty and can lead to injuries and damage to the horse's eyes if hay seeds drop into them. They are difficult to fill, especially for shorter humans! They also reduce yard management flexibility in that they may be too high for smaller ponies.

Hay nets, while awkward to fill, can be a useful alternative and the smaller-meshed type can be used for hydroponically grown cereals and moist, packed forages, to slow down their consumption. Tie hay nets so that they will be above the level of the top of the horse's leg when empty. It is quite astonishing how many valuable competition horses are injured every year due to getting a foot caught in a hay net or other feeding equipment, let alone more humble critters! A common error is to forget that as deep litter beds build up, the hay nets need to be hung correspondingly higher.

### Field hay feeders

Ensure that horses using field racks cannot get a foot caught if the rack legs cross over as a part of their construction. Also check that the horses cannot bang their heads or get them trapped in a circular feeder designed for cattle. Care should be taken in the selection of circular feeders, as more gymnastic horses can catch their legs and heads in openings which would not be a danger to cattle.

Various attempts have been made to develop tube-type feeders, rather like large flutes with feeding holes on the top, openings at the end for the hay to be pushed in and drainage holes in the bottom. Although I have seen some very useful prototypes, these never seem to catch on. Again, hay nets can be used in fields but they must be tied high enough for safety and on a very secure post or tree. If there are several horses in the field, there should always be one more hay net than the number of horses or ponies, to prevent bullying. This also applies if hay is to be fed in heaps on the ground and there should always be one heap for each animal in the field plus an extra one. The location of the heaps should be moved regularly to reduce poaching and, if possible, heaps and feeders should be placed on slightly elevated ground so that drainage is better.

**Purchasing hay**

If you buy your forage from a farmer with surplus stocks, it is quite likely that he will have had it analysed and will be able to tell you the exact feed value (and pH level [acidity] if appropriate).

It is to be hoped that forage merchants will increasingly follow suit and price their products according to such an analysis. It is in the interest of horse owners to be prepared to pay a premium for forages which are *known* to be of a good feed value, whereas at present many so-called 'good' hays, 'racehorse' hays and so forth, while they might be clean, are, on analysis, of very low nutritional value and considerably overpriced. I have seen expensive alfalfa (lucerne) hay imported from Canada which had half the feed value of Yorkshire meadow hay bought in the same year by the same yard.

It is worth costing your forage purchases against interest rates when deciding whether to buy in bulk to assure continued supply or in smaller quantities. As prices tend to rise through the winter, it can even pay to borrow money (e.g. via a bank) at known interest rates, especially if there has been a poor hay crop and prices may rocket as the winter progresses. Obviously, the availability of adequate storage facilities will be a consideration.

## *Tower Hayage*

Haylage is the registered trademark of Howard Harvestore. This, and similar products, which are cut at an earlier growth stage than forage for hay and are moister, can be fed to horses kept on farms with a tower silo. The main disadvantage is that hayage cannot easily be sampled for laboratory analysis and the product can be quite variable through the crop, with pockets of spoilage, especially in less sophisticated silos.

## *Moist, Packed Forage (MPF)*

These are of two kinds, the fermented type and the non-fermented type.

The **fermented** products can vary in feed value and the plastic packaging must be kept intact to ensure correct fermentation. It is therefore essential that the bags are not punctured or gnawed at by rodents. Although such products can be exceedingly useful for horses with respiratory problems, they tend to have a high protein content and/or soluble carbohydrate content. However, in correctly made material the water soluble carbohydrates (WSC) should have undergone fermentation to produce volatile fatty acids, thus reducing the pH and preserving the material. The WSC levels should be down to 2–5 per cent by the time the product is fed. The high protein levels apply especially to the lucerne/alfalfa types but also with many of the grass ones. In practice, this has caused a number of problems with horses, apart from making the overall protein content of the diet too high for performance horses, and very careful consideration should be given before selecting such a product as the main forage source for the performance horse.

Some of the problems experienced are more likely to be due to very high soluble carbohydrate levels with possible concurrent low mineral levels, and a number of physiotherapists and vets have noticed a high incidence of muscle problems, including azoturia, in horses being fed these products. This is often the result when horse owners have not fully understood how rich these materials are and have not reduced their concentrate feeding levels to compensate but it has to be said that this does not entirely explain the incidence of these problems.

Some of the more enlightened manufacturers are now marketing lower-protein products and a number of vets and physiotherapists have confirmed that these lower-protein materials have not been related to these problems. Although they are aiming this product at ponies rather than performance horses in their marketing, these are usually the products I would select for competition horses. The possible problems which might follow from over-feeding protein have been outlined on page 127.

In any case, MPFs are lower in fibre than hay on an as-fed basis and tend to be eaten quickly. Although they have a very high feeding value which quickly satisfies the animal's nutritional requirements, many horses tend to get bored and feel unsatisfied, so it is a good idea to feed another, bulkier, dust-free forage to dilute the bagged forage. A useful example would be molassed chaff.

The other type of moist, packaged forage (MPF), which is usually packaged in some sort of plastic bag, is the **non-fermented** material, which tends to be of more consistent feed value and have a lower protein content. I find this ideal for performance horses as it has the benefits of reduced respiratory challenge by moulds and dust because it is a moist forage, without the potential disadvantages of excessive protein levels. Avoiding subclinical respiratory stress is one way in which you can ensure that your performance horse has the best possible opportunity to achieve its maximum potential.

In general, both types of moist, packaged forage should be fed within four days of opening in winter and two days in hot weather, as spoilage can occur rapidly.

All of these products are of higher feeding value than most hay and it is often possible to reduce concentrate feeds somewhat if they are used but it is also a good idea to find some other way of satisfying the horse's requirement for bulk. You should also be aware that if you are reducing the total feed intake, you may also be reducing the horse's intake of vitamins and minerals and this should be taken into account.

## Silage

This is effectively 'pickled grass' and has been made since Roman times. Silage is cut much earlier in the growth cycle than grass for hay and at a more nutritious stage, although it contains more moisture. It is important that the acidity (pH) is as low as possible to prevent spoilage and that air is effectively excluded while the silage is made and stored. 'Wilted' silage, i.e. silage which has been wilted in the field after cutting and before collection, is usually drier and of a higher feed value on an as-fed basis than non-wilted silage.

**Additives** may be used to help to preserve the crop and trials have shown that proprionic acid ones are safe for horses if used with care and provided the vitamin E level in the diet is adequate. Some of the additives which have recently come on to the market, including biological ones which are related to probiotics (i.e. silage inoculants), may be even more suited to silage destined for horse feeding but no specific trials have yet been conducted on this so you should check the product labels and discuss this point with the manufacturer and/or a knowledgeable vet or nutritionist.

These inoculants have been selected and developed for cattle where meat or milk is the intended end-product and while one would expect them to be safe for horses, it should be remembered that the strains of inoculant chosen have been selected for feeding to ruminants whose digestion of forages is somewhat different to that of the horse. The best additives for cattle may not necessarily be the best ones for horses and vice versa. This is a rapidly growing subject and one worth watching.

Silage may be made in 'clamps' (usually walled heaps) which can either be cut and carted to the horse, or eaten directly off a self-feed face. If the horses are self-feeding, care should be taken that they do not overeat, e.g. by restricting access. If yarded with cattle, ensure that the horses do not prevent the cattle from eating. Horses and ponies can become very possessive about silage and find it extremely palatable once they are used to it.

With **big-baled silage**, which tends to be drier, it is again essential that air is excluded and the bags are protected from mechanical damage or damage by vermin. However, because it is harder to exclude all the air than when in a clamp, it is probably advisable to use a preservative. If in doubt, have the material analysed and check that the pH (acidity) value is below 5.5 so that diseases such as botulism (which has resulted in the death of horses fed unpreserved, bagged silage in the past) can be avoided.

The botulism organism cannot produce toxins if the pH value is below 5.5 throughout the clamp or bales. For this reason, clamp silage must be evenly compacted and bales carefully made, with preservatives evenly applied to avoid pockets of a higher pH value. A number of organic preservatives are available and most inoculants could also be regarded as organic.

Introduce silage gradually, like any new feed. Many horses dislike it at first but once they are used to it, they may be reluctant to go back on to hay. If they have a mix of hay and silage, they will usually eat the silage first.

As silage is a very moist material, in most cases it is a good idea to dilute it with hay, feeding straw (oat or barley) or chaff. In the case of broken-winded horses, use cubed (i.e. dust-free) straw, grass or alfalfa (lucerne), or molassed (i.e. dust-free) chaff to increase the fibre allowance.

Silage may be made from grass, grass and clover, oat and vetch or even from whole-crop maize or ensiled brewers' grains. These latter two are sometimes used by farmers in layers in the clamp to enhance the preservation and nutritive value of both.

All can safely be fed to horses provided they are introduced carefully and are fed as part of a balanced diet.

## Straw

Straw can be a useful feed for horses provided it is free of visible moulds and dust. For the performance horse, however, it is most likely to be used to provide a source of additional roughage, perhaps as chaff, and as a forage source when the horse is not actually working. Organic straw is especially useful. (It is interesting to note that thatchers have found that organic straw lasts for years, even decades, longer than pesticide-treated straw!) If you have a horse which is highly sensitive or has suffered from a respiratory virus, you may find that the presence of residual pesticides on some straws can cause problems and you should be aware of this possibility, particularly if the horse has developed chronic obstructive pulmonary disease (COPD), or has mysterious skin lesions which are difficult to eliminate. This may also apply to pesticides on straw used for bedding and, indeed, to chemicals on shavings.

While related to grass, unlike hay which consists of leaves and stems (unless it is threshed hay left after the production of grass seed – i.e. effectively 'grass straw', a useful product for chaff), cereal straws consist mostly of mature stems with very little leaf. This material has become lignified which means it is not digestible to any great extent by horses, although microbial fermentation will release a certain amount of nutrients and produce heat which may be useful for resting horses in winter. Its main benefit is as a source of roughage to 'exercise' the gut, as a substrate for gut micro-organisms and as chaff to keep the ration open.

**Oat straw** from spring-grown oats is preferable as it has a higher feeding value than other straws and is quite often more nutritious than some so-called 'horse' hays that appear on the market.

**Barley straw** may also be used provided it is not full of awns.

**Wheat straw** is not generally fed on its own, although it may be used in compound cubes to increase the fibre level and dilute the ingredients if they are too rich. Some horse owners complain if they see straw listed as an ingredient in cubes but it is quite often necessary to dilute cubes in the interest of good feeding practice.

Pea straw or pea haulm is a **legume straw** which may be found in some compounds. This tends to be too dusty to feed as a long fibre and may contain high levels of pesticides and desiccants.

## *Nutritionally Improved Straw Cubes (NIS) (e.g. Viton)*

These are also a useful horse feed, particularly for children's ponies and resting horses. They are most likely to be fed to performance horses either as an ingredient in cubes (in which case the compounder will regrind them and mix them with the other ingredients) or as one of the ingredients in a coarse mixture. Basically, they are made of cereal straw which has been ground up and chemically treated to release the nutrients bound up by the fibre of the straw so that the horse can digest them. Some types also contain urea to increase the protein (nitrogen) levels. Urea can be fed to horses provided it is carefully introduced – in fact, it is safer for horses than for cattle but it should not be overfed or rapidly introduced. If it is being used, it is also important to ensure that the horse is getting adequate supplies of the limiting amino acids (see page 20).

## *Dried Grass, Dried Alfalfa/Lucerne, Molassed Alfalfa Chaff*

These products are available as meal, cubes, molassed chaff and, in some areas, wafers. They are highly nutritious when compared to hay and other forages and if used as a forage source they usually need diluting with chaff or straw. Available in various grades, the meals are sometimes more palatable, though dustier, than cubes but cubes are usually accepted if they are *lightly* soaked before feeding when first introduced, a practice which can be phased out once the horses are eating them happily.

When diluted, these feeds form a useful alternative forage for horses with respiratory problems or when the usual forage sources are of poor quality or in short supply. They are also extremely useful when mixed with the concentrate ration to balance cereals as they tend to balance out a number of vitamin and mineral deficiencies in cereals, while providing protein of a reasonable quality and a good source of energy.

It is a good idea to use suppliers who specialise in the horse market as they tend to take more care in the manufacture of the product, avoiding over-heating which may reduce the nutritional value for horses and cause palatability problems. A number of growers and driers now produce cubes and pellets in sizes specifically suited to equine consumption. Some imported products are of poor or variable quality.

Both dried grass and dried alfalfa (lucerne) cubes are often found as an ingredient in compound horse feeds which have been cubed and as a loose ingredient in coarse mixes.

Although these products have a number of similar characteristics and both are dehydrated forage crops cut at a highly nutritious stage, they come from completely unrelated plant families, dried grass being more closely related to cereals, whereas alfalfa is a legume. These differences are important to the horse owner for a number of reasons.

While the alfalfa (lucerne) crop is capable of obtaining or 'fixing' nitrogen from the air for protein formation, and therefore requiring little or no artificial fertiliser in its production, grass is unable to do this and grass grown for dehydration is very heavily fertilised indeed, particularly with nitrate fertilisers. There is increasing concern that this may have an adverse effect on the horse and it may be prudent to restrict the use of dried grass products for broodmares, youngstock and horses convalescing from specific illnesses.

While the alfalfa crop does not require heavy applications of fertilisers, the areas and climate in which it may be grown are much more restricted in the UK than those for grass and most alfalfa crops will be found in eastern regions of Britain. However, developments in plant breeding techniques are already bringing about an expansion of the crop and it is likely that British-grown dehydrated alfalfa will become more widely available. We may also see a related crop, sainfoin, available in dehydrated form in the future and this would be an excellent addition to the horse's diet. Another related crop, fenugreek or 'Greek hay', makes a super horse feed. It has never caught on as a forage crop in the UK, although the seed is used in spice mixes and in flavourings for horse feed and herbal conditioners.

**Dried grass** and dried alfalfa are especially useful for feeding to breeding stock and youngstock because they both contain comparatively high levels of beta-carotene, the precursor of vitamin A and an essential nutrient in its own right, and folic acid, a vital B vitamin. In addition, alfalfa is a very good source of available calcium. Youngstock will also benefit from the high levels of copper and other trace elements it contains.

Both feedstuffs contain highly digestible and good quality fibre and, along with sugar beet, make an excellent balancer for cereals. In fact, I would go so far as to suggest that there is a place for good quality alfalfa cubes, either as a forage supplement or in the concentrates in the diets, on most stud farms at some time of the year if not all the time, provided the varieties selected by growers are of the low oestrogenic-activity type. Alfalfa (lucerne) and certain clovers have oestrogenic activity, in other words they produce substances similar to the female sex hormone and this may be associated with abnormal oestrous cycles in mares.

**Grass cubes** and **alfalfa cubes** can both be fed in free access out of doors when grazing is of poor quality in order to top up the feeding value, especially in times of drought when summer grass growth is poor.

Both can also be used with sugar beet to make a nutritious mash which is infinitely more beneficial than an indigestible, unbalanced bran mash and may be particularly useful for convalescent horses and broodmares after foaling (when a bran mash, which is short of calcium, could actually be detrimental).

## Grazed Grass

The feeding value of grazed grass is a huge topic. One of the biggest problems is working out its likely feeding value and just how much benefit the working horse is obtaining from it.

It should also be remembered that the feed value of grazed grass varies enormously through the year. It may need supplementing with straw in spring when it is sappy (to prevent scouring) and grass/alfalfa cubes in periods of drought to prevent loss of condition.

The factors affecting the feeding value of grazed grass are beyond the scope of this book. Providing you take good care of your grazing, however, the benefits of 'Dr Green' should *never* be undervalued.

## Concentrates

Concentrates, also referred to as 'hard feed' or (incorrectly) as 'corn feed', provide a more concentrated energy source (mainly from starch) than forages. This is especially useful for horses in hard work, in cold weather, with impaired digestion (e.g. some elderly horses) or with a limited appetite (finicky feeders).

For the high-performance horse, even when on good grazing or forage, some form of concentrate feeding will almost certainly be necessary. This is because concentrate feeds contain less fibre than forage feeds. While a certain amount of fibre is highly desirable, as the horse's nutrient requirements increase, particularly its energy requirements, the nutrients in forage become spaced out to too great a degree to allow the horse to obtain sufficient energy and nutrients in the amount of feed (i.e. dry matter) it can reasonably eat. Although the forage level fed to the performance horse is, in many stables, much too limited, leading to various digestive and temperament problems and other metabolic disorders including filled legs, it would not be desirable for the high-performance horse to eat too much bulk as this would spend a considerable time in the digestive system and might press against the heart and lungs, potentially impairing performance. There is, however, little danger of this happening with the unsuitably low levels of forage being fed in almost all racing and all too many competition yards in the UK.

The term concentrates may refer to both 'straights', which are individual feed ingredients, and compounds, which are blends or 'straights' manufactured by feed compounders.

## The Effects of Processing on Concentrates

### Rolling

Rolling, to crack the seed coat and allow the horse's digestive juices to enter, is necessary for barley but not for oats or maize which can be fed whole. Any benefits from rolling these may be lost as rolled cereals rapidly deteriorate in feed value. However, very young or very elderly horses may have difficulty in chewing whole oats or maize. Never buy more rolled cereals than you can use in two weeks at the most and always buy them freshly rolled or, in larger yards, consider rolling them yourself on the premises every day or so.

### Micronising

Micronising is a way of cooking feeds (rather like producing popcorn) which are then rolled before feeding. In general, this increases the feed value by increasing digestibility by 3–20 per cent, so micronised feed should never be fed weight for weight to replace the same non-micronised material. It is, therefore, important that micronised feeds are fed as part of a balanced diet. They may be particularly useful for finicky feeders or elderly horses and any animal with impaired digestion.

### Extrusion

Extruded (gelatinised) feeds are cooked to a porridge and flash dried. They appear as irregularly shaped 'lumps' of feedstuff or may be further processed for other animals into specific shapes which are supposed to be attractive to the customer! They may be used as individual feed ingredients or as a mixed feed to form a new way of producing a compound as an alternative to pelleting. We are likely to see a lot more of them in the horse-feed market in the future. This process tends to increase the digestibility of the ingredients but has the advantage that they are eaten more slowly than other concentrates, resulting in fewer digestive upsets and problems associated with boredom. They may be particularly useful if concentrates are being fed on a free-access basis in yards or paddocks.

Some feeds need to be processed in order to remove or destroy anti-nutritive factors or anti-metabolites. For example, raw soya beans contain allergenic, goitrogenic and anti-coagulant factors in addition to protease inhibitors. The correct toasting and cooking of the beans, as in micronisation, destroys these factors without detracting from the protein quality. Whole wheat can also be fed when processed in this way.

Both micronising and extrusion may adversely affect the vitamin levels during the cooking process and continued research is needed to establish the precise details of this, although amino acid levels may be improved. The whole question of the desirability, or otherwise, of giving cooked feeds to horses, especially breeding stock and youngstock, is also in need of further research.

### Boiling

Boiling cereals, e.g. barley, is generally a waste of time. There is little enhanced digestibility and if boiled feed is not given at every feed, this constitutes a sudden change in feeding because boiling changes some of the components. Barley can be fed more easily rolled and is preferable in this form. Think how indigestible porridge can be, no matter how tasty it is, before you inflict boiled barley on a tired or sick horse.

## *Cereal Concentrates*

The most commonly used concentrated feedstuffs for horses are cereals, i.e. oats, barley, maize (corn), wheat products (micronised wheat, breadmeal, wheatbran and wheat feed) and, less frequently, sorghum (milo), various rice products and even millet. You may even see some newly reintroduced ancient grains such as triticale, kamut and spelt, especially in compound feeds. Cereals are all related to grasses and cereal feeds are all based on the dried seeds of these different grass-related plants. It is important to remember this, particularly in the very rare instances of cereal intolerance in horses, because it is sometimes possible to resolve the problem by feeding a completely cereal-free, and sometimes grass-free, diet, usually on a temporary basis.

Which cereal is mainly used will depend to a great extent on which part of the world you are in but the cereal most widely fed to horses worldwide is probably maize (corn), although some would argue for sorghum (milo). However, as far as performance horses in the Western world are concerned, it is probably correct to say that maize is the most widely fed cereal, with oats coming a close second. (Maize grows better in hotter, drier areas; oats in cooler climates.)

### Oats

A favoured feed for horses, the oat grains in a sample should be large, plump, dry, clean and of even size, which will tend to mean that they have dried evenly and there is less likelihood of spoiled and mouldy grain. Clipped oats have a lower fibre content because some of the husk has been removed and are only economical if the digestible energy content is raised by more than the cost of the clipping, or if they are for an animal with an extremely restricted appetite (in any case, they are probably not the best choice as a main ingredient for this type of animal). Rolled oats should be sweet and not too floury when you plunge your hand into the sample, nor overrolled. A light cracking of the husk is all that is desirable.

In the UK imported oats are usually of good quality but barely justify the expense and may be contaminated in transit with prohibited substances which could cause problems for the performance horse. If you cannot easily obtain a good sample of nice, clean, heavy oats, you should consider using an alternative such as a compound or rolled barley or a combination of other concentrates.

Oats are not 'God's gift to horses', although because they are effectively slightly diluted, compared with other cereals, due to their high fibre content, and are relatively low in starch when compared with legumes, they tend to be more 'idiot proof' in the hands of less-knowledgeable feeders. However, they can have a 'heating' effect on some horses, which is possibly an allergic response to a protein unique to oats, to a combination of proteins or, more likely, to phenolic compounds.

It is dangerous and counter-productive to persist in feeding oats to a horse that becomes temperamental and hyperactive when they are fed, as it wastes both horse's and rider's energy. The horse will probably concentrate less on the job in hand, which could lead to poor performance, and accidents frequently result. Feeding an additive containing a clay-like compound called sodium montmerrillonite (e.g. Thrive) can help to alleviate this effect, probably because it 'mops up' toxins produced by this allergy, more correctly referred to as a feed intolerance) but they are not suitable for long-term use. If you have a horse with this type of problem, therefore, you should seriously consider using an alternative energy source. While feeding something like Thrive can work very well, it only masks the problem and does not remove it. Over a long period, its use could also alter the trace element balance and availability in the diet too much. I prefer to keep this type of very useful additive for relatively short-term emergency use to solve specific problems while a longer-term solution, including an overall change in the diet to something more suited to that individual horse, is established.

Oats can be fed whole, cracked, cut, rolled (preferably very lightly), micronised or extruded.

**Naked oats** or **oat groats** (husked oats) are both highly nutritious, low-fibre feeds which should be fed with care *and* added fibre!

While oats are generally a good source of energy in the form of starch and have particularly digestible fibre as cereals go, they are very low in the amino acid lysine. They are also low in calcium, with a poor calcium to phosphorus ratio, and contain phytate which can lock up calcium in the rest of the diet. The higher oil content than barley means that oats spoil (become rancid) faster when rolled than barley, although this oil will enhance coat condition in horses that are deficient in essential oils. The pronouncements of various horse owners in the past – that horses *must* have oats when they are in fast work and cannot do fast work on barley and other cereals – are merely an indication that those horse owners were unable to produce a balanced ration and has nothing whatsoever to do with any special qualities that might be ascribed to oats.

### Barley

Barley can be fed cracked, rolled, cut, steam-flaked, micronised, extruded or boiled but *not* whole. It is preferred by many horse owners to oats. It is much easier to buy a good sample of barley than of oats, as it is more widely grown. It also tends to be less 'heating' than oats. Barley has a slightly higher digestible energy content than oats so it should not be substituted on a weight-for-weight basis but should be incorporated into a balanced diet. The fibrous husk is much harder and less digestible than that of oats, which is why barley cannot be fed whole.

The superstition that barley can cause liver or kidney problems is an old wives' tale for which there is no evidence whatsoever. Barley is low in lysine, has a poor calcium content, a poor calcium to phosphorus ratio and, because of its lower digestible fibre content, it is probably a good idea to break up the concentrate ration with chaff, dried alfalfa or sugar beet. This is a good idea in any case, even with oats, but is perhaps more important with barley, wheat (and breadmeal) and maize, which have lower levels of natural fibre.

### Wheat

Wheat is not usually fed untreated as it tends to form an indigestible glutenous mass in the stomach, which can cause colic. However, it has been widely used in the past, particularly for cavalry horses, and if it is to be fed it is a good idea to feed the ration well mixed with chaff to break it up and also well damped to prevent separation of the grain from the chaff.

While wheat could be fed to horses in the form of a grain, it would need to be fed with great care and considerable expertise and is certainly not recommended for use by novices. However, processed wheat is increasingly available, both micronised and extruded, in which forms it can safely be fed, preferably with chaff. Higher in protein and energy than oats and barley, it should be introduced with care and the ration balanced appropriately.

As with all cereals, it is low in calcium and the calcium to phosphorus ratio is poor. Although when processed it is a much safer feed, it is extremely important that care is taken to maintain the fibre levels fed with it.

## Wheat products

### Wheat bran

As flour mills have become more efficient at extracting the flour, bran has diminished in feed value over the years. This is one reason why strict adherence to traditional feeding methods will not achieve the same results that it did in the past and modification of the diet is necessary on an informed basis.

Wheat bran, which is the outer husk of the wheat grain, is a source of very indigestible fibre. Unfortunately, it has a *very* poor calcium to phosphorus ration and contains particularly high levels of phytate which can lock up calcium, both in the bran and from the rest of the diet, making it a very unbalanced feed source.

For this reason, I prefer not to feed it to broodmares and youngstock and consider chaff a much better-balanced and more desirable roughage source. However, even this may not be necessary if the diet contains reasonable levels of grass/alfalfa meal/cubes and/or sugar beet.

Because of bran's highly fibrous nature, bran mashes are extremely indigestible and should not be necessary if the overall diet is balanced, contains adequate forage and chaff and is in keeping with the level of work. Bran mashes are also nutritionally very unbalanced and, unless fed at each feed, constitute an undesirable sudden change in feeding.

For sick horses or those laid off due to snow etc., increase the forage ration. If you are already feeding dried grass/alfalfa and/or sugar beet, you can make a nutritious, palatable (but revolting-looking!) mash from these. For sick horses in particular, a bran mash, rather than being an aid to recovery, is, in many cases, likely to prolong the period taken for recovery. It is rather like 'whipping the nutritional carpet out from under the horse's feet' just when the sick or tired horse most needs it. If you feel you *must* feed a bran mash, make sure that you add 50 g (2 oz) of limestone flour for each kilogram ($2\frac{1}{4}$ lb) of bran to rebalance the calcium levels. Also add a suitable vitamin/mineral supplement – *after* the mash has cooled so that the heat does not destroy the vitamins.

If horses are resting but expected to go back to work after a rest day or bad weather, give significantly reduced amounts of each of the other working-ration ingredients at each feed to keep the appropriate digestive micro-organisms and enzymes ticking over.

If, for example, you are feeding three feeds per day, the normal management of working horses on a rest day should be to cut out the total amount of one feed (but *do not* cut out any feed time entirely) and spread the remaining ingredients out over the three feed times. You can also increase the forage allowance. For a Sunday rest day, ideally you would start this at the Saturday night feed and go back to a normal feed on the Sunday night, or Monday morning if you feed early or work the horse later.

With regard to broodmares, the common practice of giving a bran mash immediately after foaling is, again, likely to cause problems in some cases as this is just the time when the broodmare is in particular need of readily available calcium in her bloodstream. A mashed feed containing her usual feed ingredients or, if she is used to them, a mixture of alfalfa meal/cubes and sugar beet, with her usual vitamin/mineral supplement, would help her to recover rapidly and ensure that the milk produced is of the best possible quality for the foal.

Horses that are fed too much wheatbran, wheat feed, wheatings, sharps or middlings without added calcium may suffer serious, mysterious multifocal lameness, epiphysitis in youngstock (big knees), bone fractures (including sore shins) and even nutritional secondary hyperparathyroidism, i.e. big head or miller's disease, giving a characteristic fibrous swelling of the progressively demineralised bones of the face which, when the growth has settled down, sounds hollow when tapped.

It is also possible that calcium deficiency, for whatever reason, will help to turn an acutely laminitic pony into a chronic sufferer, so a bran mash is the last thing you should give to a pony with laminitis. Starving laminitis-prone horses can also have a similar effect as the resulting mineral deficiencies can lead to hormonal imbalances which may prolong the laminitis. As a rule of thumb, if you must feed bran and are not giving significant amounts of calcium-rich feeds, such as dried alfalfa cubes, alfalfa hay/chaff or sugar beet feed, you will need to add 50 g (2 oz) of limestone flour per kilogram ($2\frac{1}{4}$ lb) of bran for adult horses – more for youngstock.

### Breadmeal

Breadmeal is marketed in the UK under the proprietary name of Bailey's

No. 1 Meal and Bailey's No. 4 Cubes (cubed breadmeal with added molasses for palatability and some added minerals). It is also popular, particularly in showing circles, in Australia and other parts of the world.

It is an excellent source of 'non-heating' energy. It contains more protein than other cereals and has a higher lysine content. Again, the calcium: phosphorus ratio usually needs balancing and, as it is low in fibre, it is usually a good idea to feed it with chaff, dried grass or alfalfa, NIS cubes or sugar beet feed.

It is safe to feed to children's ponies if they require additional digestible energy (DE), as it does not appear to hot them up, and is an excellent concentrated energy source for high-performance horses. There is absolutely no reason why a performance horse cannot have breadmeal as its sole cereal-energy source. Although to humans a horse which is 'jumping out of its skin' appears to have a lot of energy, in fact this is often a manifestation of nervous tension and may well mean that the horse is not concentrating on the job in hand. It will, therefore, waste valuable work-energy in messing about, running backwards at the start of a course and fighting the rider, who is also wasting energy which may become particularly crucial later when riding across country or for long periods in endurance riding. This will have a knock-on effect in that the tired rider will further tire the horse. The aim should be to supply energy and other nutrients in a form that will enable the horse to concentrate on the job in hand and utilise effectively the maximum amount of available energy from the diet for performance.

Initially, some horses are not keen on the taste of breadmeal, so molassed breadmeal pellets are also produced which can be fed to them instead. Breadmeal cubes or pellets are not a compound feed which has been balanced and should be considered as a cereal source along with oats, barley and maize. They cannot be compared in isolation with any form of horse and pony nuts, competition cubes and so on.

### *Wheatgerm*

This is a vitamin-E-rich supplement which proves rather expensive for livestock consumption.

### Maize (corn)

Maize is sometimes fed on the cob in the USA, which increases the fibre level and is, therefore, safer. The grain may also be fed whole, steam-flaked, micronised or extruded. For the worldwide horse population as a whole, it probably vies with sorghum as the most widely fed cereal.

Maize supplies more digestible energy on a weight-for-weight basis than either oats or barley and is lower in fibre, so it should be introduced very gradually and preferably fed mixed with a rich fibre source such as chaff. Many people, misunderstanding the concept of balanced rations, say that maize puts weight on. It will only do this if it is fed on a weight-for-weight basis compared with lower-energy feedstuffs such as oats or barley. If the total ration is formulated to contain the same amount of digestible energy as an oat- or barley-based diet, it will not lead to any additional weight gain. This is called an 'isoenergetic or isocaloric diet' (iso = the same) and enables us to compare like with like.

Maize is generally a poor source of lysine, although some varieties are specially bred to contain more lysine than other cereals. Again, the calcium content and calcium:phosphorus ratio are poor. Maize is, however, a very good source of concentrated (starch) energy and provides useful amounts of vitamin A.

### Sorghum (milo)

This is not widely available in the UK except as an ingredient for concentrates but is fed as an ingredient of home-mixed rations in various parts of the world and can certainly be included in the diets of performance horses. Its feeding characteristics are similar to those of maize.

## Non-cereal Concentrates

Non-cereal concentrates come from a range of plant families and may include sugar beet feed, dried grass or alfalfa (discussed under forages above), legumes and pulses (which are the dried seeds of legumes), such as soya, peas and beans. Others include by-products which are mainly found in compound feeds, including palm kernel meal, locust bean meal, cottonseed cake, groundnut cake, rapeseed (canola) meal, linseed cake and soya bean meal, most of which are the meals and cake left after various plant oils have been extracted. (Soya and linseed are often fed with the oil left in.) Other materials, such as dried apple pomace, which is quite widely used in some areas of the world and distillers' dried grains, along with linseed, vegetable oils, tallow, meat and bone meal and fish meal, milk powder, manoic (cassava or tapioca), molasses and malt syrup, are all used as concentrate feeds for horses.

In general, healthy, mature horses on reasonable quality forage do not require the higher-protein-containing concentrate feeds such as soya beans, peas, beans, linseed, meat and bone meal, fish meal or milk powder, although some of these may be useful for broodmares in late pregnancy and early lactation and for youngstock. Specific amino acid supplementation combined with a lower, crude protein diet is probably more appropriate for the horse in hard work.

Many of these concentrates are processed in some way, usually in an attempt to make them more digestible or, in the case of soya or linseed, rendering them safe to feed. They may be rolled, flaked, micronised, extruded (gelatinised) or boiled and, in future, may also be irradiated. (See also grassmeal/cubes and alfalfa [lucerne] meal cubes on page 59.)

### Molassed sugar beet feed

This is a very underutilised feed in the horse world, often only used to 'damp the feeds' when, in fact, it could be used as a significant digestible energy source. It is particularly useful for competition horses as the molasses gives an immediate release of energy while the unusually highly digestible fibre can act as a reserve, slow-release energy source.

Molassed sugar beet feed is rich in available sodium and potassium salts (it is a maritime plant and therefore salt-loving) and is an excellent source of available calcium. This makes it especially useful as a source of natural electrolytes and for horses prone to 'tying-up' (see page 233).

Apart from the physical advantages of damping down the ration, the supply of water sugar beet brings to the performance horse is important and the incorporation of a reasonable level of water into the concentrate feed in this way will help to prevent the problems of dehydration. At normal feeding levels, soaked sugar beet will not cause problems due to bulkiness.

Up to 2.5 kg (5½ lb) of sugar beet feed per day (unsoaked weight) may be fed, especially if there is a shortage of good forage, although for horses up to 500 kg (1,100 lb) in bodyweight, the usual maximum level is 1.5 kg (3 lb 5 oz) per day (unsoaked weight).

The shreds or pulp should be soaked in *twice their weight* of cold water for *twelve to eighteen hours* before feeding.

The nuts or pellets must be soaked for *24 hours* in *three times their weight* of cold water.

Do not use hot water to soak sugar beet pulp or nuts as the destruction of nutrients and even dangerous fermentation may result. The use of hot water does not speed up soaking time. Likewise, do not soak more than you can use in one day, especially in hot weather. If leaving beet to soak in freezing weather, you should attempt to prevent it from freezing, otherwise incomplete absorption of water may occur. Surrounding the bucket with slabs of straw or an old rug, or putting in a cut-to-size piece of polystyrene packing to float in the bucket may help.

Do feed any spare liquid as it will contain soluble nutrients and is very nutritious. It will also help to make the ration more palatable.

Where sugar beet is used as a significant source of digestible energy in the diet of the performance horse, it may be noted that the droppings are smaller. This is perfectly all right and is simply because the fibre is more digestible than in most other concentrates given to horses. This means that while the horse is gaining the benefit from the physical qualities of the fibre as it passes through the gut, it is also able to obtain more nutrients from the fibre during its passage and this means that there is less material left at the end to form the droppings!

As has been mentioned above, when making up a ration based on cereals it is a good idea to include some molassed sugar beet feed and/or dried alfalfa to improve protein quality and calcium levels, as well as dried grass or chaff to keep the ration open by maintaining fibre levels. The weight of chaff may be deducted from the forage amount if you are rationing accurately.

The benefits of the available potassium levels and other salts in sugar beet should not be ignored and may be particularly useful to horses who are prone to tying up and also to lactating broodmares.

### Soya beans and soya bean meal

Full-fat soya beans cannot be fed to horses in their raw form as they contain a toxin. However, with the advent of micronisation and extrusion processes, it is now possible to use full-fat soya processed in these ways and it is now included in a number of proprietary coarse mixes and compounds. Having said this, however, unless the rest of the ingredients are of very poor quality indeed, it is unlikely that mature performance horses will benefit to any great extent from the use of full-fat soya as other sources of concentrated energy, such as vegetable oils, may be used without the possible disadvantage of drastically raising the crude protein content of the overall diet. Although soya is a good source of lysine and other amino acids, as only relatively small quantities can be used (to avoid overfeeding crude protein), these do not necessarily make a significant contribution to the diet. If enough is fed to put the amino acid level right, then the crude protein content of the diet will be too high. I would, therefore, prefer to use alternative amino acid sources for mature horses.

Soya bean meal is the by-product left after most of the oil has been extracted, so it is lower in energy content than full-fat soya (although still relatively high) but very high in crude protein content.

There is quite often a case for feeding soya bean meal to broodmares and very young stock as part of a balanced ration as their crude protein requirements are somewhat higher than the resting or working mature horse. Care should be taken to ensure that the diet is balanced and this is particularly crucial for youngstock. If necessary, expert guidance should be sought from a qualified animal nutritionist as it is very easy to push a ration out of balance or to continue feeding a ration which may have been balanced for a six-month-old youngster but is completely wrong once the animal has reached nine or twelve months old.

Having said this, I prefer to use as little soya as possible on the stud, especially around conception time, as there are certain anti-nutritional factors in it which may (and this is purely informed conjecture at this stage) be one of the reasons why the fertility levels in some equine breeding stock are so poor in comparison to other domestic livestock. I therefore look for the bulk of my protein from such materials as low-oestrogen, activity-type dried alfalfa cubes and other amino acid sources and, if necessary, only top up with small amounts of soya. I should be more than happy to change this policy if it could be proved that these factors are not, in fact, causing any problems.

### Peas and beans

Peas and beans are generally fed steam-flaked or micronised. They are frequently an ingredient of coarse mixes and can be fed as 'mixed flakes' in traditional rations. They are palatable and a useful source of protein, containing about 24 per cent, and a particularly potent source of lysine.

Winter and spring varieties of field beans (*Vicia faba*) and the field pea (*Pisium arvense*) are grown in the UK and can be fed safely to horses. Beans and peas of unknown origin must be processed before feeding to horses as they can contain many toxins.

### Linseed and linseed cake (flakes)

Linseed is the seed of the flax plant. It contains fairly high levels of rather poor quality protein (i.e. it is very deficient in limiting amino acids, including lysine) but is rich in oil and mucilage. The flakes are a by-product left after much of the oil has been extracted.

As a protein source, linseed is not very desirable but the oil can enhance coat condition. However, as linseed *must* be cooked before feeding, it is far easier to obtain the protein from a better-balanced source and feed 1–4 tablespoons (25–100 ml) of corn oil or some other pure vegetable oil per day to enhance coat condition.

In fact, purified, feed-grade linseed oil may form part, or all, of this allowance. Certainly, the essential oils contained in linseed have considerable beneficial effects on the health and condition of the horse and these are very visibly demonstrated in the improvement in coat condition found in many horses, particularly those who are already deficient in essential oils, otherwise known as essential fatty acids (EFAs).

Whole linseed must *never* be fed raw as it may contain hydrogen cyanide (prussic acid), a deadly poison. However, this is destroyed by first soaking the linseed for 24 hours, then boiling it vigorously for a couple of minutes and, finally, simmering it for a couple of hours. (A great deal of time and effort for not much benefit!) The amount of 225 g (8 oz) of dry linseed requires around 2 litres (4 pt) of water.

Alternatively, it may be covered with water and cooked in a microwave oven for twenty minutes. One enterprising manufacturer is now marketing ready-cooked linseed (Glint) on the horse market, so if you are particularly keen to use linseed and can justify it economically, this is perhaps the simplest method.

After cooking, the resulting linseed jelly and linseed tea should both be fed and the tea can be further diluted to make it go further. Linseed jelly and tea will also provide essential oils but this is a rather laborious way of obtaining them.

Feeding a linseed mash (i.e. a bran mash with added, cooked linseed) once a week is a sudden change in feeding and therefore undesirable. It should be fed daily or not at all. Many people like to give their horses a 'change' but it must be remembered that horses are not humans and do not have the same priorities when it comes to feeding. The odd Polo mint, carrot or apple is one thing but major dietary changes, such as mashes, are quite another.

**Linseed flakes** or **cake** is the residue when whole linseed has had the bulk of its oil extracted. It may often be seen in coarse mixes and may be available to home-mixers as an ingredient. As it still contains a fair amount of oil, it will enhance coat condition and increase overall proteins and energy levels but amino acid supplementation will be necessary.

## Salt, Limestone, Dicalcium Phosphate and Vitamin/Mineral Supplements

Try to divide these among the daily feeds to gain the most effective use and feed at least on a daily basis. Feeding any of these supplements once or twice a week is largely a waste of money. Although the horse will still derive *some* benefit, this hardly constitutes a balanced rationing programme.

Mix all supplements and additives well into the (damped) feed to ensure even distribution – pre-mixing first with a little sugar beet pulp or similar helps. Do not add hot water to vitamins as it will destroy them.

For endurance horses only, some competitors have found that cutting out limestone for five days prior to competition is helpful. This practice is thought to encourage the horse to mobilise its own calcium resources when dietary resources would normally run out over very long distances. They recommence feeding calcium immediately after the competition. I would expect this to be worthwhile only for 120–160 km (75–100 mile) events and am not yet fully satisfied that it is a valid practice. *Do not* cut down on vitamins, minerals and salt which should all be given daily right up to (and immediately after) the competition.

I am not at all happy with the technique of cutting out limestone and would certainly not recommend it unless I was absolutely sure that the horse had a very adequate calcium status which is difficult to measure as blood calcium levels are a poor indicator. I feel it would be preferable to look at using more easily absorbable calcium sources and to check the overall trace element balance. If the non-limestone technique is to be used, it is vital that arrangements are made to stable the horse on site for a day or so after the event so that consumption can be restored. Otherwise, if long journeys are involved, transit tetany may occur.

## Other Feeds

### Succulents

Succulents such as carrots and apples are a welcome treat for stabled horses. Carrots should be cut lengthways and apples quartered. Mangolds (mangelwurzels) may also be used and are especially useful for horses with a tendency towards developing stable vices through boredom, as they can be suspended from the ceiling for the horse to play with.

### Eggs

Eggs are not really suitable as they contain a compound called avidin which locks up the vitamin biotin. If you do feed them, do not give more than three per week and, ideally, also feed the shell (crushed) for its calcium content (use only cleaned eggs for this). If you are feeding several horses, run the eggs (shells and all) through a food blender or liquidiser first.

### Hydroponics

One feedstuff which has not been mentioned is hydroponic cereals (usually barley grass). These are an extremely useful source of a succulent feed that is suitable for performance horses and may be fed (including roots) in the mats which form when it is grown or put through a chaff cutter and added to the concentrate feed. Hydroponic 'grass' is produced by germinating barley seeds in lighted trays under humid growing conditions in a specially designed unit. I would like to see future consideration given to adding micronutrients to the water in which hydroponic cereals are grown to enhance their feeding value. Hygiene in the growing units is important to ensure that there is no formation of potentially harmful moulds.

Good planning is essential to ensure a continuous, adequate, but not excessive, supply of the material. This feed is especially worth considering for horses stabled all the time or with access to only very poor pasture or 'leafing areas'. Portable units are available for horses on the competition circuit.

## Compound Feeds

These rations are manufactured by a feed compounder and are balanced to a greater or lesser extent depending on the knowledge and back-up facilities of the manufacturer and how reliable the company is. Unfortunately, horse feeds are often a long way down the list of priorities for a non-specialist manufacturer as they represent a small volume of sales in comparison to cattle feeds. If there are breakdowns in manufacture or problems with transport, these can affect quality and supply.

Compounds may be fed in the form of a coarse mix (sweetfeeds) or cubes/nuts/pellets. These are similar to the coarse mix but the ingredients are ground and formed into pellets. A new development is 'formed' feeds, made up of extruded ingredients. These are already widely available in the USA and are likely to become increasingly common in other parts of the world. Coarse mixes and sweetfeeds do not keep as well as pellets, as their ingredients are more exposed to oxidation by air. They are also more prone to separate out in the sack and should be carefully mixed to ensure that each feed contains the full range of ingredients.

People often say they do not like compound feeds because they 'can't see what is in them' but, in fact, you cannot see what is in an oat either, nutritionally speaking, and unless you are having all your feed ingredients analysed, it is far more likely that the compound feeds will be better balanced than the majority of home-mixed rations.

This is partly because even if the home-mixer has a reasonable understanding of a balanced diet, unless ingredients are being analysed they cannot compensate for variations in different batches. For example, one sack of oats may contain 6 per cent protein, while the next sack may contain 16 per cent! If both are fed at the same rate, fluctuations in performance will be inevitable although not immediately obvious. Because of their superior facilities, feed manufacturers have the ability to adjust the ingredients in the ration to compensate for variation, or even turn away batches of ingredients that do not match up to the standards required. Samples from the two different sacks of oats mentioned above may look remarkably similar and the only way to be really sure would be through a laboratory appraisal.

However, some of the ingredients, additives and processes used in modern manufacturing can give cause for concern and any responsible horse owner should attempt to be well informed and up to date on this subject. Bear in mind that if you buy on the basis of price alone, you many very well get what you pay for! Quality control and optimum nutrition are more expensive but may also be more economic than least-cost formulation for minimum nutrient levels!

## Complete Diet Cubes

Here the whole diet, forage and concentrates, is pelleted together by the compounder. In practice, diet cubes are usually fed with a little chaff (molassed or damped for COPD-affected horses) or long forage (MPF for COPD horses) to prevent boredom. They may be useful for horses in transit, for competition horses being moved around a lot and especially for COPD-affected horses. They are, however, somewhat inflexible and it may be more appropriate to use a combination of dried grass, dried alfalfa and NIS straw cubes and molassed chaff for forage or an MPF and the appropriate grade of concentrate cubes for performance horses or for feeding a COPD-affected horse.

The complete compound cubes can be extremely useful for elderly horses with missing or damaged teeth, as they can be fed soaked.

## Concentrate Cubes (Pellets) and Coarse Mixes

These compounds are generally formulated to be fed safely along with hay. Diluting them with anything other than chaff or molassed chaff, which has been subtracted from the forage allowance, will unbalance them. Examples include horse and pony, hunter, competition, stud, racehorse cubes or coarse mixes.

If they are fed diluted with oats, barley, wheat bran, sugar beet, etc., the vitamins, minerals (including calcium) and salt they contain will also be diluted. Diluting compounds is not normally good practice but the least disturbing diluter, if one is needed, is molassed sugar beet feed. Conversely, adding a few cubes to a cereal mix will not 'balance the ration' as many people seem to believe.

Always feed according to the manufacturer's instructions as different brands of the same type have different nutrient densities and should be fed at different rates. Bear this in mind when evaluating the cost of different brands. Although most brands will contain added vitamins and minerals, their levels may vary considerably – from the absolute basic which the manufacturer can reasonably get away with, up to the maximum levels believed to be required by performance horses.

Virtually all manufacturers will claim that it is not necessary to add a vitamin/mineral supplement when feeding their product. However, when feeding the high-performance horse, there is sometimes a case for feeding, if not a broad-spectrum supplement, perhaps specific vitamins and minerals for a specific purpose. Obviously, this should only be done with full knowledge of what is in the proposed supplement and what is contained in the compound and you should take expert advice first. Although the staff of some feed manufacturers may be perfectly capable of giving you this advice, be very selective about who you believe and who you do not and consider consulting an independent nutritionist who is not trying to sell you something! Some veterinary practitioners are also sufficiently knowledgeable on the subject of equine nutrition to give this sort of advice but do not assume that all are as it is not generally part of their training.

## Cereal Balancers and Protein Concentrates

These are compounds specially designed to be fed as a cereal balancer. Most contain around 26 per cent crude protein and for a mature horse 0.5 kg or 1 lb per day, with oats, is ample.

Some are recommended for use at 25 per cent of the concentrate ration but if they contain a 26 per cent crude protein content, they usually give excessive protein levels in the diet.

This type of product is very useful and it is to be hoped that an 'energy balancer' such as bloodstock conditioner, with less emphasis on the protein, will become more widely used. This type of product is usually designed to balance the energy, protein, calcium, phosphorus, vitamins, minerals and possibly salt for the whole ration. Read the manufacturer's instructions for the brand you choose, however, as some may in fact suggest inclusion of a separate vitamin/mineral supplement. In addition, extra salt may be required for horses in hard or fast work.

While such products are extremely useful for performance horses, they are also particularly useful on the stud because, when introduced at a constant level to youngstock but balanced with increasing amounts of cereals and other ingredients, most brands will ensure a reasonably balanced ration throughout the growth period, without complicated adjustments to the ration being required. Provided the entire regime is initially set up as a balanced ration and the quality of the added ingredients, such as cereals and forages, is checked on a regular basis, these products can provide a versatile and reliable means of ensuring optimum nutrition on the stud.

Given a horse-owning public who like to buy compounds but to feel they are mixing a feed as well, these balancers ought to be the most popular compounds. However, instead of using the right product for the job – one designed for this very purpose – horse owners and managers still cling to using compound cubes and then unbalancing them by diluting them. The absence of 'horse sense' in the horse industry is sometimes quite breathtaking!

### Feeding compounds

Always make any transitions from home-mixed rations to compounds, or from one brand or batch of compounds to another, gradually. Never wait until you run out before ordering a new lot.

If necessary, you can often combine types of compounds, e.g. horse and pony with racehorse, but do check their compatibility with the manufacturers first.

## Herbs and Other 'Natural' Supplements

There has been a resurgence of interest in the feeding of various herbs and spices in recent years, some of which certainly have a place in the diet of the performance horse and on the stud.

### Comfrey (Symphytum spp.)

For many years comfrey has been fed cut and wilted on Thoroughbred studs and is a very useful source of vitamins, minerals and proteins for youngstock. It is also beneficial for mature and, particularly, elderly horses. It is thought to have certain therapeutic effects when digestive and arthritic conditions occur and, from practical observations, it has certainly been my experience that this can be the case. I have seen a number of animals, who were condemned to finishing their lives on a variety of anti-inflammatory drugs and painkillers, actually coming off these drugs and resuming work when fed on combinations of comfrey and garlic and would certainly consider using these with a problem horse. However, they are certainly not a cure-all and should be used judiciously.

Questions have been raised recently about the safety of some varieties of comfrey when fed in large amounts but the research done has been most unsatisfactory and incomplete and has not been borne out in the practical feeding of horses. The work was based on rats (fed on comfrey up to 200 times their bodyweight!), plus anecdotal 'evidence' from humans who do not appear to have been using the product properly. However, if you are concerned about this, you can still obtain the benefits of comfrey by using comfrey oil and poultices externally, or by using homoeopathically potentised comfrey without the possibility of adverse side effects. I have, as yet, seen no evidence whatsoever to dissuade me from feeding comfrey to horses in my care and would point out that many of those who have suggested that there are problems have a vested interest in promoting drug use.

## Garlic (Allium sativum)

Garlic oil and whole plant garlic have also been used as an expectorant which, when fed, loosens mucus and can be most helpful after coughs and colds and for COPD-affected horses. There are a number of brands on the market and many owners have commented to me that although some brands are more expensive, they do appear to be more effective, so that using a cheap product is false economy. Cheaper products may, in fact, blend the garlic with an inert base, thus reducing the actual amount of garlic included by weight.

Garlic oil has been prescribed in the past by doctors for patients with circulatory problems because it helps to keep the blood more 'slippery'. This may well be beneficial to horses with problems involving the circulation, including laminitis and navicular disease. Again, this has not been scientifically proven but many owners are convinced that they have seen an improvement when such products have been used.

An added benefit is that feeding garlic seems to help to keep flies away! This may be particularly useful for show animals and dressage horses and also for any animal prone to sweet itch or which has an open wound of some sort. Again, I have seen this work in practice but would not necessarily expect it to work for every animal. You should obtain a good quality product with good allicin levels for maximum benefit.

Garlic may also have anti-infective properties, an aspect which is now being continuously and very promisingly researched.

## *Raspberry Leaf (Rubus idaeus)*

The only other single herb which I have used routinely is raspberry leaf, usually made into a tea and poured on to the feed or added to the drinking water (if the horse will take it). It is useful for feeding to brood-mares, especially for a first foaling, for a month or so before foaling to help to relax the pelvic-floor muscles and to facilitate an easy parturition. Many human mothers swear by this herb and stud managers have remarked that it has been beneficial for mares who are prone to difficult foaling for certain reasons. It should *not* be used in the early stages of pregnancy.

I have also found it useful for mares that are 'marish' and difficult when on heat, especially if they are touchy about the belly – but I usually give it in conjunction with added vitamins, minerals and essential oils.

Having said all this, I would be very reluctant to consider herbs in general as cure-alls and am also rather concerned that they are often presented as being particularly safe because they are natural. It should be remembered that many drugs are either derived from plants or are synthetic copies of plant materials and that some herbs contain very concentrated ingredients indeed. They should, therefore, only ever be used in an informed fashion and care should be taken when adding them to other feed ingredients with which they may well clash. Some herbal remedies contain the deadliest poisons known, so horse owners should beware a false sense of security.

Some self-styled experts in the herb-lore field, many of whom gained their experience dealing with humans, are not qualified to prescribe herbs for horses which may metabolise them in a completely different fashion. Many herbs offered for horses have a diuretic action (i.e. they make the horse urinate) and this may be very undesirable for the performance horse as it could lead to dehydration in competition and resulting problems.

However, I am fully satisfied that both comfrey and garlic can be fed in reasonably large quantities to the majority of horses, either specifically for therapeutic reasons or as part of a balanced ration. I would willingly use other herbal remedies under the guidance of a master herbalist with an understanding of equine physiology and the problems of prohibited substances. There are many other useful herbs, such as golden rod (*Solidago virgaurea*), devil's claw (*Harpagophytum procumbens*) and cleavers (*Galium aparine*) but they *must* all be used in an appropriate and informed fashion. Overuse can, in fact, reduce their effects. For herbs which may contain prohibited substances, it is best to use them homoeopathically potentised for com-petitive horses.

## *Other Natural Supplements*

Many of the above comments also apply to such materials as seaweed, wheatgerm and brewer's yeast. Whatever it may say in the manufacturer's instructions, it *is* possible to overfeed these materials and they certainly should not be fed *as well* as a full dose of a broad spectrum vitamin/mineral supplement, as overdosing will occur. I do not really see them as a viable alternative to a broad spectrum balanced supplement for the performance horse (although they may, perhaps, make a useful adjunct) as their feeding value can fluctuate considerably depending on the time of year, which is rather unsatisfactory when one is trying to obtain peak performance from a horse. However, I would certainly use them for general riding horses and on the stud as part of a balanced approach.

## **Analysis of Commonly Used Feedstuffs** (As Fed)

NB: these are average analyses and will vary from batch to batch of feed. The figures are offered as a guide only.

## Analysis of Commonly Used Feedstuffs

| | Digestible energy (DE) mJ/kg | Crude protein (CP) % | Crude fibre (CF) % | Calcium (Ca) % | Phosphorus (P) % | Ca:P Ratio | Amino acid lysine % |
|---|---|---|---|---|---|---|---|
| hay – meadow | 10.24 | 8.5 | 32.8 | 0.41 | 0.15 | 2.70:1 | – |
| hay – good | 11.00 | 10.0 | 30.0 | 0.45 | 0.20 | 2.25:1 | – |
| hay – average | 8.50 | 3.0–8.0 | 38.0 | 0.20 | 0.30 | 0.66:1 | – |
| barley straw | 7.07 | 3.7 | 48.8 | 0.24 | 0.05 | 4.80:1 | – |
| oat straw | 8.17 | 3.4 | 39.4 | 0.25 | 0.07 | 3.60:1 | – |
| Hygrass (hayage) (MPF) | 11.58 | 13.1 | 39.2 | 1.00 | 0.03 | 3.30:1 | 0.16 |
| *(Other hayages vary considerably in CP but tend to have a lower DCP value.)* | | | | | | | |
| dried grass meal/nuts | 10.66 | 14.0 | 26.0 | 0.90 | 0.03 | 3.00:1 | 0.80 |
| dried alfalfa (lucerne) meal/nuts | 9.70 | 16.0 | 24.0 | 1.40 | 0.20 | 7.00:1 | 0.64 |
| chaff (see hay/straw) | | | | | | | |
| sugar beet** | 15.43 | 10.6 | 14.4 | 0.80 | 0.08 | 10.00:1 | 0.66 |
| oats | 14.02 | 10.9 | 12.1 | 0.07 | 0.37 | 0.19:1 | – |
| barley | 15.73 | 10.8 | 5.3 | 0.05 | 0.37 | 0.14:1 | 0.48 |
| maize | 17.31 | 9.8 | 2.4 | 0.05 | 0.60 | 0.08:1 | 0.30 |
| breadmeal (Bailey's No. 1) | 14.90 | 15.0 | 1.3 | 0.24 | 0.28 | 0.86:1 | 0.30 |
| wheatbran | 12.31 | 17.0 | 11.4 | 0.12 | 1.43 | 0.08:1 | 0.68 |
| non-heating H & P cubes* | 10.10 | 10.5 | 14.0 | 0.45 | 0.20 | 2.25:1 | 0.68 |
| H & P not from a national compounder* | 10.00 | 10.5 | 16.0 | 1.40 | 0.65 | 2.15:1 | 0.25 |

* Compare these two and you will see how important it is to follow the individual manufacturer's instructions.
** *Must* be soaked before feeding. (Shreds: twelve hours/pulp: eighteen hours/nuts or pellets: 24 hours. Do not soak longer, especially in hot weather, as fermentation may occur.)

# 4    Working Out a Ration

The following is a simplified and workable method of working out nutrient requirements for horses and ponies, which is suitable for all but the most finely tuned ration and training programmes. It was adapted from the NRC method developed by Jeremy Houghton-Brown and others but has been amended and updated by the author. The more accurate formulae for working out requirements are given on page 88.

Be prepared to sit down with a simple calculator for half an hour. This could well save money and lost time due to lay-offs and poor performance later!

## Rationing in Nine Steps

### 1 How Big is the Horse or Pony?

It is bodyweight and condition in relation to frame size that are significant, rather than height.

There are various ways to estimate a horse's bodyweight.

- Weighbridge (remember to deduct the weight of tack and handler) – It is useful to establish the exact initial weight at a public weighbridge or in a purpose-built horse weigher, even if you will be using a tape thereafter. This will give you a guide as to how accurate the tape is for your individual horse, provided, of course, that you check the actual weight against the weighbridge weight at the same time. The weight of cobs is notoriously difficult to estimate (although a tape may give a useful guide to changes once you have a weighbridge base-weight. Donkeys are impossible!
- Weigh tape (e.g. Equitape) – You read an estimation of weight directly off the tape.
- Tape measure and tables – To estimate your horse or pony's

bodyweight, take the girth measurement at a quiet time, right around the barrel; the tape should lie in the girth groove and just behind the withers. Read off the measurement (or weight on a weigh tape) when the animal has finished breathing out. (Watch the flank – it is useful to stand a dark horse against a light background and vice versa.)

The following tables are offered as guidelines for use with a tape measure or even a measured piece of baler twine, although it is best to check cob-types initially on a public weighbridge to find which table applies to them. This table illustrates that a mere 1.23 cm (about $\frac{1}{2}$ in) change in girth can mean a 5–6 kg (14–15 lb) change in bodyweight! This may not be visible to the naked eye but could be indicative of an undesirable progressive weight loss or gain.

Once your horse or pony is fit, you should feed it to maintain bodyweight throughout the season. Check the weight or heart girth at least once a week, at the same time on the same day if possible.

A number of formulae are available, which involve taking measurements of body length from various points but I have found that these are not significantly more accurate for the majority of horses and are often less so. At best, all of these measurement methods are estimates not an accurate representation of weight. However, what they can do is give an indication of bodyweight *changes* and alert the horse keeper to alterations which may well not be visible to the naked eye. Cattle weight tapes and 'horse tapes' based on cattle ones are not at all accurate for horses.

## 2 How Much Forage Per Day?

As a rule of thumb, the following ratios of forage to concentrates (shown on page 88), by weight, usually apply:

*Ponies and cobs*

| Girth (in) | 40 | 42.5 | 45 | 47.5 | 50 | 52.5 | 55 | 57.5 |
|---|---|---|---|---|---|---|---|---|
| Girth (cm) | 101 | 108 | 114 | 12C | 127 | 133 | 140 | 146 |
| Bodyweight (lb) | 100 | 172 | 235 | 296 | 368 | 430 | 502 | 562 |
| Bodyweight (kg) | 45 | 77 | 104 | 132 | 164 | 192 | 234 | 252 |

*Cobs and horses*

| Girth (in) | 55 | 57.5 | 60 | 62.5 | 65 | 67.5 | 70 | 72.5 | 75 | 77.5 | 80 | 82.5 |
|---|---|---|---|---|---|---|---|---|---|---|---|---|
| Girth (cm) | 140 | 146 | 152 | 159 | 165 | 171 | 178 | 184 | 190 | 199 | 203 | 206 |
| Bodyweight (lb) | 538 | 613 | 688 | 776 | 851 | 926 | 1014 | 1090 | 1165 | 1278 | 1328 | 1369 |
| Bodyweight (kg) | 240 | 274 | 307 | 346 | 380 | 414 | 453 | 486 | 520 | 570 | 593 | 611 |

These tables are based on the work of Glushanock, Rochlitz & Skay, 1981.
50 kg = 112 lb.
There is no satisfactorily reliable method of estimating the bodyweight of donkeys.

### Mature horses in work

|  | Concentrate % | Forage % |
|---|---|---|
| Light to medium work | 25 | 75 |
| Medium work | 50 | 50 |
| Hard work | 60 | 40 |
| Hard, fast work* | 75 | 25 |

(* in exceptional circumstances only. If you *must* use this low level of long forage, you should try to feed dried alfalfa, dried grass or sugar beet with the concentrates.)

25 per cent forage by weight is the *absolute minimum* for healthy gut function. In cold weather increase concentrate levels or, better still, nutrient density, remembering that the actual process of digesting forage by fermentation helps to maintain body heat. You can, of course, also add rugs and bandages.

### Broodmares

|  | Concentrates % | Forage % |
|---|---|---|
| First three months after foaling | 55 | 45 |
| Third month to weaning | 40 | 60 |
| Weaning to 90 days before foaling | 25 | 75 |
| Last 90 days of pregnancy | Gradual rise from 25% to 55% after foaling | Gradual decrease from 75% to 45% |

*Youngstock*

|  | Youngstock destined to race in second/third year | All other youngstock |
|---|---|---|
|  | Concentrates/forage % | Concentrates/forage % |
| Creep feed (from 3 months) | 100/0 plus milk | 100/0 plus milk |
| 3-month foal | 80/20 plus milk | 75/25 plus milk |
| 6-month weanling | 70/30 | 65/35 |
| 12-month weanling | 55/45 | 45/55 |
| 18-month long yearling | 40/60 | 30/70 |
| 2 year old | 40/60 | 30/70 |

## 3 Work Out Digestible Energy (DE) Requirement for Maintenance

$$\text{This} = \frac{18\,\text{mJ} + \text{bodyweight in kg}}{10\,\text{kg}}$$

So, for our 500-kg horse this $= \dfrac{18 + 500}{10} = 68\,\text{mJ per day.}$

## 4 Work Out Digestible Energy (DE) Requirement for Production

For **work** per day, for each 50 kg of bodyweight add mJ of digestible energy (DE).

| | |
|---|---|
| Light work | + 1 e.g. one hour walking |
| | + 2 e.g. walking and trotting |
| Medium work | + 3 e.g. some cantering |
| | + 4 e.g. schooling, dressage and jumping |
| Hard work | + 5 e.g. hunting 1 day/week |
| | + 6 e.g. hunting 2 days/week |
| Fast work | + 7 e.g. three-day eventing |
| | + 8 e.g. racing |

For **lactating** per day, for each 50 kg bodyweight add:

for first three months + $4\frac{1}{2}$ mJ of DE

for next three months + $3\frac{1}{2}$ mJ of DE.

NB: all diet changes must be gradual, particularly for lactating and pregnant broodmares.

For **pregnancy** per day, add:
+ 12% for the final three months of gestation.

For **growth** per day add:
youngstock over one year – feed at maintenance ration for their expected weight at maturity
up to one year – provide 13 mJ of DE per kilogram of feed and feed to capacity.

**A working example**

We have worked out that the total daily energy requirement for our particular 500 kg horse is 128 mJ DE/day.

8.75 kg of our 9 mJ hay will supply:
$9 \times 8.75 = 78.75$ mJ DE (say, 79) from hay.

So our concentrate needs to supply 128–79 mJ DE:
128–79 mJ DE = 49 from concentrates.

We have decided to give 1 kg/day (unsoaked weight) of sugar beet, which has a DE content of 13 mJ (*as fed* but before soaking). So, after 1 kg of sugar beet, our concentrates need to supply:
49–13 = 36 mJ of DE.

Say we want to use oats and our sample has a DE of 12.5 mj (as fed):
$$\frac{36}{12.5} = 2.88 \text{ kg of oats.}$$

## 5 Adjusting the Ration

We now have a ration of:
8.75 kg of hay rounded to 9 kg
1.00 kg of sugar beet (unsoaked weight)
2.88 kg of oats rounded to 2.75 kg.

In practice, I would round this up or down to give manageable amounts, then find the percentages that these represent.
On a calculator key in the following:

$$9 \text{ kg hay} = \frac{9}{12.75}$$

$$1 \text{ kg sugar beet} = \frac{1}{12.75}$$

$$2.75 \text{ kg oats} = \frac{2.75}{12.75}$$

**Answer**

| | | |
|---|---|---|
| (total hay) % | = | 70.6% of total ration |
| (total sugar beet) % | = | 7.8% of total ration |
| (total oats) % | = | 21.6% of total ration |
| Total | = | 100.0% |

supplying 128 mJ DE/day.

(If your calculator has a memory, you only need to key in 12.75 once, then press:

weight of hay (e.g. 9) + memory % =

On many calculators you will not need to press the '=' key.)

## 6 Check the Protein Level

Find the protein level of your feedstuffs by laboratory analysis or from tables, and make the following calculation:

crude protein % of feedstuff × weight of feedstuff = protein contribution of that feedstuff to the ration.

For example, say our hay is 8% crude protein, sugar beet 11% and oats 10.9%.

On the calculator:

| | | | |
|---|---|---|---|
| Hay | 8 × 70.6% | = | 5.6 CP |
| Sugar beet | 11 × 7.8% | = | 0.86 CP |
| Oats | 10.9 × 21.6% | = | 2.35 CP |
| Total CP in diet | | = | 8.8% |

which is reasonably near our target of 8.5%

## 7 Check Other Nutrients

In the same way, you should at least *check* the calcium, phosphorus and lysine levels and as many other nutrients as you have time for or are concerned about. I cheat a little and use a computer to assess all the known nutrient requirements of each individual horse (including all the vitamins, minerals and several amino acids). By hand this would take an inordinately long time. Of course, if you do not want to get bogged down, you could always feed hay and cubes as guidelines as their ration levels will have been worked out for you already by the feed compounder.

## 8 Check the Need for Supplements

Do not forget salt and consider the need for a vitamin/mineral supplement.

A sample table of nutrient levels in various feedstuffs is on page 84.

It is preferable to have your main inputs, i.e. forage and, say, oats, analysed for their actual feed values as they can vary enormously. I have asked 'experts' to pick out samples of good horse hay and the analysis has ranged from 3 to 15 per cent crude protein! Oats can vary by nearly as much.

## 9 Monitor Your Programme Through the Season and Adjust as Required

Monitor the horse's bodyweight and performance and amend the feeding accordingly. If the horse is overweight, work out the ration requirements for 5–10 kg (11–22 lb) maximum less than actual weight. When the horse has lost that amount, recalculate the ration. Excessively rapid weight loss is not good for the horse and 'starvation' slimming can precipitate hyperlipaemia (see page 221), chronic laminitis and protein, vitamin and mineral deficiencies. (The requirements for vitamins and minerals for maintenance remain virtually the same so when you cut down digestible energy to achieve weight loss, make sure you are not underfeeding the other nutrients. Sudden weight loss can also cause hormonal disturbances, e.g. resulting in a tendency to put on weight even more easily (human slimmers should be encouraged to avoid 'crash' diets for this very reason). Chronic laminitis can be caused by endocrine (hormone) disruption.

Keep weight loss steady and slow and do not waste a winter slimming campaign by letting the horse put it all back on when it is turned out in the summer!

# Part 2
# Practical Considerations

# Introduction

While pretty well all equines will *survive* on the same type of feedstuffs, if we are to obtain optimum health and performance, whether it be for a child's pony or an Olympic three-day eventer, it is important that we try to establish a suitable feeding regime containing suitable feedstuffs. These must be selected with the particular requirements of the individual horse and its intended activities in mind, not forgetting the abilities of its rider or handler.

The *raison d'être* of the domestic horse is that it should provide its owners, riders, handlers and, where appropriate, spectators, with pleasure. Any horse whose health, temperament and trainability are constantly being compromised because of poor or inappropriate feeding and nutrition can be a constant headache rather than a pleasure to own and handle. The welfare of the horse can be seriously compromised by inappropriate nutrition, which is not simply inadequate or excessive feeding, and the safety of both horse and rider will become an issue if the horse is overexcitable or fatigued, stumbling and therefore accident-prone, due to inappropriate nutrition.

In addition to this, any horse which becomes ill or has an accident due to inappropriate nutrition, or whose convalescence after an unrelated illness is delayed due to wrong feeding, will inevitably cost the owner considerable time and effort, quite apart from the poor quality of life of the horse itself.

# 5   Feeding Leisure Horses, Cobs and Ponies

The specific requirements of the leisure horse are that its feed should maintain it in a healthy condition and it should be safe for, and capable of, the work that is required of it. The feed programme should suit the capabilities and schedule of the person doing the feeding and should be economic. As with any food, if it is not also palatable to, and digestible by, the specific horse in question, it is of no value whatsoever.

The conditions in which leisure horses and ponies might be kept may range from a patch of weeds next to the motorway (with all the resultant nutritional deficiencies and high loads of toxins from vehicle exhausts, which require extra nutrients to detoxify them) to being turned out on lush pasture with dairy cows and all the variations in between, along with a part-stabled arrangement or full-time stabling.

From a health viewpoint, most equines used for leisure could be kept out, although it is accepted that suitable grazing is not always available in all areas and for working horse owners, who may have to do a considerable amount of their horse-care activities in the dark in winter, a cleaner, stabled animal may be easier to manage provided it can be exercised daily. An ideal arrangement for these animals is to be kept part out and part corralled in a sort of enlarged bull pen where they have the freedom to wander and stretch their legs in the open air on a prepared surface. However, this is only likely to be possible for someone who owns their own property. If you do, I would very strongly recommend that you consider this system for both leisure horses and competition horses.

Twenty-four hour per day confinement, with perhaps a half-hour ride on weekdays in the winter and maybe two hours a day at the weekends, is an extremely abnormal method of keeping horses. Owners should not be surprised if they encounter repeated physical and mental problems which can prove extremely expensive and time-consuming for the owner and unpleasant for the horse. If this is the best life you can offer a horse or pony, you must seriously consider whether you have the facilities to keep one.

Dual-ownership is sometimes an answer to this if you can combine with somebody who is available at different times of the day or even different times of the year, e.g. a teacher who is available in the summer holidays sharing with a parent during term time.

Whatever your arrangements, the horse's physical and mental welfare must be your priority, followed by your own satisfaction and pleasure as a horse owner. If you do not have the facilities to satisfy these criteria, please consider whether you should keep a horse right now.

## Horses and Ponies Kept at Grass

For the grass-kept horse or pony, the type and amount of supplementary feeding required will depend largely on the quality of grazing available. A bare, weed-infested, all-too-typical horse paddock may provide just about enough digestible energy, inadequate essential amino acids, and a definite deficiency in minerals and vitamins (very possibly made worse by an additional load of toxins from ingesting poisonous weeds and vehicle exhaust or industrial fumes). Both fumes and weeds may very considerably increase the horse or pony's micro-nutrient requirement in order to detoxify such materials. However, it is a sad fact that the type of owner who accepts this kind of environment for their horse or pony is not usually the sort of person who will bother to try to redress the balance.

Most fields of this type tend to be rented or grass liveries, rather than owner-occupied, and this further complicates the situation as there may be other pony owners involved and the actual pasture management by the grazing owners may range from zero upwards. I would urge all owners of equines kept at grass liveries to try to persuade the pasture owner to institute specific rules with regard to parasite control of the horses kept on the land, especially new arrivals, and to *enforce* these rules. If the paddock owner will not bother with any other pasture management, try to get together with the other horse owners to form teams to remove poisonous weeds such as ragwort, bracken and mare's tail, check fencing and boundaries for any poisonous, overhanging trees and, if possible, collect droppings, although I am aware that this may be asking too much. The biggest problem is that there is usually somebody who will not get involved so that the other owners soon resent doing all the work and eventually go on strike. The ones who really suffer, of course, are the horses and ponies.

Bearing all this in mind, the one thing you can have control over is what additional feed your horse or pony receives. In this type of grazing, I would particularly suggest that, even if your horse is doing no work at all, you should endeavour to keep up the level of minerals, which will help it to withstand the other stresses imposed by this type of management. You can do this by giving a small feed, even a scoop of sugar beet used as a carrier for a full dose of minerals. A few pony cubes will not supply the full daily dose of vitamins and minerals required. The other alternative is to use a vitamin/mineral biscuit-type supplement which can be fed alone or even used when catching up the horse or pony. You should also ensure that the pony is obtaining adequate salt, whether from salt licks in the field (there should be several in each paddock) or in supplementary feeding.

A horse or pony which is being worked off a horse-sick pasture will, almost certainly, require some sort of supplementary feeding based on the amount of work it is doing and accepting that it may be obtaining very little useful nutrition from the pasture. I would again encourage you to be generous with supplementation. If you are feeding compounds, you should consider whether you need to add additional supplementation for this type of pony. Consult the manufacturer to ensure that any products you use will be compatible. Be suspicious about nutrient status if the pony is sluggish or irritable, or tends to stumble a lot, even if the coat looks good and the bodyweight is acceptable.

Horses and ponies on well-managed pasture that is free of toxic weeds, not influenced by environmental toxins, is regularly topped, has its lime status routinely checked and attended to when necessary, and is prefer-ably fertilised with organic or Conservation Grade fertilisers (which, while avoiding the sudden flush of growth that is obtained with inorganic fertilisers, provides good levels of minerals to replace those removed from the pasture), may well be worked quite hard with very little supplementary feeding. Even the most intensively worked horses, i.e. endurance horses, compete at quite high levels of competition while kept at grass, although, of course, they do receive considerable supplementary feeding (see page 143).

Where possible, salt licks should be provided at all times and it may also be useful to give some sort of mineral supplement, especially if there is a known specific mineral deficiency, such as of selenium, in your area.

(You can obtain such information from your local Ministry of Agriculture office or even local agricultural merchants.) Where large areas are affected, it is quite often possible to obtain salt licks which have been mineralised, e.g. with additional copper or selenium, and it is always a good idea to choose a salt lick containing iodine. However, you should note whether or not your horse or pony uses the salt lick as not all animals will use them adequately.

When there is a flush of spring grass, it is a good idea both to restrict grazing and to give additional oat straw or hay to keep up the fibre levels in the diet and to prevent scouring.

On the other hand, at the height of summer, when the grass may be fairly bare, it can be useful to feed supplementary dried grass cubes. Alternatively, if you are worried about the high levels of nitrates used when the grass is grown for dehydration, you can feed alfalfa (lucerne) cubes which are relatively hard and can be fed on the ground except in the wettest weather and which will provide a very good complement to pasture.

If you are working the horse or pony, it is not a lot of use just feeding it on a Friday night ready for a weekend's work. If this is the only way you can organise matters, you should use something like dried alfalfa (lucerne) or grass cubes. Having been on pasture, the horse should be able to cope with this rather better than a sudden feed of cereals or nuts which its digestive tract and the digestive micro-organisms it contains will not be prepared for and will not, therefore, be able to utilise very efficiently. Alternatively, in order to keep the gut in a state of readiness, you could feed a very small amount of 'weekend feed' daily and increase this on the Thursday or Friday. You might find the easiest method is to use a compound cube or coarse mix which contains grass meal or nuts, or alfalfa meal or nuts. Again, it is particularly important that mineral levels are maintained.

It is not really reasonable to leave the horse or pony with no specific exercise during the week and then gallop around for four hours a day with friends or at gymkhanas and shows at the weekend. If you want to work the pony hard at the weekend, you must give it reasonable levels of exercise, above and beyond being free to roam in its field, to maintain muscle tone and bone density during the week. It is hardly fair to impose an exercise regime on a horse or pony that leaves it feeling stiff and sore every Monday morning!

It should also be remembered that, while being at pasture is ideal for the pony's digestive tract as it has evolved as a trickle feeder, if you are going to give supplementary feeds it is most important that these are small and frequent, as a bucketful of pony nuts on a Friday night will come as something of a shock to the system.

As winter approaches, you should bear in mind that while there may be quite a lot of grass about in the autumn, it may be of very poor nutritional value and can be quite sappy. It is often a good idea to feed some long fibre and you should certainly look carefully at the mineral intake. Again, if the horse is working, supplementary feeding may be required.

As winter progresses, native ponies may be fine in all but the very worst weather without any additional feed at all (including hay) but this will be very dependent upon the quality of your grazing. You should still bear in mind the provision of minerals, and good quality oat straw can be quite useful as the digestion of fibre produces quite a lot of heat and can help to keep the pony warm. However, you should beware of allowing the horse to develop a 'hay belly' which is the result of feeding too much poor quality forage. The caecum becomes increasingly distended as the forage stays in the gut for longer and longer periods while the horse's system vainly attempts to extract some reasonable nourishment from it. A horse with a hay belly is not fat, it is usually desperately malnourished. It is also probably rather uncomfortable and will certainly not welcome doing any work on this kind of diet.

An extremely useful means of providing micro-nutrients to horses and ponies at grass who are resting or are in light work, is the use of feed blocks or range blocks (USA), which can be distributed about the field for the ponies to lick and nibble. They should be suspended or placed in containers which prevent the horses from taking bites out of them. If you find that they are disappearing at a more rapid rate than the manufacturer's suggested intake, you should consider whether additional supplementary feeding may be required.

These blocks are particularly useful for 'pocket-money ponies' because where a child might eke out a sack of pony nuts because their father complains about the feed bills (thereby significantly underfeeding micro-nutrients), blocks do not have to be purchased as frequently and, in some cases, the pony is more likely to get what it actually needs. Again, however, if the ponies are using them too quickly, it is probable that they need some sort of additional supplementary feeding.

Native ponies have evolved to live on poor quality grazing where, in normal circumstances, they would have the ability to range widely, find natural salt licks and nibble an enormous range of herbs of their own choice, which would provide them with a rich source of minerals and some vitamins. However, when we bring them into lowland situations on restricted areas of grazing they are likely to run into problems. They may have a paddock which looks a lot like a piece of moorland but the degree of choice available to the pony has been restricted and it is not able to pick out the nutrients it requires so we have a responsibility to supplement them.

The other side of this problem is that we may, instead, be putting them on land that is far richer than the type of land on which they have evolved. Even if it has come from a lowland stud, genetically, the domesticated horse or pony will still take thousands of years to evolve in order to be able to cope with lush grazing.

This subject is dealt with in considerably more detail on page 224 under laminitis – the most common result of these changes – so I will only say here that the most commonly imposed management technique for ponies on lush grass is to restrict their grazing. It is vital to remember, however, that if you restrict grazing to reduce carbohydrate intake, you are also reducing mineral intake and you must take the responsibility for supplying this in another form. Otherwise, the whole situation becomes a vicious circle because mineral deficiencies can further unbalance the endocrine (hormonal) system of the pony, rendering it more prone to obesity, problems with the thyroid gland and other increasingly severe metabolic disorders. The use of starvation paddocks is not a management tool, it is a mismanagement tool. I call them 'Winnie' paddocks as the ponies often whinny for food and their owners (and, unfortunately, often their vets) seem to be close relatives of Winnie-the-Pooh, 'a bear of very little brain'! Such ponies do not need starvation; they merely need to have their grazing on lush grass restricted.

If horses and ponies are plagued by flies in summer, they may do less grazing while they spend time stamping, swishing and even galloping about. In a bad year this can significantly affect both their digestible energy requirements and, because of loss of grazing time, the amount of energy they obtain from their pasture. In this case you will either have to adjust your feeding or bring them in during the day. Elderly horses and those pastured without a fly-swatting companion are especially vulnerable. Feeding garlic can help to discourage flies and this is especially useful if the horse is kept out while recovering from a minor wound or suffers from sweet itch.

The mineral nutrition of ponies which are prone to sweet itch is also particularly important, especially their intake of zinc. Even if a lack of minerals is not a causative factor, the problem calls for a higher than normal mineral, sulphur amino acid and essential fatty acid intake in order to bring about good quality tissue repair and hair growth.

Paddocks should always be provided with an area where horses and ponies can shelter from strong sunlight, whether this is a group of trees or a specially constructed field shelter. Many owners have noted that their equines will use field shelters more readily in the summer than in even the worst winter weather.

Ready access to good quality water supplies is also vital and, if you are providing water in buckets, it should be borne in mind that the expected intake would be an absolute minimum of 36.5 litres (8 gal) per day, even for ponies. Just because your pony never drinks that much, do not *ever* assume that it is not going to need to. At least this much fresh water should be provided daily.

In winter it should be remembered that horses and ponies with a decent coat and/or rug will not be too bothered by even the coldest weather. What causes them real problems is wet and windy weather. However, if the grass is frosty or covered in snow, then supplementary feeding, whether just hay and feed blocks or hay and concentrate feeds, will obviously become essential.

It is also vital that the ice on water troughs is broken at least twice a day. Dehydration is a common cause of colic in grass-kept equines in icy weather. Again, some form of shelter, including big stout hedges to shield the horses against the prevailing wind, is essential and may significantly affect your horse or pony's feed requirements.

By the middle of winter, the pony may well have used up all its fat-soluble vitamin reserves and, even if it is not doing any work, it may be useful to provide some form of vitamin supplementation. If you are sure that it is already receiving adequate minerals, you could introduce cod liver oil at the recommended feed rate until the spring grass returns.

However, if you are feeding compounds at the recommended rate and not diluting them with other feed, or use a proprietary cereal balancer combined with cereals (again at the recommended rate) and if you use a reputable brand, a horse or pony that is resting or in light work should be receiving more than adequate levels of these nutrients. After all, they tend to be cheaper ingredients so most manufacturers will readily incorporate in adequate quantities! Again, you should not forget about the salt which, even when compounds are adequately supplemented, provides useful 'insurance' measure.

## The Part-in, Part-out Horse or Pony

The most convenient method for many owners/riders is to keep the horse or pony part-in and part-out and the ideal system, from the horse's point of view, is to be in during the daytime in summer and at night in the winter.

It is important, especially with laminitis-prone ponies, that ponies and horses are not left standing in for twelve hours with nothing to eat because their gut has evolved as a trickle feeder. If the pasture is very lush, you can leave them in with good-quality, clean oat straw or stemmy hay (as these are relatively low in nutrient value) and a salt lick, even if you are giving no other supplementary feeding. It is a good idea to put the forage in small-mesh haynets so that it is eaten slowly.

If the horse or pony is in light work, you may supplement this diet with grass nuts or alfalfa (lucerne) nuts or a mixed chaff, such as Dengie Hi Fi, and perhaps a little compound feed. You may also wish to provide some succulents such as mangolds (mangelwurzels) or peeled carrots (sliced length-ways). A working diet may be formulated based on the information on rationing given on pages 85–93, making allowances for the quality of the grazing.

Unfortunately, the actual digestible energy obtained from grazing is virtually impossible to quantify but if you consider this to be the forage portion of the diet and take into account how much forage you are feeding in the stable, you should, over a period of time (particularly if you monitor the horse's bodyweight on a weekly basis with a weight tape), gradually be able to obtain some estimate of how much DE the grass is supplying, but do remember that the grass will vary as the season progresses. If you work out the horse or pony's full requirements and then note how much hard feed you are actually giving in order to maintain bodyweight and performance, and then deduct the one from the other, you may obtain a rough guide to the feeding value obtained from the pasture. It is interesting to note how this alters over the year.

Again, when there is a spring flush of grass, it is a good idea to feed additional long fibre in the field to reduce the likelihood of scouring as this new grass is effectively treated by the digestive micro-organisms as a 'new' feed and it takes them some time to get used to it.

## The Stabled Leisure Horse

First ask yourself if the horse really does have to be stabled all the time. If it is at livery, can you move it? Being permanently stabled is a grim existence for a creature which has evolved to roam freely on the plains and steppes (even if it is now a 'created' breed like the Thoroughbred). Unfortunately, evolution has barely even begun to catch up with people's management of the horse's body systems.

If you keep the horse in all the time, no matter how well you look after it you are likely to encounter various physical and mental problems. Even when I am told 'it doesn't bother him', I would say that *this* in itself is probably a mental problem. It is the mark of a horse which has given up being a horse and resigned itself to being some sort of automaton. Of course, you may be quite happy about that because the horse is 'easy to manage' but to an outsider it makes a very sad picture.

However, if this is the system that you and your horse are stuck with even after you have tried your best to find some way to keep it part-in/part-out, you should at least endeavour to turn it out somewhere for an hour or so a day, even if this is in an indoor school or, better still, an outdoor manège.

Even more than your fellow owners with outdoor horses, you are now fully responsible for every single nutrient that your horse obtains and also for the physical attributes of its diet – the fibre content and the amount of succulents it receives. You may have to take its temperament into account if it responds to this system of management by constantly 'jumping out of its skin'. You will need to be especially careful to feed non-heating feeds and feeds which satisfy the horse's natural craving for bulk. Otherwise you are likely to have a creature which is climbing the walls and eating its rugs and any passing people or parts of the stable that it can get hold of.

While possibly subject to a genetic predisposition, most stable vices will be triggered by boredom, watching other horses (particularly weaving and windsucking) and a craving for fibre. If you do not want these vices to develop, you should consider very carefully how you are going to satisfy your horse's requirements.

If vices have already developed, then you may have a major problem on your hands in trying to break them. Weaving bars and cribbing straps are likely to add to the horse's frustration and are no real answer. You can discuss with your vet the possible use of naloxone to block the endorphin release which repetitive aberrant behaviour stimulates (such as weaving). These endorphins, which are related to morphine, are addictive which is why it can be so difficult to break these vices even when the horse is given a more interesting lifestyle. You may have the additional problem that windsuckers which grasp a stable door, or any other projection, may have severely impaired digestion because they take great gulps of air into the digestive tract. Furthermore, both windsuckers and crib-biters (effectively 'trainee windsuckers') may sustain considerable damage to their teeth so that it may become necessary to feed only soaked feeds and mashes.

The provision of stable toys and hanging up mangolds (mangelwurzels) for the horse to play with and nibble at can be useful, and forage fed through a small-mesh net can slow down consumption and keep the horse busy, although I would imagine also somewhat frustrated, for longer periods. This is especially vital if you have to feed moist, packed forages (MPFs) because your unnaturally kept horse has also developed respiratory problems!

A fresh, clean water supply must be available at all times but it should be remembered that water absorbs ammonia released from urine in the stable and can become 'flat' and unpalatable, so just topping-up buckets is not sufficient. Automatic waterers should, if possible, be of the metered variety so that you can keep an eye on the horse's water intake, as a drop in intake or excessive thirst can be early warning signs of developing illness. It is, of course, important to ensure that the pipes do not become frozen in the winter. All water receptacles should be kept scrupulously clean and be scrubbed regularly. If it becomes necessary to use a disinfectant of some sort, use dairy hypochlorite and rinse the receptacle thoroughly afterwards.

Ensure that stable ventilation, especially for horses which are kept in all the time, is excellent and, if necessary, install fans in the roof ridges to improve it. You can check ventilation by using smoke bombs but take advice from your local Ministry of Agriculture buildings consultant and do not even *think* about closing the top door of the stable! Re-breathing warm, moist air in a stable full of straw dust and moulds is a perfect recipe for developing respiratory problems. It is also a pretty good method of mental torture for the horse is an animal which did *not* evolve as a cave dweller or a creator of burrows, nor did it in any way show any inclination to live indoors in the wild, unlike other domesticated animals such as the dog or cat!

If the stable needs wood treatment or painting, use non-toxic materials such as Livos or Ecos and keep the animal elsewhere for a few days, or even weeks if toxic creosote or other treatments are used.

Feeding should be based on the information given on page 87, with considerable emphasis placed on it being dust-free and on its potential amusement value and provision of succulents throughout the year, whether these are root vegetables, fresh cut grass, hydroponic cereals or slightly wilted comfrey. In the past, horses on the 'British standard diet' of oats, wheatbran and grass hay were frequently deficient in a number of vitamins, particularly those most usually associated with fresh green feed material, such as folic acid (deficiency of which can lead to chronic anaemia) and minerals such as calcium.

Even in light work, because of their unnatural management conditions I feel that the majority of stabled horses will benefit from good quality supplementation, whether this is part of a compound feed, a cereal balancer or specifically added as a proprietary supplement and/or herbal blend to home-mixed rations.

Most stabled leisure horses can be kept quite happily on good quality forage with a little supplemental alfalfa (lucerne) cubes, sugar beet, a salt lick and a good quality source of vitamins, minerals and amino acids. If they need additional digestible energy and do not hot up on oats, then you can use whole oats or rolled barley. Alternatively, you can use a good quality high-fibre compound, although these are, of course, less flexible than home-mixed rations, particularly if you intend to do more work at the weekend. Simply cutting down the amount you feed will also cut down any supplements which the compound contains. Diluting compounds with cereals or any other feedstuffs simply unbalances them, so if you want to mix your own feeds and also use a compound to 'balance the ration', choose a properly formulated cereal balancer or use the compound in the way that was intended when it was formulated by the manufacturer (i.e. usually with hay alone). Home-mixed rations for horses in light work will probably require the addition of 25–75 g (1–2 oz) of salt per day plus a trace mineralised salt lick which should be available at all times in the stable.

Keep feeding receptacles clean. If you have a horse that worries and dashes backwards and forwards from the manger to the door when it is eating, buy a hook-over-door feeder so that it can see what is going on while it eats. If you have a finicky feeder and have tried altering the feed to tempt its appetite, you could consider removing a brick or cutting a hole through to the next stable so that it can see and hear an adjacent horse eating. Make your hole 'patchable' in case of infectious diseases later on in the yard!

Bear in mind that a horse that is not kept out, or that is ridden in the dark in winter or wearing an exercise sheet, does not receive adequate sunlight on its back to convert vitamin D in the skin and, unlike grass-kept animals, may require year-round supplementation.

Try to ride, at least lead-out or, at worst, use a (preferably free-style) horse walker at least twice a day. If you can take the horse outside to groom it, which will at least give some sort of change of scene, all the better. This is especially important if the horse suffers from COPD when it should be taken out of the stable while it is being mucked out and moulds are being disturbed, and groomed outside with its head upwind (unless badly affected by pollens and moulds in the 'hay fever' season). Any horse will benefit from this type of management and it will help to reduce the likelihood of respiratory problems developing.

Many people still seem to believe that stabled horses do not get worms but it is worth bearing in mind that encysted parasites can be carried on hay and that a significant worm burden can be picked up by a horse grabbing the odd snatch of fresh grass in fields, verges and at show grounds where other horses have dunged.

All too often one sees leisure horses and ponies, and their owners and riders, having a grimly rotten time because of inappropriate feeding. I see children's ponies which are forever suffering with laminitis, are constantly inattentive or naughty because they cannot cope with oats or are sluggish and stumbling because they are so full of toxins or short of minerals and other micro-nutrients that they cannot co-ordinate. I see cobs which are obese due to the overfeeding of digestible energy and a serious lack of minerals, and horses which are bad tempered in the stable and either sluggish and inattentive or overexcitable and inattentive outside. Either way they are no pleasure to own. Leisure horse owning, riding and driving is *supposed* to be fun!

It is so sad to see somebody, who has for years aspired to owning their own horse, desperately trying to make the best of a bad job when, often, a simple change of feeding could make their leisure a pleasure. Unfortunately, so many animals or horse owners are at the mercy of every 'expert' who comes along (i.e. anybody in a pair of jodhpurs, most probably leaning on a field gate or stable door) and are taken in by the overzealous blandishments of a feed rep or confused by the frank lack of interest in the subject maintained by all too many vets. A day at a small country show or a visit to a livery yard can be a depressing spectacle indeed.

So, if you find yourself in difficulties with the feeding of a stabled leisure horse, close your ears to all the 'experts' if they are confusing you. Start with a clean sheet. Sit down and work out your horse's actual requirements and remember, when you are choosing your feedstuffs, the importance of fibre and satisfaction, the entertainment value of feeds and feeding practices, the possibility that some problems may have arisen because your horse may be allergic or intolerant to certain feeds, or that certain health problems may impose specific requirements (see below). Look very carefully at the micro-nutrient content of your feedstuffs and find out your horse's actual bodyweight (on a weigh bridge if possible) and monitor it weekly with a bodyweight tape. Bearing in mind this unnatural management situation, whatever you do, remember that wherever you can emulate natural conditions you will have a better chance of keeping your horse fit, healthy and happy and you should be happier too!

# 6 Feeding Professional Working Horses

The heading of 'professional working horse' is given here to include animals used in riding schools, by the police and military, as well as draught, farm and forestry horses. (See the section on competition carriage driving [page 151] for notes on the essential differences imposed by driven rather than ridden work.)

Where horses are kept for professional purposes and are expected to earn their living, while consideration must be given to their particular requirements if competing or if they have specific, health-related problems, the overriding considerations (especially when larger numbers of horses and increasingly small numbers of staff are concerned), are the economy of the rations chosen and the convenience related to their mixing and feeding. One of the most often neglected aspects of feeding this group of horses is making sure that the diet received is suitable for the work the animals are intended to perform. They are expected to work for prolonged periods without lay-offs due to feed-related injuries or ill-health, and must be fed to ensure reduced convalescence times after illness. The general standard of the diet must be set with a view to maintaining health and performance.

While the private owner, whose horse may work hard at the weekends but rest during the week, may get away with feeding their horse a mildly deficient diet for prolonged periods, a working horse whose diet is chronically deficient is likely to have a significantly shortened useful lifespan, may become increasingly bad tempered or inattentive and dull, may be prone to unnecessary accidents due to stumbling and lack of co-ordination and will generally not be a sound business proposition. It is a very sad truth that by saving only a few pence a day you can lose a significant degree of the usefulness of the horse and possibly, ultimately, lose the horse for all practical purposes. It is worth bearing in mind that the most economical feed is not necessarily the cheapest by weight.

If you grow your own hay and it is not very good, then it may be better to sell it or do a swap with somebody who may need poor nutritional quality hay for some reason. If this does prove necessary, you should also take a good hard look at the management of your hay pastures. If you are stuck with poor hay, you must take this into account when formulating the concentrate rations for your horses and ponies. It is certainly well worth a professional yard having its hay, and any cereal that provides a major component of the diet, analysed.

It is also worth bearing in mind that forages and cereals grown on the same type of land as that on which the horses graze will tend to suffer from the same mineral deficiencies and unless you have a very expensive and detailed analysis done, you will not have this information in front of you. A hay swap with a similar establishment in a different district (with a financial adjustment based on analysis) is not a bad idea. Managing your hay pastures and any horse-grown cereals as well as possible, using organic or Conservation Grade fertilisers which provide good mineral nutrition, will also help to even the score if you are going to use your own produce.

If you can sit down for between half an hour and two hours with a piece of paper, a calculator and some basic information and formulate a ration which saves you just 10 pence a day per head for a yard of 20 horses, you will have shaved a visible £732.00 per year off your feed bill and, quite possibly, an unquantifiable, considerably larger amount on vet bills and loss of income on just one of those horses. If, in the course of your calculations, it becomes possible to identify specific shortfalls in your horses' diet, then you might very well spend that 10 pence, and more, on supplementation or on instituting other adjustments which may add to the performance, longevity and economy of your yard as a whole.

The professional yard needs to keep its diets as simple and manageable as possible. They must be fairly idiot-proof, especially if large and varying numbers of personnel are involved but, at the same time, they must be reasonably flexible to accommodate the individual traits and requirements of different horses in the yard. Larger yards, which undertake to teach students, may also wish to use different types of ration programme as part of their student training. Provided this is carefully targeted, it could well repay the time and trouble involved as it facilitates more individual feeding of those horses which require it.

While compound cubes and coarse mixes may be very useful when set against increased labour costs and are possibly better balanced rations than home-mixed feeds (although this is by no means always the case), it has to be remembered that they are formulated for the *average* type of horse in each category. When you are feeding a large group of horses there will always be those which are inclined to be under- or overweight on these rations, or under- or overenergetic. Because of the differing requirements for nutrient density of individual horses, simply adjusting the weight of compound fed will not always solve problems because a reduction in total compounds will also reduce the levels of vitamins, minerals and other nutrients given, while an increase in the total amount will, of course, increase all the nutrients.

Unfortunately, most people still fail to appreciate that the majority of compounds are formulated for use with hay or hay and chaff alone and continue to dilute them with their own ingredients, or, alternatively, use diets based mostly on their own ingredients but add a few nuts or a couple of handfuls of coarse mix to 'balance the ration'. What they are actually doing is unbalancing both the compound and the straight ingredients they are feeding, rather as if you tried to repair a Ford tractor with Massey Ferguson parts. Both the Ford and the Massey Ferguson may work perfectly well on their own but when you try to combine them, if they work at all they are unlikely to work at their maximum level of efficiency!

Mixing your own feeds may be time consuming but it does allow for some flexibility within a range of ingredients as you will be able to vary their proportions. A riding school with one of the healthiest diets of this type I have encountered, with possibly the lowest vet bills, uses a combination of rolled barley, soaked sugar beet, dried alfalfa cubes, chaff and hay, varying the proportions as necessary and adding a basic but well-balanced vitamin/mineral supplement to the diets of harder working and fully stabled horses. All horse and ponies have access to salt licks in both field and stable and additional salt is given to any horses in hard work. Quite apart from anything else, the use of the vitamin/mineral supplement is likely to offset any long-term individual nutrient deficiencies which may be incurred through the unvarying diet and as the horses are all stabled at least partially if not full time, it will ensure that the nutrient deficiencies inherent in this form of management do not become a problem.

For those who wish to use a compound feed but also to add their own ingredients, by far the most suitable method is to choose a proprietary cereal balancer which is designed to be diluted with your own oats, or possibly barley, and fed with hay and perhaps some chaff. This enables you to adjust the amount of cereals fed and to provide the necessary balancer to achieve the desired results. Considering people's penchant for messing about by adding things to compounds, I am always surprised that these products, which are specifically designed for the purpose, have never really caught on. Excellent results can be obtained from good products of this type and I think it is in the interest of both horses and horse managers that they become more widely used in the future.

Where full-time stabling is necessary, the old adage about feeding something succulent daily should be remembered and the use of hydroponic cereals may be the most convenient method for large numbers of horses.

There can be a tremendous build up of dust, moulds and ammonia in larger yards, so special attention should be paid to ventilation and using low-dust bedding and forage.

Lastly, please feed according to the amount and type of work done. The potential antics of ceremonial cavalry horses fed a proprietary racehorse mix may be hilarious to onlookers but this is dangerous for the riders, by-standers and the reputation of the cavalry concerned. Such rank stupidity *has* happened. If you stop and think, it need not happen in your yard.

# 7   Special Considerations when Feeding Competition Horses

Broadly speaking, the competitive horse should be fed just like any other horse, that is as an individual. As with any other horse, during a period when the horse is resting you need to establish its maintenance requirements, to use as a base line. It can save a considerable amount of time, and prevent difficulties, if you then take the trouble to attempt to quantify the amount and type of work which is being done, both in training and in competition, not forgetting travelling to and from competitions.

This may seem like a lot of unnecessary effort but, certainly at the higher levels of competition, the fine tuning of the training programme, together with the rationing regime, can not only help in spotting problems before they have time to develop fully but can bring considerable benefits in relation to performance, recovery from both minor and major injuries and increased resistance to disease.

For a competition horse, lay-offs due to infections and injuries can prove expensive but with an appropriate nutritional input, a sensible training programme and the timely intervention of a physiotherapist, osteopath, chiropractor, acupuncturist or radionics practitioner, these can be minimised. These techniques, *including the nutrition*, are all drug-free, which is particularly relevant for the competition horse as the possibility of residual prohibited substances can be a problem when the horse returns to work.

A number of chronic illnesses can largely be controlled by management and nutritional means, e.g. chronic obstructive pulmonary disease (COPD). Drug-free homoeopathic techniques, in conjunction with dietary manipulation, can often solve apparently intractable problems. Selected herbal products also most definitely have their place. They should be chosen with care, however, as some herbs are potent sources of prohibited

114

substances and in the high-performance horse which, with the exception of the endurance horse, may have a tendency towards acid urine, they may subsequently appear in sufficient quantities to show up on a dope test.

A basic homoeopathic first-aid kit for the treatment of minor accidents and injuries, including grazes, bruises and shock, should have a place in every competition yard. Unfortunately, most people leave homoeopathy until it is a choice between that and the knacker's yard but, even so, homoeopathic vets still have a reasonable success rate in returning these 'basket cases' to full, or even improved, competitive work!

## Prohibited Substances

Basically, prohibited substances are chemicals which may be intentionally or inadvertently administered to the competition or racehorse and which are deemed by the ruling bodies of the sport concerned to have a potential for altering the performance of that horse in a manner which would be unfair to the other competitors (and also, where appropriate, to the betting public) and/or potentially harmful to the welfare/performance of the horse itself.

For example, while, when administered at a low level, painkillers may dull pain to a certain extent and enable an event horse to proceed in a bold fashion and not be deterred by odd knocks and bumps, at a higher dosage they may allow the horse to proceed when it is suffering from a relatively serious injury or disorder. This could well result in the horse being crippled or even in an accident that is fatal to horse and/or rider when the injured part gives way under the stress of competition.

Other substances which may be administered are those which can act as a stimulant, theoretically increasing the horse's ability to perform by 'hyping it up' or increasing its aggressiveness and, therefore (theoretically), its competitiveness. The so-called benefits of substances of this type are highly debatable as are such materials as anabolic steroids, which also build muscle, as there is little correlation between muscle mass and athletic performance (you do not see many weightlifters winning races!). The other side of this coin is the type of substance which slows down the horse's reactions, reducing speed and/or stamina and making it sluggish and dopey.

As a nutritionist, it is my experience that a large number of competition horses are either being overstimulated or rendered dopey due to unbalanced feeding and an ill-informed fitness programme but that is another subject which is discussed in broad terms throughout this book. Both chemical stimulants and chemical depressants may be administered intentionally to a competition horse but what we are most concerned with in this section is to give some guidelines to horse managers to enable them to avoid the inadvertent administration of prohibited materials.

It is useful to remember that most drugs in use today are either derived from plant material or are synthetic copies of chemicals derived from plants in a purified form. It is not therefore surprising to find that a lot of stimulants, depressants and other pharmacologically active chemicals occur naturally in plants which we may then feed to our horses or apply to them in some other way, for example as ointments, poultices or inhalants. The horse may also inadvertently ingest such materials itself when it licks paintwork, chews fences which have been treated with certain preservatives, eats various plants which contain pharmacologically active chemicals (including alkaloids and glycosides) or gets loose and comes into contact with materials which it would not normally be exposed to (drugs, slug pellets, pesticides, even ornamental plants).

The problem with many of these materials is that the rules governing their appearance in the urine and/or blood of the competition horse were formulated when intentional doping was a major problem and analytical techniques were relatively crude. Basically, the Jockey Club of the UK decided that certain proscribed substances should simply not be present in horses' body fluids and that racehorses should not be fed any substances which could not be defined as 'normal and ordinary feeding' (which they described as oats, bran and hay only if you pressed them hard enough for a definition). The Federation Equestre International (FEI) and, indeed, the governing bodies of many equestrian sports in many countries, then adopted these, or similar, rules.

This was all very well at first but, gradually, two things were happening. First of all, different feeding stuffs were being moved around the world, particularly for use in compound cattle feeds and, as a result of this, both compounds and straights (oats, barley, etc.) were becoming contaminated (either at the feed mill or while being transported in ships and lorries) with materials (e.g. cocoa bean meal) which contained prohibited substances such as the stimulants caffeine and theobromine. These were then, quite inadvertently, turning up in racehorse feeds and, of course, those of other competition horses.

This meant that increasing numbers of positive dope tests were made due to the presence of either caffeine or theobromine and, to a lesser extent, other substances, when, in fact, it was quite probable that the amounts concerned were insufficient to stimulate a mouse, let alone a thumping great Thoroughbred!

While the 'big, bad feed compounders' were continually being blamed for this problem, trying to find contaminants of this order of magnitude at a mill is rather like trying to find a pinch of snuff in a haystack (sometimes literally, as nicotine is also a prohibited substance!). Although many of the manufacturers spent a great deal of money and completely reorganised their mills and transport, positive tests were still occurring. They also took out some pretty hefty insurance policies but the main result of all this frenzied activity was probably to increase the price of the feed and little else.

As a wider range of feedstuffs was becoming available to the horse owner, many of which were capable of producing a far more appropriate ration for the high-performance horse, it became questionable whether it was reasonable to expect people to stick to an oats/bran/hay guideline or 'be prepared to suffer the consequences', especially after a number of oat samples were also analysed as positive!

The second aspect of this was that, as time went on, the analytical techniques being used became increasingly sophisticated, which generally meant that they could detect smaller and smaller amounts of various substances. Even more significantly, these techniques were now picking up other substances which nobody had thought to worry about previously. Ironically, nowadays the really serious, intentionally administered drugs are *not* well detected and electromagnetic interference is also a technological possibility so, in fact, this sophisticated technology has actually encouraged the real crooks to use even more sophisticated methods to beat it!

The upshot of all this is that more and more feed-related positive tests have been called over the years, causing problems in the industry and bad press in the eyes of the general public.

In the last few years, therefore, both the Jockey Club and the FEI have introduced arbitrary minimum levels of theobromine and four other substances to try to weed out the insignificant, inadvertently administered positives. It is to be hoped that the industry can now be less paranoid about caffeine and theobromine, although good mill and transport hygiene will still be important (particularly in view of the fact that the higher levels of these chemicals can be harmful). It should also be remembered that human foodstuffs, including tea, coffee, cocoa and chocolate, should not be made available to the competition horse. This does not only mean that you should not feed Mars Bars to your competition horse but that you should not dispense powdered coffee or eat chocolate flakes in the vicinity of feed bins. It might not be a bad idea either to wash your hands after handling such materials. This may sound silly to many people but, even with the minimal levels set by the ruling bodies, we are dealing with such trace amounts that it is quite possible for a horse to lick a chocolate-covered toddler and then show up positive and lose its Olympic medal. Make the stable yard a chocolate/coffee/cocoa/tea/cattle feed-free zone. At the very least, it will do wonders for *your* diet and health!

There are one or two other worthwhile measures which the competitive rider can implement.

- Buy compound horse feeds only from manufacturers and merchants who operate a 'clean mill' policy and who are aware of the problems of prohibited substances and take these into account, both in their manufacturing and in their transport and storage of raw materials and finished products. Ask them for a written guarantee of this and keep it somewhere safe.
- The above also applies to the purchase of straights, including oats, both from the feed compounders and neighbouring farmers who should not store them adjacent to pig, poultry or cattle feed which might contain substances which are both prohibited and dangerous to the horse, including various growth promoters and so forth.
- From about one month before the commencement of the competitive season and thereafter until the results of any tests taken are known, it is well worth taking about 0.5 kg (approx. 1 lb) as a sample from each batch of feed purchased and marking it with the number of the delivery note plus any bag labels with batch numbers available. If a positive test is called, you then have your own reference sample of feed should any legal action ensue and you can also be seen to be taking steps to avoid the problem if a decision has to be made about your culpability and how to penalise you. Ensure that part of the sample comes from near the bottom of the bag where smaller particles collect.
- Apart from the points about not allowing coffee, chocolate and so

forth in the feed room and where feed is being dispensed or fed, points about feed storage in relation to farms supplying hay and cereals should also be borne in mind in your own yard.

- You should also be aware that certain pasture and hedgerow weeds can contain narcotic substances (of course, these may also appear in conserved forages) and you should do your best to eliminate these as they may not only show up as a positive in a dope test but can also be extremely dangerous for the horse. (See comprehensive tables in *Pasture Management for Horses and Ponies* by Gillian McCarthy.)
- Discourage visitors to field and stables from giving titbits, not only of the coffee/chocolate nature but also various types of mints (see reference to menthol below). Stick to peeled carrots and washed apples!
- Keep small samples of any supplements and additives you give as mentioned above, including those given by syringe or in water, as it is quite likely in the future that increasing numbers of positives will be called, not because of caffeine and theobromine but because of substances used as preservatives, flavourings or colourants in various feedstuffs (see below).

Apart from materials administered in feed, there is a whole range of substances, which the horse may have applied to it or injected into it, which can lead to a positive dope test. In general, 'clearance times', i.e. the time it takes for a drug to leave a horse's system, have been worked out for many drugs which may be prescribed for horses but as horses may vary significantly in their metabolic make up and as many of these tests are performed on resting ponies, not fit competition horses, these figures are not always reliable and it is advisable, if possible, to extend the period allowed before competing with a horse given such a substance. It is quite possible that the antioxidant nutrient status of the horse will significantly affect such clearance times.

It is, of course, vital that the vet is made aware that you are planning to compete in any way with a horse that they are treating so that they can modify any drug therapy programme, if possible, or at least ensure that you are aware of potential problems.

Many horse owners will be aware that certain substances which are applied as ointments, creams or lotions can end up in the bloodstream and result in a positive test being called. There are also ointments which are known not to pass into the bloodstream and are therefore often considered to be safe. The problem is that ointments do not always have to pass through the skin to get into the body. For example, the horse may lick the area which has been treated or even rub against the stable or a fence post and then lick or chew that so, unless steps are being taken to prevent this happening, you cannot assume that *any* ointment which contains a prohibited substance is safe for use on the competition horse.

One major problem in this whole field is that although these substances may appear in the blood or urine of the horse, they may not be present in the same form in the material which has caused them to appear. That is to say that various chemicals, which a horse might ingest or have applied to it in some way, may then be acted on during metabolic processes in the body and, as a by-product, or even the direct end product of these processes, other chemicals may appear (metabolites) which are prohibited substances. A number of glycosides (a type of plant chemical) fall into this category.

This means that you can analyse the feed, ointment, drug powder or whatever until you are blue in the face but unless you are aware of all the possible metabolites (maybe thousands) of all the chemicals in the original substance, you have very little hope of predicting whether the prohibited substance is going to turn up in the blood or urine. Although the manufacturer or producer of whatever material you want to feed or apply to your horse may well be able to screen for such substances as caffeine and theobromine, there are many others which they and you simply cannot test for and neither can the authorities, which makes it very hard to advise the poor horse owner.

For the few substances which might be tested for their metabolites, this testing is again likely to be done on resting ponies due to the expense of conducting experiments and the natural reluctance of owners and trainers to subject valuable animals to tests which may exclude them from competitive work if a positive result comes up. There is a world of difference between the metabolites produced by a resting pony and those of a fit performance horse and even between a resting, fit performance horse tested prior to competition and one tested immediately afterwards when its urine becomes more acid, resulting in various glycosides showing up which would not otherwise appear. (This latter point raises interesting questions about dietary manipulation which can have significant effects on urine acidity and may well be a further benefit of fine tuning the diets of performance horses.)

While a limited amount of data is available with reference to proscribed drugs (although a lot of the advice relating to this is on the lines of 'we do not really know so don't take a chance; don't use it'), many people are becoming increasingly aware that there is a large number of herbal materials, particularly ointments but increasingly feed additives and supplements, which can have a highly beneficial effect on all manner of problems ranging from wounds, swellings and bruising to respiratory disorders.

Many people take the view that 'if it is herbal it is harmless' but as very many drugs are plant derivatives, it is not hard to see that herbs can have powerful pharmacological effects. I fear that quite a number of them fall into the category of materials which will not appear when the herb, ointment or whatever is tested but could well turn up as metabolites which are proscribed substances in blood and urine testing.

I raised this matter with the authorities – the Jockey Club and the ruling bodies of various equestrian sports – all of whom referred me to the FEI. The latter, while as helpful as it could be, said that while we know so little about these materials it is not possible to say that any of the available 'home treatments' are safe from the prohibited substances point of view. Sadly, this means that the excellent arnica and calendula creams, even homoeopathic ones, are out, although extensive use over the years of comfrey (*Symphytum*) as a feedstuff, ointment and even poultice seems to indicate that this is safe provided other ingredients (e.g. in ointments) are inert in this context. In my experience, raspberry leaf (*Rubus idaeus*) has been used to relax horses who have been subjected to testing and so far none of them has come up positive. (NB: for other reasons raspberry leaf is *not* suitable for continuous use.)

Due to the changing accuracy of the equipment used for testing, a substance which is safe today could well cause a positive test to be called in the future. For this reason, the best advice I can give is that you should not assume that just because something is 'natural' it is safe in this context and you should check with the manufacturers of any material you wish to use. Do your best to research any natural ingredients, including herbs, which you wish to utilise, as well as keeping abreast of developments as they occur and consulting the ruling body of your sport if you are in doubt. I know that this is not terribly helpful but at least if you are aware of the nature of the problem from the viewpoint of the ruling bodies and manufacturers of various products, it should help you to make reasoned decisions on this matter.

One example of the confusion which can arise was a well-publicised problem in the racing world in 1989, involving a positive call for what proved to be camphor, an ingredient in many ointments, leg-washes and inhalants, not to mention cough sweets and certain mints and other confectionery often given as titbits. The amounts contained in most of the above-mentioned items would probably not affect your horse's performance and many people would wonder why this is considered to be a prohibited substance at all. However, Mr M.A. Atock, head of the veterinary department of the FEI, points out that camphor has been used by certain unscrupulous people in the show jumping world to make their horses' shins more sensitive and thereby to encourage them to pick up their feet. As camphor applied in this way would appear in the bloodstream, it is necessary for them to test for this. Unfortunately, it has not yet been possible to set appropriate minimum levels which, strictly speaking, means that, under current rules, many of the leg washes, ointments and other materials gaily splashed about as a matter of course before, during and after competition in many spheres could, in fact, lead to a positive dope test and should therefore be avoided completely. This is rather unfortunate as many of these materials must be extremely refreshing to the horse, although it is true that even this benefit could, I suppose, be considered to have a potential to affect the horse's performance by changing its attitude and willingness to work. However, it is pretty sad if the tired competition horse cannot be allowed the equestrian equivalent of 'relaxing in a Radox bath'!

It is probably a good idea to avoid using such materials prior to competition, between the days of events such as horse trials and endurance rides or during show jumping competitions and to reserve them for the end of the show, provided another show or competition will not follow within less than seven to ten days, although a safe clearance time for most materials is about three weeks. If and when minimum levels are set, it may be possible to use them. In the meantime, try Epsom salts or sea salt as a leg wash.

One practice which people sometimes use when travelling several horses together is to apply Vick or something similar to their muzzles to discourage them from nuzzling each other and possibly fighting. As Vick is a source of camphor, this practice should obviously be avoided.

It is also important to remember that two ointments containing the same active ingredients may vary in their degree of absorption through the skin. For example, if one contains DMSO or MSM – only the latter of which is innocuous from a prohibited substances viewpoint – this may well increase the degree of absorption of an active substance into the bloodstream and lead to a positive test being called.

Currently a number of topical (for application to the body surface) preparations are available (such as sprays, ointments, creams and lotions) which contain disinfectants and which may be used without contravening the rules of racing as they stand at the present time. These include proflavin, centrimide, chlorhexidine, chloroxylenol, gentian violet and fentichlor (an anti-fungal agent). Good old salt and water is also an extremely useful disinfectant which promotes healing and causes less tissue damage than several of the above.

With regard to homoeopathic treatments, many of which seem to be very effective for a number of disorders, an independent analyst has indicated that it would be unwise to give a racehorse or competition horse any homoeopathic topical treatment (i.e. plaster or ointment) within less than four or five days of racing or competing, although oral administration above the 6c potency would be safe as there is no material dose (i.e. no actual molecules of active ingredient) present.

To put this section into perspective, the FEI had 96 positives from 1981 to 1988, of which 76 were for drugs, and it is suggested that many of these may well have been due to inadequate withdrawal periods being allowed for prescribed medication. A spokesman for the National Trainers Federation has pointed out that most of the recent positives in racing 'have arisen from substances in common use in stables such as leg washes, harness cleaners and disinfectants'.

If you have spent months, or indeed years, getting horses ready for a top class competition, whether it be an Olympic three-day event, a 160-km (100 mile) endurance ride, a Grand Prix show jumping final or a show class at Olympia, it is obviously a disastrous end to your long campaign to be disqualified, and possibly penalised further, because of a positive dope test. With this in mind, it *has* to make sense to do everything in your power to avoid inadvertent administration of prohibited substances, not to mention, of course, intentional administration!

It is to be hoped that, in time, a sufficient body of data will have been collected to enable us to begin to understand which materials must be avoided and what we can safely use and that a list of the latter will include some of the many useful herbal ointments and creams available for topical application to minor scratches and bruises. In the meantime, much can be done in fine tuning the diet and in the dietary manipulation of specific nutrients to improve the temperament and, ultimately, the performance of the horse, in particular when combined with an appropriate fitness programme. A number of minor disorders are, in fact, better treated using various nutrients and other feed additives, including probiotics, sodium montmerrillonite and organic feed sources such as MSM (methyl sulphonyl methane), without contravening any rules or compromising the horse's health and welfare. In fact, such techniques are more likely to enhance the latter than compromise it.

For those who wish to look into this subject in greater detail, the standard work is still *Drugs and the Performance Horse* by Thomas Tobin, although, as this has not been updated since 1981, it should not be taken as the sole source of reference.

## Practical Rationing for the Competition Horse

Before the start of a competition, it is a good idea to rough out both your fitness programme and how you intend to feed to maintain that programme.

Of course, it is easier if you know your horse well and have been developing suitable rations over a period of time. With a new horse, on the other hand, it is desirable to find out what it has been consuming up to date. A new horse is an unknown quantity, particularly when its previous diet is not available (even if this is known, *your* hay will not be the same as the previous owner's hay). It is therefore a very good idea to keep things simple and feed good quality forages. It is also often beneficial to give a five to ten-day course of probiotics, both to counteract the effects of any stresses related to being in unfamiliar surroundings, passing through a sale yard, travelling long distances, etc. and also to facilitate the horse becoming accustomed to new feedstuffs as rapidly as possible. Compared to the cost of feeding a competition horse, the cost of a short course of a good quality probiotic, which has been correctly stored, can merely be counted as a useful insurance.

In this way you are working *with* nature to help the horse to settle in as quickly as possible instead of against nature by using the potentially toxic purges and 'condition powders' which are still used in many yards when horses are brought up in order to 'cleanse them'. In my opinion, this is, quite frankly, a cruel and unsound practice. It also slows up the process of acclimatising a horse to a new diet and surroundings and this includes any horses which have been 'roughed off' and are being brought up to go back into work.

'Roughed off' is an unfortunate term as horses which are resting should by no means be allowed to become rough but should be kept in reasonable condition and, if possible, fed small amounts of their usual working rations while they are at pasture in order to acclimatise the appropriate digestive micro-organisms and maintain fitness of the gut. It is important that the pasture they are turned out on is well looked after. Even if this is a relatively rough area, it must not be allowed to become sour and overrun with weeds, some of which may be potentially poisonous. At the very least, low-level toxicity can account for loss of performance and susceptibility to disease.

It is a good idea to plan out a simple basic ration which includes ingredients that you intend to use as the horse becomes fit but which, initially, may consist only of good quality hay as the horse starts long, slow, distance (LSD) work. As the season progresses, you should have in mind a diet for the mid-fitness stage and the sort of diet you are aiming for when the horse is fully fit and competing. Apart from anything else, this will enable you to order any materials you require early so that you are not making last-minute alterations, and to lay in adequate supplies of good quality hay and cereals if these are required so that you are not making any sudden changes through the course of the season.

The table on page 88 gives a rule of thumb guide to the relative proportions of forages to concentrates but individual variations should always be taken into account. However, I would reiterate that no matter how hard the horse is working, the more fibre you can reasonably feed it, the better. If this means buying forages of a higher nutritional quality for competing horses because of limitations in appetite, then I would far rather do this than try to balance a ration based entirely on poor quality forages with higher quality concentrate. Forages play an important role in maintaining the physical fitness of the gut itself. This needs to be functioning at an optimum level to enable the high-performance horse to derive as much goodness as possible from its feed, and provides a substrate, or feed-stock, for the digestive micro-organisms which play such a vital role, both in digesting fibrous feed and in supplying various vitamins and energy sources (volatile fatty acids or VFAs). These are increasingly thought to play an important part in the functioning of the immune system and the overall health, well-being, resistance to disease and, indeed, recovery of the horse.

It is generally better to have at least a token amount of all the ingredients from the final diet added in at an early stage to allow the horse and its digestive micro-organisms to become accustomed to them. The week before your first one-day event or endurance ride is no time to be changing the diet or pursuing culinary experiments. Having said this, if, for some reason, things are not going well with the diet you have chosen during the season, as long as you make transitions carefully and sensibly, it does not make sense to wait until the next season to sort things out when a few simple adjustments may improve the horse's performance, safety and well-being.

Maintenance requirements for any horse of a particular size will be relatively similar but the type of work the horse is doing can affect the type of feedstuffs it is sensible to choose. Other influences on these are the past history of the horse in relation to parasite damage, disease and injury, its temperament and, of course, whether it is a poor or good doer. Having said this, many purportedly poor doers on oats, bran and hay-type rations, frequently become perfectly good doers when they are fed a ration which actually suits them! It is sad to think that they may have become labelled as problem horses by people who cannot be bothered to take the trouble to look into just how one can make appropriate changes to the diet instead of messing around randomly, altering ingredients, changing the proprietary brands used and perhaps using somewhat dubious supplementation for no particular reason rather than following a well-thought-out and logical plan of action.

Research over the last few years indicates that horses doing longer-distance, slower work may benefit from the addition of fats and oils to their diet, provided this is accompanied by suitable antioxidant nutrients, including vitamin E, selenium and choline, to enable them to utilise the additional fats. The object is to prolong the glycogen reserves in the muscles, encouraging the horse to utilise triglycerides as an energy source once blood glucose levels have been exhausted.

It is probable that there is little benefit in doing this for horses in shorter, faster work, unless there is a particular reason why you have to keep their carbohydrate intake down, e.g. for some reason they are allergic or sensitive to cereals, or are prone to laminitis. The latter example may be a problem with competition carriage driving *ponies*, who may, in fact, require relatively high digestible energy levels in their diet but may tend to become laminitic if given too many cereals.

## The Protein Fixation

Whenever I talk to horse owners about feeding, their first concern is often, 'What is the protein in the feed?' Speakers at horse keepers' meetings still stand up and say, 'The most important thing is to have enough protein in your feed.'

An alarming number of horse keepers and self-styled 'experts' seem to think that the terms 'energy' and 'protein' are interchangeable. I think it is time to clear up some of these confusions and misconceptions once and for all when applied to the nutrition of mature riding/driving horses in competition or high-performance work such as hunting.

The point many horse owners are missing is that protein levels are almost certain to be adequate on most rations and that the dietary factor they should be worrying about for hard-working horses is energy.

Check the bodyweight weekly, at the same time each week. An energy deficiency will show itself as reduced performance/staying power, either on a day-to-day basis or by deterioration over the season and by loss in bodyweight as fat reserves and glycogen (carbohydrate) are used up. The horse may become bad tempered, irritable, sluggish and, ultimately, prone to disease.

Once your horse is fit, you should feed to maintain bodyweight at an even level. You will soon discover that your horse has an optimum racing/ competing weight and that variations of 50 kg (110 lb) or so can result in reduced performance – not quite clearing that last pole, time penalties on the cross-country section, etc.

A horse may *appear* to be bursting with energy and still lose weight. This is especially likely if you feed a lot of oats which have a 'heating' effect on many horses, causing energy to be wasted as nervous energy. The horse that runs backwards at the start of a cross-country phase, or fights its rider, may look spectacular to the uninitiated but it is wasting both its own and its rider's energy.

For the serious competitive horse, I tend to use barley rather than oats, along with maize, fat/oil and often Bailey's Bread Meal as main energy sources. I steer clear of oats unless the horse tolerates them really well, which, of course, many do.

This is a very simplistic view and, of course, energy is not the only factor. Even if your horse has all the energy it needs in its diet, it may not be using it properly if, for example, it has a parasite problem, a deficiency or imbalance of vitamins and/or minerals or, indeed, amino acids (specific protein constituents).

The first thing to remember about protein is: 'Don't worry about it.' It is the major nutrient most likely to be in excess in the ration of an adult horse – often by two to three times as much as is needed. The question 'Am I giving him enough protein?' should really be: 'Am I feeding the correct amount of energy and is my ration balanced?'

A recent article in a feed manufacturer's magazine talked about 'The exaggerated stress on the importance of proteins by the early pioneer biochemists. It seems ironic that even after 150 years of additional research and nutritional knowledge, the importance of protein in the diet is still being exaggerated' and, I might add, in some instances commercially exploited by feed manufacturers.

*'It must be good – it has extra protein!'* – not true! When calculating rations for horses, I have, for a long time, felt that, apart from my built-in 'safety margin', any excess nutrient in the diet, even if it has no known bad effects (e.g. excess energy = fat horse!) must be counter-productive because the horse has to use metabolic effort to break up and dispose of the surplus.

For a riding school plodder that may not matter too much but for a high-performance horse, where a jump a fraction of an inch higher, or a speed a fraction of a second faster can win or lose the competition/race, every fraction of metabolic effort needs to be channelled into the performance.

This common-sense 'gut feeling' has been increasingly backed up by my knowledge as a nutritionist and biochemist, and by my observation as a horsewoman, that excess protein can lead to excessive sweating (including 'breaking-out syndrome'), increased urination and possible kidney damage (in the long term).

Research in New Jersey, USA has indicated that the degree of excess protein fed can adversely affect flat racing performance; i.e. too much protein can lose you races and, presumably, reduce performance in other high-performance competitions.

Many racehorse, hunter and competition cubes contain considerably more protein than the horses need, even if fed with quite poor hay (which you should not be feeding to a competitive horse anyway) but manufacturers cannot be entirely blamed, as pressure from feed buyers is for more protein.

The manufacturers often attribute a reluctance to change to 'consumer resistance' – i.e. you will not buy it. Let your feed representative know you will and are anxiously waiting for him to bring you a lower-protein, high-energy competition/racehorse cube.

Dr Jean Mayer, a top US human nutritionist, has pointed out that one of the most common misconceptions among human athletes is that exercise uses up protein. It does not. Exercise uses up carbohydrates and fat. Get that clear in your mind and you will not go far wrong!

So keep your soya, linseed, skimmed milk, beans, peas, fishmeal and meat-and-bone meal for your breeding and youngstock and do not overload your competition horse's digestive system by giving them to it. Buy it the best hay/oats/barley or balanced proprietary feed you can afford, back it up with a good vitamin/mineral supplement and make sure you get your salt and calcium (limestone) levels right.

## Maintaining Fitness and Stamina Throughout the Competition Season in Both Horse and Rider

Most reasonably experienced horse owners have a fair idea of how to get a horse to a stage of at least basic fitness suitable for the activity for which it is being prepared. Unfortunately, once they have reached the desired level of fitness, often by using complicated and carefully worked out fitness regimes, they seem to forget it, relying on the competitions themselves, plus schooling, to keep the horse fit.

The same sort of thing happens with feeding. The ration is carefully built up and increased in nutrient density (i.e. made more nourishing weight for weight) and balanced for each stage of training until it reaches the desired competition level. Then the horse's diet is 'set', more or less, for the season.

Believing that the horse's fitness and feeding requirements will remain the same throughout the season is a mistake. The horse you have at the beginning of the season will be physiologically quite different from the one that subsides gratefully into its paddock at the end – if it makes it through sound to the autumn. It is worth noting that the same applies to the rider.

Whether you are preparing a horse to compete in flat racing or endurance riding, dressage, show jumping, eventing or showing, you should bear in mind that, apart from the specific and very different requirements of each sport, it will need stamina to sustain a competitive edge and also to withstand all the stress, travelling, exposure to alien disease organisms and incidental ups and downs of competitive work, right to the end of the season.

## The 'Forgotten Athlete'

The rider needs to be as fit as the horse. A fatigued rider fatigues their horse, has slower reaction times and can cause – or at least fail to prevent – accidents.

A graphic illustration of this is to look at any group of flat-race jockeys. Most of them do quite a lot of fitness work these days but, because most have a poor understanding of nutrition and have to keep their weight down, they eat an inadequate and unbalanced diet and are frequently dehydrated.

Happily for them, they usually generate enough adrenalin to keep them functioning during a race. What you do not see is that, by the end of the season, many are like zombies, sleeping all day as someone else drives them to the racecourse. They are also constantly prey to colds, flu and other infections as they become depleted in protective vitamins when they lose their body fat reserves.

This is an extreme illustration of the rider as a 'forgotten athlete' but it is a syndrome common to all horse sports: just watch any major horse trials on TV and you will see a tired rider 'sagging' as their tired horse slogs through the finish. Compare this with the spectacular recovery as a fit rider 'lifts' a horse out of a difficult situation. You can plan to be like the latter rider – fit and ready for anything. What a waste if all that training and preparation of the horse fails because the rider is dehydrated or fatigued, maybe simply because they ate a high-protein steak meal instead of high-energy, high-carbohydrate pasta the night before the competition. Of course, it is not quite as simple as that but the point is that you need to build, and then maintain, fitness and stamina in the horse *and* rider.

## Equine Energy Boosting

Assuming that the horse is receiving sufficient protein with its constituent amino acids, the vitamins and minerals it needs to utilise its feed and function efficiently and that it is having as much fibre as is compatible with its work levels to keep its gut functioning correctly, the big variable requirement, especially on a day-to-day level, is the available energy, measured as digestible energy (DE) in the diet. The horse may obtain this from:

- carbohydrate – i.e. starches (mainly) and sugars
- excess protein – expensive and inefficient

- to a lesser extent from volatile fatty acids (VFAs) produced during the digestion of high-fibre feeds by digestive micro-organisms
- dietary fats and oils.

Once these have been digested and absorbed, the energy source either circulates throughout the horse's body as blood glucose, ready for immediate use, or as circulating fatty acids; or is stored as glycogen in the muscles and liver, or as fat which may be remobilised and circulated as free fatty acids (FFAs). The importance of this is that the energy is present in different forms which you can plan to use in the optimum way.

On a day-to-day basis, the horse will use the blood glucose first. To maintain blood levels of this the body will, if necessary, mobilise stored glycogen, including glycogen from the muscles. Use can be made of free fatty acids and these can, in fact, be useful in delaying the mobilisation and breakdown of the muscle glycogen.

In many activities, notably endurance riding and possibly drag hunting and eventing, you can take advantage of this by feeding a certain amount of oil or fat to prolong the muscle glycogen reserves.

It is a good idea to do this, both on a daily basis and over the season, because, after a hard competition, it can take up to three weeks to replenish the muscle glycogen reserves with traditional diets. Even if horses are not competing hard every three weeks, most people will, one hopes, be training their horses more frequently in between. If, in addition, you take into account the fact that simply travelling in a vehicle can take as much out of the horse as the competition itself, you can see that, cumulatively, over the season, unless something is done about it, the horse is likely to become progressively depleted in the very vital energy reserves that come into play especially at the crucial end of an event. You could often add to the sentence 'he fell at the last' – 'because his diet wasn't good enough'.

Very high fat/oil diets will require extra vitamin E and probably choline but if no more than four tablespoons a day are being given, there should be no need for extra vitamins provided a good background level is already available in the diet.

In most cases, the average British-trained horse continues to get fitter through the season, to start with at least. As its body fine tunes and becomes more efficient, it uses its energy systems more efficiently. However, after a while the show jumper may start to become careless, the event horse tires and has to take the easy routes, or gallops to the finish as though it is chest deep in mud and even the dressage horse starts swishing its tail, grinding its teeth and losing suppleness.

Worse still, the horse may be prone to stumble or fall as a physically tired horse is far less likely to get itself out of trouble easily. Injuries are likely to be more serious to fatigued, overstressed tissues. In addition, a tired horse is likely to notice pain from knocks and scrapes more and, consequently, may be less bold. As the horse becomes stressed it may react by becoming bad tempered or sour.

A brief lay-off may help the horse to replenish its diminished reserves. Alternatively, a change of activity may sharpen it up mentally – this is desirable as part of the fitness schedule anyway. However, surely it is better to prevent the horse from getting into this state in the first place!

Apart from the depletion of glycogen described above, other factors which can occur, both in the short term at a competition and in the long term over the season, are progressive depletion of vitamin and mineral reserves, leading, for example, to sore shins (star fractures of the cannon bones), sore muscles (probably available magnesium depletion) and progressive dehydration due, in particular, to lack of potassium and sodium (table salt) and poor watering practices.

The latter can lead to the early onset of fatigue as the blood becomes 'thicker' and less able to flow freely through the peripheral circulation – the tiny blood capillaries that deliver oxygen and nutrients to the muscles and remove carbon dioxide and waste products which can cause cramp if they build up. A tendency to tying-up is often linked to this problem and can be progressive through the season.

If the vitamins and minerals the horse needs are being progressively depleted, this could affect the efficiency of its various enzyme systems, hormone balance and immune system, particularly as the horse becomes more stressed.

### Female Factors

With mares there is a further variable. It is quite likely that the micro-nutrient requirements, especially for essential fatty acids (EFAs), minerals, including magnesium, and B vitamins, may increase at certain times in some mares.

Mares who become difficult and intractable when on heat are probably suffering from 'equine pre-menstrual tension' and there are reasonable grounds for attempting to alleviate this by trying increased levels of high-quality vegetable oil, magnesium and B vitamins for a time, and possibly vitamin E. If this does not help, however, do not continue to feed these supplements. I have also found that feeding raspberry leaf can alleviate some of the symptoms *as a short-term measure*, particularly to mares who tend to become touchy about the belly, and will kick.

Obviously, an uncomfortable or even mentally distressed mare will not give of her best when she competes and could thus lose a large chunk out of the season when she is on heat. It is therefore worth trying to sort this problem out. If the problem is very serious, your vet should check that there are no problems such as cystic ovaries etc.

The same applies to lady riders! *Any* rider who is short of magnesium is likely to have less-effective muscle function and slower mental reactions; women can take supplements and raspberry leaf tea or tablets as well to stop period pains. Horse and rider (or driver) compete as a team and all members of the team need to be at their best!

## Stamina Checklist

Specific feed requirements will vary from horse to horse, sport to sport and season to season but the following is a checklist which applies to most situations and can be followed throughout the season. Check it out at regular intervals and you will have a good chance of maintaining fitness and stamina.

- *Ensure that the diet is balanced* and adequate for the stage of training and work. Adjust for changes in forage or in the quality of other ingredients.
- *Do not run out of feed*. Make transitions to a new batch or brand gradually or the horse will lose ground as it adjusts. Consider using a probiotic for five to ten days to help to ease the horse through any major changes.
- *Make sure the horse has unrestricted access to clean water* whenever possible and, in particular, is given time to drink its fill on arrival at a show and before leaving afterwards.
- *Monitor your horse's bodyweight regularly* – even an estimation tape will give you some idea of weight changes. When comparing actual (weighbridge) weights, remember that protein (muscle)

is heavier than fat. Losses of up to 50 kg (110 lb) can occur on the day of competition due to dehydration but these should be rapidly replenished.

- *Have a salt lick* or loose-salt box available at all times as an added insurance but do not rely on this as the sole source of dietary salt. A 500-kg (1,110 lb) horse will need 50–100 g (2–4 oz) per day from feed/compounds or added as table salt.
- *Consider offering electrolytes* after a hard competition, training session or even a journey but always offer them as a drink *alongside* plain water. Force-feeding electrolytes, in feed or as a paste, can actually cause dehydration and should only be used as a last resort in unusual cases. Horses cannot store electrolytes.
- *To replenish glycogen reserves*, do not feed glucose, dextrose or sucrose (table sugar) to horses or humans as this can lower blood sugar if wrongly timed. Fructose (fruit sugar), honey or carbohydrate-loading materials, such as carbohydrate polymers (e.g. *Hyspeed-H* from Natural Animal Feeds or *Equine Energiser* from Equine Products) and possibly dimethyl glycine (DMG Paste from Horse Health Products), are useful to replenish glycogen reserves after the event and to encourage the horse to eat up. They can be used beforehand under expert guidance. The horse should be receiving plenty of B vitamins to utilise all this extra carbohydrate.

  Forget bran mashes after the event – they slow recovery time – but, provided the horse is used to it, extra sugar beet pulp given daily will help to replenish carbohydrate, electrolytes and water and can be used as a carrier for normal supplements and carbohydrate polymers if these are used.

- *Do not forget about vitamin D*. Bear in mind that a stabled horse, especially one mostly exercised early or late in the day, wearing exercise sheets, or worked indoors, will not be having its vitamin D reserves fully replenished by the action of sunlight on the skin and this will be further compounded by feeding old or badly harvested hay. Two-year-old hay should be avoided.
- *Feed green feed*. Stabled horses also benefit from fresh succulents such as carrots and green feed, or at least dried alfalfa, as a source of beta-carotene and folic acid, commonly deficient in cereal-based diets. Hydroponic cereals are very useful in this context.

- *Remember that overloading and excesses are also a form of malnutrition.*

- *Too much digestible energy* leads to obesity. Dressage horses are supposed to be equine gymnasts but some British competitors, even at the highest levels, hamper their horses with obese physiques that can only make it harder for them to perform well. This is ludicrous, wasteful and even cruel and betrays a degree of ignorance which will continue to keep us knocking at the door of consistent top international honours in this field.

  Top-class dressage is extremely hard work and you do not see many grossly overweight ice skaters, gymnasts or ballet dancers trying to perform while carrying up to 20 per cent of their own weight as additional padding. Obesity will stress the joints unnecessarily and can lead to stiffness and injury.

  The acceptance of such a large number of obese show horses as being suitable for various pursuits is also a scandal in view of the suffering and health problems this causes but until judges, the veterinary profession, welfare groups and owners refuse to accept this situation, agonising laminitis, potentially fatal hyperlipaemia and other disorders will be the fate of all too many show animals. Just like lameness in dressage, obesity should be viewed as an unsoundness and lead to elimination.

- *Too much protein* also causes problems as it has to be metabolised wastefully, may cause dehydration, breaking-out in night sweats, filled legs (when combined with too little fibre), skin rashes and other increasingly apparent problems. Do not risk overloading horses with protein – it is expensive and unnecessary, especially if quality amino acid requirements are met. Most adult horses need no more than 8–10 per cent in the overall diet.

- *Too much of most vitamins and minerals* can also cause problems, for example excess iron does not 'boost the blood' but can cause lethargy. Follow dosage recommendations and remember, if one scoop is good, two scoops are not necessarily twice as good.

- *Keep the horse's environment good* with clean air, an ioniser if necessary, good ventilation, clean, suitable bedding, stable toys, an interesting outlook and as much time turned out (in a sand manège if necessary) as possible. A bit of sun and Dr Green can work wonders but do put on protective boots.

A good environment and good-quality air will save the horse from wasting valuable resources and reserves in fighting off infections.

- *Watch the water quality.* There are so many chemicals and so much chlorine in mains water in some areas that this may lead to health problems, scouring or even dehydration due to a reduced appetite for the water. Consider water filtration if this becomes a problem. It can make a dramatic difference but is relatively expensive so has to be a last resort. You could try 'borrowing' a tank of water from elsewhere and using it for a week if you suspect this is the problem.

## Fluid Balance and Electrolytes

If an imbalance of any type is causing pain or confusion or even difficulties with eyesight, hearing or co-ordination, the results may be perceived as a change in character, temperament or behaviour.

The fluid and electrolyte balance will also be affected by when and what the horse eats. For example, if the horse has just eaten a large fibrous feed (such as hay), fluid may be drawn back out of the bloodstream and into the large intestine, which will affect the results of blood tests, especially for electrolytes and red blood cells (RBC) or PCV (packed cell volume or haematocrit).

This is why it is important, when taking a blood test, that your vet knows whether the horse has just eaten and what type of meal it had. If results are to be compared, they need to be taken under similar circumstances.

Electrolytes may also be measured in sweat and in urine – especially to see if there is an excessive loss – but these can be difficult to collect and interpret.

Electrolytes are basically mineral salts present in body fluids and cells in a highly active form which can be readily moved about the body and used by the horse. They are present in varying amounts in feed, occur naturally in minute amounts in water and can be bought as proprietary products.

All horses need adequate amounts of electrolytes but as the horse becomes stressed by work, heat, travelling or various illnesses, it becomes more crucial that the proportions and availability are assured.

Alfalfa (lucerne) is a good source of natural minerals and sugar beet is an especially rich source of available potassium if you also feed all the liquid it was soaked in. Grass and hay also contain useful amounts but this will depend on the quality of the soil they are grown on. It is also probable that soaking hay washes out some of these soluble nutrients. Hay tea was, in fact, an early form of electrolyte drink.

All horses should have access to a trace-mineralised salt-lick in both field and stable. However, unless horses are kept on desperately deficient pastures or fed poor hay, those in light work are unlikely to need additional electrolytes unless they are ill, or in exceptional weather conditions.

In harder work, a diet based on a mix of cereals (oats/barley/maize/ Bailey's No. 1 meal) and non-cereals such as sugar beet and alfalfa, or molassed chaff (molasses is a rich source of potassium) with 25–100 g (1–4 oz) of added salt, depending on work rate, and a good broad-spectrum vitamin and mineral supplement, will usually provide sufficient electrolytes. Do not use dishwasher salt as this does not contain iodine and you may prefer sea salt to table salt as the latter may contain chemical flowing agents which affect the requirements for vitamin $B_{12}$ and molybdenum in some horses. Alternatively, hay and a good-quality proprietary compound which contains added minerals and salt will be fine.

However, if you start diluting compounds with ingredients other than specially formulated cereal balancers, this unbalances the mixtures of minerals and salt that the manufacturer has added.

As far as giving additional electrolytes is concerned, if your horse's daily diet is reasonably balanced this should only become necessary for very hard work such as endurance riding, eventing and other competitions, especially in very hot or humid weather or after prolonged journeys in a box or trailer when the horse may lose a lot of electrolytes in sweat.

A major factor in fluid imbalance is simple dehydration. In extreme cases, this can be tested for by pressing the gum and noting the capillary refill time or by a skinfold test, although these tests are not 100 per cent reliable. Your vet should be able to show you how to do them properly. A blood test can also show chronic dehydration provided it is taken before a large forage feed and not immediately afterwards.

Water is needed as a medium to transport nutrients, including electrolytes, around the body; to bathe and lubricate cells, tissues and organs in body fluids including blood and lymph; to lubricate joints, eyes, nose and lungs; to facilitate digestion and so forth. A chronically dehydrated horse will probably be dull, have a staring coat and perform badly as its muscles fail to function adequately (because they are receiving good supplies of oxygen and nutrients but poor removal of toxins). It may even be prone to colic, an all too common phenomenon in dehydrated grass-kept ponies in winter when the water freezes, or in horses whose owners have failed to rehydrate them adequately before boxing them when returning home from hunting or a competition.

Ample supplies of clean, fresh water are, therefore, vital. Stable water should be changed frequently. Buckets and troughs should be scrubbed out regularly.

## Administering Electrolytes to Horses

I would only use syringe-type electrolytes in exceptional circumstance and for horses proved to require them but which, for some reason, will not drink free-choice ones. I would not add electrolytes to feed (effectively force-feeding) and there is no point whatsoever in 'loading' electrolytes by feeding extra before a competition as:

- They are not stored.
- This could lead to dehydration before the horse even starts as the horse needs to 'dilute' excessive levels of electrolytes and may then become short of water. Think how thirsty salty food can make you.
- The horse wastes 'metabolic effort' in getting rid of them.

So we are left with offering electrolytes as a free choice in water. Plain water should also always be offered because if a horse is dehydrated but does not need the electrolytes, it may refuse to drink and become further dehydrated, or drink the mix and, because of an excess of electrolytes, again become further dehydrated. If a horse refuses electrolyte drinks when it plainly needs them, it is worth trying other brands as it may simply not like the taste!

What one must be wary of is manufacturers increasingly adding sugars and flavourings to make their drinks more appetising. I would be a bit suspicious of a horse in light work who always willingly drinks electrolytes or, indeed, any horse doing so every time electrolytes are offered. Check the horse's health and diet but also try a sugar/flavour-free electrolyte to ensure that the horse did not just like the taste. Electrolytes taste horrible if you do not need them and like nectar if you do but if their true taste is masked by other things, this can confuse the horse's natural instinct to take what it needs.

## High-energy Supplements

It is also a good idea to avoid giving too much sugar (glucose, sucrose, dextrose, etc.) to competing horses as this can lead to rebound hypoglycaemia (low blood sugar) at a crucial moment. Honey or fructose poses fewer problems, although, again, they should not be fed in large quantities. These sugars are absorbed in a different way to glucose, without the intervention of insulin, so the problem of rebound hypoglycaemia is not likely to occur.

There are now a number of high-energy carbohydrate polymers on the market, along with dimethylglycine (DMG), an amino acid which can be used as an energy source. While I would accept that dimethylglycine is a very effective energy source, I am concerned about its use long term because, unless there is an overt deficiency of glycine in the horse's diet, overloading it with one individual amino acid without balancing it with others, particularly those of the glutathione complex, could eventually lead to problems. This is certainly not a product I would use as a first choice, although I would rather use this on the day of a race or competition than resort to feeding glucose.

I prefer the use of carbohydrate polymers or energisers which are artificially formulated using easily absorbed carbohydrate which can bypass the insulin system and do not, therefore, lead to rebound hypoglycaemia. With any high level carbohydrate supplement, it is necessary to ensure that the supply of B vitamins is adequate as these are required in larger than normal quantities for the utilisation of the carbohydrates.

In the human athlete these products can be used to 'load up' the muscles with stored carbohydrate and muscle glycogen prior to a competition. However, most veterinary research suggests that the horse's muscles are already fully 'loaded' and thus glycogen loading cannot occur in horses. In addition, equines do not metabolise or, indeed, digest foods in exactly the same way and are prone to various disorders due to carbohydrate overloading, including azoturia (Monday-morning sickness) and laminitis. However, I have obtained good results from giving such a supplement on the morning of a competition and dramatically good results from giving these products immediately after competition or a hard work-out.

It has been estimated that a middle-distance, flat-racehorse takes three weeks to replenish its muscle glycogen stores on a 'normal' diet. As carbohydrate polymers probably aid recovery when given immediately after competition, the sooner they are given, the better for maximum absorption because they will rapidly replenish the stores.

They also encourage the horse to drink plenty of water and to eat up after hard work, therefore enabling it to pick up more quickly. This is particularly important for event horses, especially during three-day events after the cross-country phase, and may also be useful for show jumpers during a hard season, particularly when they are jumping several rounds a day for several days running.

Polo ponies may also benefit from carbohydrate polymers, particularly as it may then be possible to formulate a more balanced diet than the one currently used which tends to encourage azoturia and tying-up, to which polo ponies are especially prone in view of the type of work that they do, i.e. short, fast, intense bursts interspersed with a lot of standing around.

I think it is likely that we shall see more of such energy supplements in the future. However, we are only just beginning to learn how best to use them for the horse. Most of them come from research into the nutrition of human athletes and it is most important to remember that the horse is not well adapted to glycogen-loading techniques except under the very strictest supervision. However, it may well be that the more important factor, as far as the competitive horse is concerned, is to facilitate rapid recovery and, quite apart from anything else, these products *may* help to prevent the horse from becoming 'run down' as the season progresses and more prone to viral infection, for example.

It is particularly important to note that many of the nutrients that protect against infection include the fat-soluble vitamins A, D and E. If the horse is constantly drawing on its body fat reserves as the season progresses, this will also mean that it is progressively losing its protective vitamin cover. If the use of these energy supplements can help to maintain these reserves, in theory they should also help to promote the competitive horse's resistance to disease.

## Specific Considerations for Different Types of Competition

### Event Horses

For many people the event horse is the most complex horse to feed because on one hand it is required to do slow, steady, dressage work in a gymnastic but accurate and obedient fashion, and on the other hand it will be steeplechasing, going along roads and tracks, when it is particularly important that it does not waste energy by messing about, followed by galloping across country. Then there is the show jumping phase, when the entire competition may be lost through simple carelessness caused by fatigue.

Over and above maintenance, the event horse will need adequate digestible energy (DE) for all its requirements, including training, adequate fibre to maintain gut health (an absolute minimum of 4.5 kg or 10 lb a day for a 500-kg or 1,100-lb horse, and preferably more), an adequate but not excessive amount of protein (8.5 per cent in the overall diet being more than adequate and 10 per cent being the maximum level), while also ensuring ample limiting amino acids. Up to 100 g (4 oz) of salt per day may be required, either as part of a compound or added to a home-mixed diet, plus a good quality source of vitamins and minerals to ensure maximum feed utilisation and performance.

Specific nutritional problems should be addressed. With more advanced horses, it is certainly worthwhile having cereals and hay analysed. Overexcitable types may benefit from high-level vitamin E and possibly $B_1$ supplementation, and any feed-related health problems must be looked into.

The use of electrolyte drinks has been discussed on page 35. As with other horses, it is recommended that the diet, if home-mixed, is a blend of cereals with non-cereals which complement each other nutritionally. The fit event horse should have its ration divided into *at least* four feeds per day. The feeding of horses before and on rest days is discussed on page 235.

The use of vitamin shots is to be deplored, unless the horse has a very specific malabsorption problem and cannot utilise oral nutrients.

Feeding glucose can be counterproductive and lead to low blood sugar levels at crucial moments, but the use of short-chain carbohydrate polymers, such as Equine Energiser and Carbo-Boost, can be especially useful immediately before a phase and, in two- or three-day events, between phases, to hasten recovery.

Feeding sugar beet to event horses is also particularly useful as it provides rapidly usable energy, followed by the highly digestible fibre action which can effectively help to sustain energy levels through the competition where other feeds may fail. As it is very appetising, it may also encourage a tired horse to eat. Again, carbohydrate polymer drinks are useful in this context, and the sooner they can be given *after* a phase the better as they not only have a restorative action but will encourage the horse to feed and replenish depleted muscle glycogen reserves.

Most event horses, particularly novices, are fine on a forage-to-concentrate ratio of 50:50, and there are very few indeed that ever need to exceed the 60 per cent concentrate and 40 per cent forage mark. It is, of course, advantageous to use the best quality forage you can obtain. If necessary supplement this with alfalfa (lucerne) chaff. All event horses will benefit from some sort of chaff with each feed.

Monitor the estimated bodyweight weekly with a bodyweight tape. It is important to note that while muscle is heavier than fat and while, as it gets fit, the horse should become hard and lean, it should most certainly not lose condition over the season.

Watering horses is dealt with elsewhere but I would remind readers that it is particularly important that the event horse be watered adequately between phases as dehydration can lead to dangerous fatigue and worse. Any horse that is anxious to drink more than is deemed desirable between phases should, quite frankly, be judged not fit to continue. Horses that are inclined to colic after a cross-country phase may very well be suffering from dehydration, while those that break out (i.e. break into a cold sweat after having initially been thoroughly cooled and dried) may be having too much protein. Filled legs, on the other hand, are often a sign of lack of fibre, although excess protein is often a contributing factor.

It should be remembered that event horses are covered by prohibited substances rules which differ slightly from those for racehorses, but it is important to note that if micro-nutrient levels are adequate, especially those of minerals, including available calcium, magnesium, potassium and sodium, a lot of unnecessary stiffness can be avoided. Lack of some micro-nutrients can also render a horse more susceptible to pain which, while it may not be serious, may cause it to fail a veterinary inspection. An increasing number of competitors now use methyl sulphonyl methane (MSM) at low-level maintenance doses, fed regularly throughout a competition, as this has natural anti-inflammatory properties. This material provides sulphur in a natural form and it is extremely useful in the event yard. Ironically, with the reduction of emissions from power stations and coal fires over the last 25 years, many soils are now becoming deficient in sulphur, and hay crops and grazed grass may actually be suffering from a sulphur shortage. It is quite possible that the reason why so many horses seem to respond to the use of MSM is because they have an under-lying subclinical shortage of this important nutrient in a bio-available form.

Alternative therapies, including homoeopathy, can be particularly useful in the event yard but care should be taken that any herbs used are checked for prohibited substances. Acupuncture, acupressure and various physical therapies play an important role, but it should be remembered that some of the electrical physiotherapy equipment can be highly dangerous if misused in inexperienced hands and although a little may do a lot of good, a little more can do a lot more harm!

## Endurance Horses

The fine tuning of rations for endurance horses is a fascinating subject. These are the supreme athletes of the equestrian world and their management is the subject of continued research and refinement.

Endurance and long distance rides may range from 40-km (25 mile) leisure rides, sometimes with jumps and often sponsored for charities etc., to 40–64 km (25–40 mile) competitive trail rides (CTRs), which tend to be relatively fast, up to 160-km (100 mile) rides which may be either basically single-stage or over two or more days. It is not unusual for a 160-km (100 mile) ride to be completed in around nine hours by top horses.

The training and level of fitness required to achieve this sort of per-formance is considerable, and the need to build, and fuel, stamina is paramount. It is also important that the rider is fit enough for competition as well, and the nutrition of endurance riders is a matter which requires further study.

Many of the top endurance horses compete largely off grass and while their grazing may be restricted to some extent, this form of extensive management is ideal for the maintenance of their health and well-being. It means that the horse has every opportunity to stretch and loosen up between training rides so that endurance horses managed in this way are probably less likely to suffer from excessive stiffness.

While keeping these horses out makes it harder to calculate their exact requirements for supplementary feeding, they are probably the most closely observed group of competitive horses and generally have their bodyweights measured by weight tape on a routine basis so that weight fluctuations are noticed in good time. It is not desirable for these horses to be so hyped up that they are wasting energy in boiling over, and many endurance riders favour rolled barley as their principal cereal, along with dried alfalfa (lucerne) nuts or chaff, or mixed hay and alfalfa chaff, with high levels of soaked sugar beet to provide both instant and long-term energy. In many cases, high levels of oil are added to the diet, particularly for horses competing over 64 km (40 miles), in an attempt to conserve muscle glycogen and prolong stamina.

High oil diets are especially well suited to this type of aerobic exercise. While feeding up to 100 ml is relatively common, good results have been obtained from feeding between 6 and 12 per cent of the overall diet as added oil. However, recent research suggests that over 8 per cent added oil may impair starch digestion. Most oils have a digestible energy of approximately 38 mJ (megajoules) per kilogram. While there are inherent benefits in the differing essential fatty acid levels in different oils, the large quantities involved often preclude the use of better oils due to expense. However, if possible, it is better to choose pure corn or soya oil, rather than vegetable oil, which may well be rapeseed oil or a blend of chemically extracted oils, often with additives. Once you start to exceed the 100 ml level (approximately 4 tablespoons) of oil it is vital that you give added vitamin E as an antioxidant and that you choose a broad-spectrum vitamin/mineral supplement or proprietary cereal balancer with the highest levels of choline you can find. In fact, it is usually a good idea to feed such a cereal balancer to these horses if you are mixing your own rations.

For horses working at the extreme limits of metabolic capability, it is particularly important that their vitamin and mineral levels are adequately supplied in the optimum proportions, and great care must be taken in choosing supplementation. I would contend that, at the higher levels of competition, feeding compounds other than proprietary cereal balancers is not likely to be accurate enough for the majority of endurance horses. No criticism of the products is implied in this statement but they are not specifically formulated for endurance work. However, proprietary cereal balancers can be useful because they are more flexible.

It is particularly important that dietary salt levels are maintained as endurance horses tend to sweat profusely, and the majority of endurance horses are likely to require 75–100 g (3–4 oz) of salt per day *plus* a salt lick as insurance (see event horses above re types of salts). Good levels of sugar beet in the feed will also provide plenty of available potassium which is particularly beneficial.

Electrolyte drinks are widely used for endurance horses, and it is important to note that you cannot load up with electrolytes as these are not well stored, so they must be provided during the ride. I would use the paste type only in exceptional circumstances because they are, effectively, a form of force-feeding and if you overfeed electrolytes you can further dehydrate the horse. Endurance horses should be allowed and encouraged to drink at every available opportunity. If electrolytes are being offered, they should be offered *alongside* plain water so that the horse can choose and satisfy its actual requirements. It is important that electrolytes used for endurance horses are not of an alkaline formulation (i.e. containing high levels of bicarbonate) because, unlike horses doing short, fast work, which may be prone to acidosis, endurance horses may be prone to alkalosis and giving further alkaline materials can precipitate serious problems.

It is important to ensure that the endurance horse has adequate calcium. A calcium shortage can manifest itself as the thumps, i.e. synchronous diaphragmatic flutter.

Another problem which may occur if the electrolytes are out of balance is tying-up or set-fast, along with azoturia if carbohydrate levels are incorrectly judged. If the horse is prone to this type of problem, as well as giving electrolytes you should also check that it is receiving adequate vitamin E which, in some cases, may be as much as 7,000 iu per day around the time of competition, with appropriate levels of selenium to go with it.

Excessive protein levels in the diet should be avoided due to their potential for inducing breaking-out and excessive sweating which may lead to accelerated dehydration.

Animals prone to multi-focal lamenesses and muscle stiffness may well respond to enhanced magnesium levels in the diet. Generous levels of vitamins and minerals will also help to maintain skin, coat and hoof condition, all of which are exposed to abnormally high levels of wear and tear.

As endurance competitions are bound by prohibited substances rules, it is worth remembering that homoeopathic remedies can be useful. Where girth galls are a problem, homoeopathically prepared hypercal (hypericum and calendula) tincture has been found to be particularly effective.

## Show Jumpers

With the widespread availability of indoor jumping arenas, the show jumper can now expect to be competing both indoors and outdoors on a year-round basis. It is therefore important that the horse is kept both fit and interested. While compound feeds can be extremely convenient for the horse that is travelling extensively, some horses may be inclined to go off their feed and become stale which can be a problem.

It should be remembered that the extensive travelling involved can, at times, take as much out of the horse as the competitions themselves and that show jumpers, along with many other types of competition horse, are exposed to a wide variety of disease challenges which may be absent in their home environment and to which they may have little or no natural resistance. It is therefore important that the quality of nutrition provided is good, to enhance natural immunity. If the horse is receiving inadequate vitamins, minerals and essential amino acids, apart from any possible effects on performance, it may become increasingly rundown over the season and therefore susceptible to infection.

The highly gymnastic nature of the work and the considerable stresses and strains on the forelimbs in particular mean that special attention needs to be given to mineral nutrition, and to the vitamins, particularly the B vitamins, which complement this and facilitate optimum feed utilisation.

Most show jumpers are stabled virtually year-round, although a few yards practise a semi-yarded system which enables them to self-exercise to some extent and is certainly preferable to full-time stabling. While these animals are extremely valuable, it is still desirable to turn them out in the fresh air for at least some part of each day if at all possible, or at the very least to lead them out in hand. Horses that are stabled and rugged at all times may become deficient in vitamin D due to inadequate exposure to sunlight, and are also likely to be deficient in vitamins and minerals which they would normally obtain from grazing. It is a good idea to feed these horses some form of green feed, and many yards find hydroponic cereals extremely useful (e.g. barley grass) although these are, of course, less convenient when travelling. Dried grass and alfalfa (lucerne) cubes and chaff make a good alternative and can be easily transported. If possible fresh feed, including carrots, should also be provided.

It has been noticed that some show jumpers have difficulties when jumping under artificial lighting conditions and, certainly, this may be due in part to deficiencies or malabsorption problems relating to certain vitamins, including vitamin A, vitamin D and vitamin $B_{12}$. Electrical sensitivity has been mentioned elsewhere, and this can be a particular problem with fluorescent lights. Expert advice should be sought if this appears to be a problem, as a number of steps can be taken in the complementary medicine field to attempt to correct these difficulties. Avoiding stabling horses under power lines and within 50 m (55 yd) of electrical transformers and 150 m (164 yd) of substations is probably a good idea if possible.

Once again, it is best to avoid excessive protein levels and to feed as much high quality fibre as possible to maintain gut health.

In view of the high degree of concentration and obedience required, it is foolish to feed rations which overexcite these horses. If the horse tends to hot up on oats, then do not feed them!

It cannot be sufficiently stressed how important it is that these horses have adequate salt in their diet. While reasonably high levels may be contained in compound feeds, at the height of the season, when these horses are travelling a lot, they may not settle enough to use a salt lick to top themselves up adequately, and it may be more convenient to feed loose salt from a salt box. Once again carbohydrate polymers and electrolyte drinks may be offered as and when appropriate.

## Polo Ponies

Much of the research that went into setting the widely used American NRC standard for the nutrient requirements for horses was originally based on work done with polo ponies. The requirements of polo ponies are therefore some of the best researched of any group of horses and it is unfortunately a sad fact that, in the UK at least, they remain one of the most inappropriately fed groups of equines! Azoturia, tying-up, colic, breaking-out and unnecessary strain injuries are extremely common. Digestive difficulties, due to problems with teeth and therefore chewing, are not uncommon, particularly with ponies imported from Argentina, some of which have had their tongues severed by the use of unnecessarily harsh bitting. These facts must be taken into consideration when feeding them.

In polo, short, sharp bursts of activity are preceded and followed by a good deal of standing around, so the ponies may be inadequately warmed up before work and then become stiff and seize up afterwards if not suitably warmed down. Combined with inappropriate feeding, often simply based on oats and hay, this probably makes this group the one most prone to azoturia.

While the fast and intense nature of the work these ponies are asked to perform requires high energy levels, stuffing them full of as many oats as they will eat is hardly the answer. If the pony tends to hot up, feed a good proprietary cereal balancer with lower levels of oats, or rolled barley, bread meal or a combination of these. Soaked sugar beet can be a useful source of highly digestible fibre and freely available minerals, and it is extremely useful to include alfalfa (lucerne) chaff in the diet to raise the nutrient density and high quality fibre levels, particularly as these ponies are frequently not offered hay throughout the day.

Again, electrolyte drinks should be offered where appropriate, and adequate salt added to feeds. Ponies who have problems with their mouths will almost certainly not use a salt lick properly to top up their salt levels. If such ponies have difficulties in eating, then a soaked compound ration may be the best option. If a cereal balancer is used for home mixed rations, then additional vitamins and minerals other than salt should not be required. However, if you are mixing your own ration entirely, it should be borne in mind that the high degree of metabolic efficiency required for the short, sharp bursts of intense effort will require good levels of freely available vitamins and minerals which will not be obtained from a simple hay, oat and possibly bran ration.

## Point-to-point Horses

As a point-to-pointer will have been hunted, it should be relatively fit, certainly from the stamina point of view, and it is important that, while it is hunting, it is not allowed to lose condition. While hunting, the horse will probably have been on a ration of roughly 50 per cent forage to 50 per cent concentrates but, as the shorter, faster work commences in training, the ratio should gradually change to 40 per cent concentrates to 60 per cent forage. Many point-to-point yards still feed just oats and hay but I have found that the substitution of a proprietary cereal balancer for part of the oat ration can lead to a marked improvement in condition and performance.

Again, it is most important that these horses receive adequate salt and, if appropriate, electrolytes can also be added. As with all classes of horses, care should be taken to avoid azoturia and tying-up (see page 233), and it should be remembered that point-to-point horses are subject to prohibited substances rules (see page 116).

It is quite astonishing that some point-to-pointers are allowed to progress through the season increasingly failing to quicken towards the end of the race or falling in the latter part, which is simply put down to bad luck. Obviously, luck may account for some incidents, but the question should always be considered as to whether the horse is receiving an adequate and appropriate diet to maintain stamina and performance to the end of the race.

## Arab Racing

Arab racing has become increasingly popular in recent years and the Arab racehorse is likely to be fed along similar lines to other flat racehorses. This is rather unfortunate because all too many flat racehorses are fed diets which are inappropriate and outdated. That apart, it should also be remembered that most Arabs and Anglo-Arabs tend to be more efficient than Thoroughbreds at feed utilisation. Again, I have found proprietary cereal balancers with whole oats or rolled barley to be extremely useful, possibly with the addition of a little sugar beet and dried alfalfa (lucerne) and *at least* 40 per cent of the diet as forage. Electrolyte drinks and carbohydrate polymers may be offered if appropriate. Adequate salt levels should be maintained.

## Dressage Horses

While dressage may be slow, it requires considerable gymnastic ability and, certainly at the higher levels, is relatively hard work. Muscle function, joint suppleness, temperament, and therefore willingness and obedience, can all be affected by nutrient deficiencies and imbalances. While a relatively high proportion of forage may be fed, say, 60 to 75 per cent of the diet, it is important to ensure that adequate levels of micro-nutrients are provided with the concentrates.

Sadly, even at the highest levels, many British dressage horses are allowed to become, or are even intentionally kept, obese and this may, in turn, be a contributory factor to keeping them out of the very highest international honours in competition. It is simply asking too much of a horse to perform highly gymnastic feats when it is grossly overweight. It also considerably detracts from the beauty and harmony of the work which is being performed, no matter how well the horse performs it, if it is carrying too much weight.

It should also be noted that if the horse is receiving inadequate trace nutrients, apart from leading to stiffness which will affect performance, it will also lead to discomfort which may affect attitude and obedience and can, for example, lead to teeth grinding, tail swishing and subsequent loss of marks. As with other groups, if oats or, indeed, any other feeds do not suit the horse, then it makes sense to try other feeding regimes rather than battle on with one that is proving less than suitable.

## Show Horses and Ponies

Again, there is a quite incomprehensible tendency for show animals to be kept deliberately overweight and many, particularly heavy hunters and cobs, may be shown in a dangerously gross condition. Competitors engaged in showing should read the section on hyperlipaemia on page 221 as this, and laminitis, are very real and potentially life-threatening problems. Unfortunately, even in yards where ponies or horses have succumbed to these illnesses and survived, all too often their owners or handlers go back to the same feeding practices which precipitated the problem.

Until show judges give a lead and treat obesity as an unsoundness, which it surely is, and resist the temptation to place animals which are in a gross condition, it is unlikely that competitors will feed with due consideration to their horse or pony's welfare. As the show ring is also a show case for breeding stock, it should be remembered that a predisposition to obesity and its inherent health problems can be inherited. In addition, over-topped youngstock will be predisposed to developmental orthopaedic disease (DOD). The condition will also be exacerbated if the animals are overweight.

These animals should be fed according to the amount of work they are doing. It is also a good idea to pay particular attention to vitamin and mineral levels to enhance coat condition and maintain alertness, and to feed corn or soya oil at a rate of 1–4 tablespoonfuls per day, or to feed grade linseed oil (or a combination of the two, i.e. corn or soya combined with linseed) to maintain coat condition.

Linseed jelly and tea are also good sources of fatty acids but are really not worth all the trouble it takes to prepare them. Ready-prepared linseed supplements are available in some areas. The use of a good vitamin/mineral supplement is also indicated because most show animals are kept in and even native ponies are brought in at an early stage or may be rugged and given neck guards, which means reduced exposure to sunlight and, subsequently, reduced production of vitamin D which *must* be taken into account in the diet.

A number of herbal and nutrient supplements are available, which are intended to quieten obstreperous ponies and horses for showing. While these may certainly have their place, provided they are checked for prohibited substances, it should be remembered that the overall diet should be corrected initially and adequate fibre levels fed, which is often sufficient to correct any behavioural problems. The use of megadoses of vitamin E, sometimes vitamin B$_1$ (thiamine), courses of probiotics and Thrive may be tried if changing the diet and increasing the forage levels does not work. However, these should not be used as long-term solutions. Constitutional homoeopathy and, of course, correct training and riding may also help.

Many show ponies do very well on Bailey's bread meal, combined with a quality fibre source, such as sugar beet and/or dried alfalfa (lucerne), and a good vitamin/mineral supplement, and they also tend to be more relaxed and obedient on this type of diet. Owners and judges should learn to differentiate between the vital spark of a superbly healthy horse and the exaggerated stable reflexes of a deeply *unhealthy* one, i.e. between 'fire' and 'fear'.

## Competition Carriage Driving

In general, the same considerations apply as for the event horse, although the digestible energy levels required may be somewhat less. This may be slightly counteracted, particularly in team work, by the pressures of interaction with other horses but, in general, less galloping is involved than in ridden eventing.

Generally speaking, it requires less energy to pull a load than to carry one, although this is perhaps negated when going across country and pulling over rough ground or through mud and water. The health of the horses should be borne in mind, and it is important that horses are not allowed to become overweight.

Again, competitors need to familiarise themselves with preventive measures in relation to tying-up, set-fast, azoturia and, particularly in the case of pony teams, laminitis.

# 8 Feeding Broodmares, Foals, Youngstock and Stallions

The feeding management of youngstock must inevitably begin with the unborn foal and thus with the mare. An unhealthy, malnourished mare is not likely to produce a healthy, well-nourished foal, although her body will do everything in its power, by starving and depleting itself of vital nutrients, in order to do so. The owner may get away with this once but not year after year.

## Pre-conception Health

Good feeding management starts even before conception. The mare should be fit but not fat at service and it is a good idea to make particularly sure that barren and empty mares are receiving adequate vitamins and minerals for at least 30 days prior to, and 18–35 days after, service, to give an optimum chance for conception to occur and to ensure that the mare holds to service.

The nutrition and condition of the sire are also important factors, as nutrition, including vitamin and mineral status, can affect the viability and quality of the sperm. An overweight stallion, with massive fat deposits around the testes, may be less fertile as such fat can lead to localised higher temperatures which may kill a proportion of the spermatozoa. Sperm motility and viability are also affected by micro-nutrient status.

## The First Eight Months of Pregnancy

From this point on, assuming that the mare is not lactating with a foal at foot, she should be fed appropriately for whatever work she may be doing, plus maintenance of condition, bodyweight and body temperature.

Subject to the grazing available, if she is not working, a vitaminised and mineralised feedblock or a daily briquette, plus a salt lick and hay or straw if necessary, will be all that she requires until approximately three months before foaling is due. If the pasture becomes vary bare during the height of summer, it can sometimes be useful to feed alfalfa (lucerne) cubes on the ground to supplement pasture quality and provide a source of calcium and certain vitamins.

If she is working, choose a horse and pony or competition-type compound or home mix as appropriate; she does not need stud cubes/mix at this stage as they are much too rich. However, an immature pregnant filly will need her requirements for both growth *and* pregnancy to be satisfied.

It should be noted that some specific herbs are not suitable for pregnant broodmares, so consult an expert before feeding and, if you use a proprietary mix, change to a breeding mix as appropriate.

## Exercise and Massage

Even in the later stages of gestation, a certain amount of gentle exercise will help the mare to foal comfortably, maintaining the back muscles (longissimus dorsi) which take a lot of the strain of carrying the weight of the foal. It will also help to prevent oedema, or water retention, in the legs and underbelly.

There is no reason why the mare should not work until a few days before the foal is due, provided fast work and jumping are avoided and the mare is not asked to overexert herself.

Even elderly mares will benefit from being led out in hand. If they are prone to oedema, a twice-daily brisk massage (towards the heart) of the lower limbs will help an elderly mare to feel comfortable. Think of keeping the mare 'fit to foal'.

## The Last Three Months of Pregnancy

During the last three months of pregnancy (also referred to as the 'last trimester of gestation'), the unborn foal will double in size, thus rapidly increasing the mare's feed requirements, particularly for protein, calcium and other minerals and vitamins.

How much more hard feed she requires will depend on the quality of the grazing available (Thoroughbreds who foal early will need their established specific requirements met). Whereas for the first part of pregnancy an overall

10 per cent crude protein diet is perfectly adequate, she will now need to build up to 12–14 per cent crude protein until foaling time and at least 14 per cent afterwards, so that the nutrient density of the ration may be increased and she can contrive to have a reasonable intake of long fibre.

Nutrient levels for native pony mares should be treated with caution and, in some cases, may be cut by 20–25 per cent of standard (NRC) recommended rates. However, you should ensure that fibre, vitamin, mineral and essential amino acid levels are maintained on energy-restricted diets.

If you feed proprietary compounds, you can simply make a transition from, say, horse and pony cubes/mix to a good quality stud cube or mix at the recommended rates and from 75–100 per cent forage to 60 per cent forage: 40 per cent concentrates and so on (see table below). Follow the manufacturer's feeding guides as different cubes have different nutrient densities and so must be fed at different rates.

During her pregnancy the mare's total feed requirements will rise from 2.5 per cent to 3 per cent of bodyweight. In other words, she needs 3 kg (6.6 lb) of forage and concentrates per 100 kg (220.5 lb) bodyweight, thus a 500-kg (1,102.5 lb) mare will need 15 kg (33 lb) total feed per day. A pony mare's requirement will rise from 2 per cent to 2.5 per cent of bodyweight.

### *Suggested feeding chart for broodmares*

|  | Forage:concentrate ratio | Total feed kg per 100 kg (or lb per 100 lb) bodyweight (kg:100 kg) |
| --- | --- | --- |
| First 8 months of pregnancy, i.e. March to Nov. in UK | forage 75%: concentrate 25% | 2.5 kg/100 kg (2.5 lb/100 lb) 2 k g/100 kg for native ponies |
| Last 3 months of pregnancy, i.e. December to February (UK) | gradually increase up to 45% forage: 55% concentrate after foaling | 3 kg/100 kg (3 lb/100 kg lb) 2.5 kg/100 kg for native ponies |

For late-foaling mares this would be adjusted to take into consideration the quantity and quality of grazing.

Many mare owners have found that introducing dried raspberry leaf or raspberry leaf tea into the diet daily, from about a month before foaling, helps to relax the mare's pelvic floor muscles, allowing for an easier foaling, especially for maiden mares. This is quite harmless, is used by many human mothers and is recognised for this purpose by the medical profession. There is nothing to be gained, however, from feeding raspberry leaf for longer than this and there may, in fact, be some disadvantages in doing so.

If you have a mare who has had problems with foaling, or is prone to oedema, you may find it useful to consult a good herbalist or a homoeopathic vet for safe and gentle means of controlling these symptoms. A balanced diet which includes plenty of suitable fibre, adequate micro-nutrients and plenty of fresh air, exercise and, if necessary, massage, will also help to prevent these problems.

If your mare is prone to oedema and is receiving adequate fibre, you should urgently check the mineral status of her diet. Diuretic drugs should be avoided as they tend to deplete mineral reserves further and lack of minerals at this stage could lead to problems for the foal later on.

It is also important that the mare's feet are kept in good condition and shape, particularly as she becomes heavier, as the additional weight will put abnormal stresses on her feet and limbs. This will be unpleasant and painful for the mare and may cause permanent damage.

It is also a good idea to give the mare a probiotic (I prefer a yeast-free formulation) for three to five days prior to and after foaling to prevent scouring and to help to reduce any stress-related problems.

Some probiotics are available as a powder and in paste form in wormer-type syringes and it is particularly beneficial to give the newborn foal a dose of the paste as soon as possible after birth and again daily for the first five days, subject to the manufacturer's specific instructions for the product you choose. This is especially desirable if the mare tends to 'run her milk' before foaling, thereby losing colostrum, or for orphan foals, but will help any foal to stabilise quickly after birth, preventing scouring and helping to establish a healthy population of digestive micro-organisms. The powdered form can easily be mixed into mare's milk replacer or frozen mare's milk/colostrum for orphan foals or twin foals or if the mare is a poor milker.

It is important to note that coprophagy (i.e. eating dung) is quite normal in the newborn foal which eats the mare's dung to obtain gut micro-organisms which she has expelled in order to establish its own population (it is born without a resident population of digestive micro-organisms). However, a depraved appetite for its own dung or coprophagy in adults is indicative of digestive problems, the need for a probiotic and possible mineral and protein deficiency and should be urgently investigated and dealt with. Adequate parasite control before and after foaling in the mare and then the foal is also vital.

It is a good idea to monitor your mare's bodyweight regularly. Obtain an initial (barren or non-pregnant) accurate weight on a weighbridge, then check weekly with a bodyweight tape. These figures will probably not be very accurate in late pregnancy but will give a guide and also a warning of any loss of condition.

Incidentally, it is also useful to get a figure for the bodyweight of the newborn foal. Stand on a bathroom scale holding the newborn foal as soon as you reasonably can without causing distress, get someone to read off the weight and then deduct your own weight. Record this in your foaling diary. It will help to monitor and even predict growth rates and dietary formulation.

If you are mixing your own feed for your mare, it is a good idea to balance cereals with non-cereals, such as sugar beet pulp/nuts and/or lucerne/alfalfa nuts.

Cereals and cereal by-products, especially wheatbran, are very deficient in calcium and contain phytate which locks up calcium from the rest of the diet. You can add calcium (e.g. as 50 g or 2 oz additional limestone flour/kg bran) or dicalcium phosphate as appropriate but I prefer to avoid using bran on the stud. Both sugar beet and lucerne/alfalfa are rich in calcium as well as digestible energy and digestible fibre. Sugar beet contains a similar amount of protein to oats but of rather better quality and is also a source of other minerals (e.g. sodium and potassium).

Lucerne/alfalfa has all these attributes and is an excellent source of beta-carotene, the precursor of vitamin A. This has been found to be necessary for good breeding performance for mares in its own right, along with folic acid, which is often deficient in broodmare diets, especially when stabled or foaling 'unnaturally' early (i.e. Thoroughbreds).

Alfalfa also offers a number of minerals, including copper and zinc, which, along with high levels of good quality protein, are especially important for healthy bone development in youngstock and the prevention of such problems as contracted tendons and epiphysitis. Alfalfa chaff and a less rich alfalfa/grass mixture chaff is particularly suitable for pony mares and useful for working horses. In fact, dried lucerne/alfalfa may give all the added protein necessary for pony mares and other broodmares.

In addition, in home-mixed rations where a cereal balancer is not being used, the mare should receive a good quality broad-spectrum vitamin/mineral supplement containing particularly high levels of essential amino acids and fed at the recommended rate; iodised salt (table salt or sea salt, not dishwasher salt) as 0.5 per cent of the diet, plus a trace-mineralised salt lick for added insurance and either limestone for calcium or di-calcium phosphate for calcium and phosphorus depending on the rest of the diet.

## Foaling

Many people like to give the mare a bran mash after foaling but as this is highly indigestible and causes calcium-uptake problems just when the newly foaled mare has a massively increased requirement for calcium for lactation, this is the last thing you should be doing!

It is far better to give a small, normal feed after foaling, either of her usual nuts/mix, dampened if necessary with warm (not boiling) water (boiling water destroys vitamins), or, if you are mixing your own feed, make up the soaked sugar beet/dried alfalfa in a warm mash if you wish – these ingredients are especially suitable at this time. Carrots (sliced lengthways), sliced apples, etc. may be added if the mare enjoys them.

However, this is not the time for culinary experiments. Your mare should be used to her regular dietary ingredients for at least a month before foaling, although the amounts will be increasing and the proportions will change as lactation commences (see chart below).

Good nutrition before foaling not only helps to build a healthy foal but will also produce nutritious colostrum, the mare's rich first milk which provides the foal with vitamins and antibodies against disease in its local environment, i.e. those which the mare has either inherited or acquired.

Other preparations for foaling day will include checking that your vet will be available if problems arise and telling him or her that the foal is on its way; preparing your stable/barn/paddock (also ensuring that the foal cannot roll under a fence into a rain-filled ditch); and, even if this is not your first time 'in attendance', it is still a good idea to read or re-read a practical book on the subject.

You should also lay in at least a small stock of mare's milk replacer (see below) and obtain, or know the whereabouts of, a supply of frozen colostrum (at least 0.5 litre or 1 pt) preferably from the same farm, i.e. from a mare exposed to the same local disease challenges. Your vet or other breeders in the area should be able to help.

## Colostrum

Colostrum is the vital first milk, secreted by the udder for the first three to four days after foaling (parturition). It contains 20 per cent more protein and a little more fat than normal mare's milk and may be tinged orange/red. It is very rich in vitamins A and D (the anti-infective and sunshine vitamins), assuming that the mare is receiving adequate quantities of these substances. Perhaps more important, it also contains a supply of antibodies against various viruses and bacteria, thus helping to transfer immunity against disease (including influenza and tetanus if the mare has been protected) from the mare to the foal.

Colostrum also has a laxative effect, stimulating the evacuation of the meconium (accumulated prenatal faecal matter). Severe meconium colic in the foal will ensue if this is not passed within six to eight hours of birth, so the foal must have some colostrum within 12 hours of birth.

It is important to enquire about frozen colostrum because:

- The mare may die before the foal can suckle.
- It is quite common for mares to 'run milk' (that is, it drips, dribbles or even pours from the teats for hours or days before foaling). Some or all of the colostrum may be lost in this way, so the foal will then need your frozen supply (warmed to blood heat).

Colostrum from the same area is preferable because different disease challenges are present at different stables and farms and the mare will pass on antibodies for those specific diseases. That is why a young foal transported, with or without its dam, to a new home, often needs the additional protection of antibiotics and/or probiotics. If the dam is too ill to suckle for a few days after foaling, you can either milk off and feed her own colostrum or, if she is very ill or receiving certain drugs, the vet may advise frozen colostrum for the foal.

If you have a haemolytic foal, or the mare has previously had one, the foal must not be allowed to have its own mother's colostrum which has to be milked off and discarded while the foal wears a muzzle to prevent suckling and is bottle fed. (Haemolytic jaundice is a disease of the newborn foal caused by a reaction between the antibodies in the dam's colostrum and the foal's red blood cells, resulting in the destruction of the red blood cells.) After a few days the colostrum has gone and the foal can suckle normally.

If you do not have any frozen colostrum, all is not lost. The vet can give probiotics or even antibiotics and an enema (to encourage evacuation of the meconium). Cow's, sow's, ewe's or goat's colostrum is *not* suitable.

If you plan to have another foal next year, milk off a couple of pints of colostrum this year and freeze it in a well-labelled, dated plastic bottle. Do not fill it to the top as liquids expand as they freeze. A foal who receives a small amount of frozen colostrum may still need probiotic support but it does give you leeway to bridge the gap for a foal in need before the vet arrives.

### The problem foal

Here I would include orphans, twins, mares that cannot (ill) or will not (vicious) suckle and mares that simply produce insufficient milk. In all cases, the foal must have colostrum or antibiotics followed by probiotics and, if necessary, an enema, when it starts life. In all cases you will also find your supply of mare's milk replacer essential.

### Insufficient milk

You will have to give a milk replacer, following the vet's advice and the manufacturer's instructions exactly. Bottle feed the extra, as bucket feeding reduces the desire to suckle, which will further reduce the mare's milk output, and get the foal on to hard feed and fresh water as soon as possible. Start with a little milk powder and graduate to milk pellets and creep feed (see below).

### Difficult to suckle

- If the mare is ill after foaling, bottle feed the foal on the mare's milk (if the vet says this is all right) or milk replacer until the mare is well enough to suckle. Do not bucket feed.
- If the mare is vicious, first try restraining her while the foal suckles, keeping them apart (suckle hourly at least). If, after a few days, she will still not accept the foal, dry her off and treat the foal as an orphan by fostering it or raising it by hand. Bottle

feed it if necessary while you make your mind up. Homoeopathic treatment can help with some mares who are vicious due to discomfort.

In either case, think very seriously before you put the mare in foal again. Apart from problems with the mare, she *may* pass on her difficulties to a filly foal.

### Twins

A perfectly healthy mare with a normal amount of milk may produce twins but she will almost certainly not have enough milk to feed two. You can do several things here. You could take one twin away and treat it as an orphan. If one twin is more robust, it is probably best to take this one (ask your vet) and either foster it or rear it by hand. However, this is a shame unless a suitable foster mother is available and it is generally preferable to supplement the mare's milk by bottle feeding, then move on to bucket feeding, with solid feed built up as soon as possible and fairly early weaning. This will be less draining to the mare and better for both offspring. The mare will, of course, need her feed adjusted accordingly.

### The orphan foal

First of all, the foal *must* have colostrum or, failing that, antibiotics, probiotics and perhaps an enema. Bottle feed a mare's milk replacer and start an earnest search for a foster mother. Ask local vets, veterinary colleges and other breeders in the area and consider an appeal on local radio, newspapers or even TV! Your milk pellet/replacer manufacturer may also keep a register of orphans and mares available for fostering. You can also try the National Foaling Bank at Newport, Shropshire, which has dealt with thousands of motherless foals. Contact Newport (01952) 811234.

Until you find one, or if you cannot find a foster mother, you will have to feed the foal yourself. While you are still looking for a foster mother, bottle feed so that the foal does not have to relearn how to suckle. However, once you are certain you will be hand rearing, it is easier to bucket feed.

If a foster mother cannot be found and you have to hand rear a foal, you will need powdered mare's milk replacer, clean buckets, bottles, teats, whisk (for mixing), thermometer (milk is fed at blood heat, at least to start with), time/patience/helpers and, after the third or fourth day, suitable solid food. Aim to have the foal drinking from a bucket as soon as possible and eating a significant amount of solid feed by two weeks of age. Follow the milk manufacturer's instructions implicitly. These vary from product to product so read and understand them and, if in doubt, contact the manufacturer. You must avoid changing brands of milk powder during foal rearing, so be sure you can obtain a regular supply and renew supplies in good time. Consider the foal's need for companionship and warmth and do not 'over-isolate' it from other animals. If penned, a goat or ewe may prove an acceptable companion but go carefully.

Under normal conditions, a foal may suckle its dam as often as four times per hour in the first week of life, down to twice an hour by six weeks and once an hour, or less, by six months. It may suck for a few seconds to a few minutes at a time. Some liquid feeding is probably essential for a few weeks but as a foal is a slow feeder, it is desirable to encourage it to take a few mare's milk pellets within a couple of days of birth, increasing to 125–450 g per day (4–16 oz) at one week of age, depending on the brand used. Also give adequate *clean* drinking water, filtered if necessary. Skimmed cow's milk is *not* fortified for foals.

The foal should be trained to suck from a teat as soon as possible after birth when the sucking urge is strong. The foal's mouth is held open, the teat inserted and a small amount of milk squeezed from it. The milk should be at blood heat (37°C/98.6°F) and this procedure usually stimulates the foal to suck. A small, soft teat should be used (obtainable from Volac or your agricultural merchant or vet).

To teach foals to drink from a bucket or shallow bowl, the handler should allow the foal to suck his or her clean middle fingers while they are gradually lowered into the milk. Having led and, if necessary, gently pushed the foal's muzzle into the bowl, the fingers should be gently removed as the foal sucks the milk. Given that you have decided to hand rear the foal, the longer you leave training it to drink from a bucket, the harder it will be.

If the foal is very weak, it may need feeding three times per hour, being offered 150–300 ml (5–10 fl oz) at each feed. Strong, healthy foals should be fed once an hour (day *and* night!) for the first week, reducing this to every two hours if you are using your own concoction based on BST-free cow's milk. If you are using a proprietary mare's milk replacer, which will be better balanced, you can reduce feeding times to once every three hours.

With this type of product, you will be able to reduce feeding sessions to every six or even twelve hours by six weeks of age, depending on the foal's condition and consumption of solid feed and fresh water. Water should be available from the first day, very fresh, in a safe container and at a height at which the foal can see into it and reach it.

Creep feed specially formulated for foals should be introduced during week two, up to 1 per cent of bodyweight. Hay should be available from week three for the foal to pick at. After eight weeks the milk replacer can be gradually reduced and the feed (hay plus creep feed) increased to about 2.5 per cent of bodyweight. The foal can be safely weaned once it is eating at least 1 kg ($2\frac{1}{4}$ lb) of creep feed and 0.5 kg (1 lb) of good quality hay per day.

On any system, it is preferable not to wean an orphan before sixteen weeks of age, although three weeks has been achieved successfully. Always wean according to condition, not age, and ensure that the weanling is eating solids well and drinking water. Whether foals are on or off the dam, they should be wormed monthly from four weeks of age, using a product prescribed by your vet as the products that tack shops are now allowed to sell to the public are inadequate for a complete worming programme. However, if the foal is isolated from other horses, herbal vermifuges may be sufficient at this stage.

## The Lactating Mare

A lactating mare has two nutritional needs that are often neglected. First, she has an increased requirement for salt, both for herself and to pass on to the foal in the milk – from 0.5 to 1 per cent of the total diet. This works out as up to 100 g (4 oz) per day for a 500-kg (1,100 lb) mare, i.e. approximately 4 tablespoons daily if you are home mixing. This much cannot be obtained from a salt lick.

The mare's water requirement also increases quite considerably. It is logical that she will need more water to produce milk but it is surprising how often this need is ignored, especially for stabled mares. In a hot summer you should also take particular care to ensure that normal water sources in fields are not overstretched by lactating mares with foals.

Once the foal is born, the nutrient density (i.e. quality) of the mare's ration must increase in accordance with her milk production, taking into consideration the grazing available. Protein, energy, vitamin and mineral levels will all need to be enhanced, building up to a maximum level during months one to four of lactation and gradually reducing to weaning.

The mare's protein and energy requirements rise to 14 per cent crude protein (in the *total* diet) until three months, then 12 per cent until weaning. The calcium and phosphorus requirements also increase and the ratio changes slightly. The amount of limestone or dicalcium phosphate required to cover this will depend on your other feeds and supplements. Choose a supplement from those specially formulated for broodmares, one which contains beta-carotene and folic acid (folacin, folate), a vitamin which can easily become deficient after foaling especially in early-foaling Thorough-breds or those on poor pasture.

If you use stud cubes or mix, do not dilute them by mixing with other ingredients, except while they are being introduced. *Either* mix your own feed *or* use stud cubes as they are balanced for feeding with forage alone. If in doubt, ask the manufacturer.

If you prefer to mix your own feed or if you have a mare with require-ments which tend to be rather different from the average, using a cereal balancer in conjunction with your own oats/barley and other ingredi-ents, including sugar beet and alfalfa (lucerne) cubes, is a useful, flexible system. Cereal balancers enable you to adjust the nutrient density of the diet by varying the amount fed at different stages of pregnancy and lactation and the quantity and proportion of cereals and other ingredients added.

A number of products are available, with systems of varying degrees of complexity. A number of these have the added advantage that they can be used either alone or diluted to some extent as pre- and post-weaning diets for the foals themselves.

Whatever you choose to feed, maintaining the fibre levels and the stability of the gut micro-organisms of the broodmare plays a vital part in both her own health and that of her unweaned foal. These can affect all aspects of equine health, including the immune system, and, with this in mind, it is a good idea to feed some form of chaff, particularly as a substitute for bran, at every feed.

It is essential not to overload the mare's digestive system by feeding too large an amount of concentrates at any one time. Divide her ration into an absolute minimum of two feeds per day, three or four being better. For a 450-kg (1,000 lb) mare the maximum amount of concentrates at any one feed should be 2 kg ($4\frac{1}{2}$ lb).

*Suggested feeding chart for lactating mares*

|  | Forage:<br>concentrate<br>ratio | Kg feed for 100<br>kg bodyweight<br>(lb/100 lb) |
|---|---|---|
| First 12 weeks of<br>lactation, i.e.<br>March to May in<br>UK for non-<br>Thoroughbreds | forage 45%:<br>concentrate 55% | 3 kg/100 kg<br>(3 lb/100 lb)<br>(for native ponies the ratio should be<br>2.5:100) |
| 13th week of<br>lactation to<br>weaning, i.e. June<br>to August in UK | forage 60%:<br>concentrate 40% | 3 kg/100 kg<br>(3 lb/100 lb) for<br>heavy milkers,<br>condition losers<br>etc.; 2.5 kg/100 kg<br>(2.5 lb/100 lb)<br>for others.<br>(for native<br>ponies the ratio should be 2:100) |
| Weaning to last three<br>months of next<br>pregnancy | forage 75%:<br>concentrate 25% | 2.5 kg/100 kg<br>(2$\frac{1}{2}$ lb/100 lb)<br>(for native<br>ponies the ratio should be 2:100) |

These guidelines will vary depending on the mare's access to pasture and the quality of the grass. From April to June most pasture has high nutrient levels but is low in fibre and dry matter. If the contribution of the pasture to the ration is not taken into consideration the mare will be overfed.

## Weaning

As weaning approaches, the foal should be on full daily concentrate rations and good quality forage/grazing so that there is no post-weaning setback. Meanwhile, the mare's concentrates should be reduced in quantity and nutrient density so that her milk dries off quickly.

Probiotics for both mare and foal for five to ten days before and after weaning will minimise stress and help to prevent scouring. It will also prevent scouring when the mare and foal are turned out on to rich grazing or if there is a sudden flush of grass growth. (Feeding hay, oat straw or chaff at this time will also help.)

Another valuable feedstuff for both mare and foal throughout this period and up to at least two years old, is fresh (but wilted) or dried comfrey (*Symphytum*). It is a good source of minerals, vitamin $B_{12}$ and proteins to promote balanced growth. Growing two or three plants per mare and foal or yearling will be plenty. Dried comfrey can be used in the winter. Recent research on humans experiencing difficulties with comfrey has been highly misleading and there is no evidence to indicate that there is any problem about feeding it to horses. Horses' digestive systems are different in many respects to those of humans and comfrey has been widely fed to horses in large amounts for hundreds of years.

## Normal Foal Feeding

Although many people regard mare's milk and nibbling hay or grass to be sufficient up to weaning, it is worth remembering that, for optimum growth, milk is deficient in a number of nutrients, e.g. iron (Fe). Although milk may be sufficient for native ponies which are highly efficient at utilising their feed, provided both mare and foal are wormed regularly, other young-stock will survive but are not likely to thrive without some supplementary feeding.

Many people are frightened to allow youngsters to grow too fast as they fear developmental bone abnormalities. These are often attributed to 'too much protein' but, in fact, this is very rarely the case. Developmental bone abnormalities are more likely to be due to the youngster receiving too *few* of the minerals and trace elements needed to build a strong skeletal structure and the vitamins and essential amino acids to facilitate this and to build muscles and energy. Trials on several hundred Thoroughbred youngsters in Australia and America showed that the ones on a high-protein (quality amino acids), energy, mineral and vitamin diet had fewer metabolic bone disorders, such as epiphysitis and contracted tendons, than those on 'traditional' diets at slower growth rates.

What must be avoided is giving too much digestible energy so that the foal or youngster puts on weight due to *fat* rather than quality *growth*. This strains the bones and joints and causes many problems, as is often the case with youngsters prepared for sales or shows.

It is a good idea to introduce the foal to creep-feeding (pre-weaning feeding) early, say, at three to four weeks, ideally using a proprietary creep mix – the mare's stud cubes are rarely nutritious enough, especially if you are breeding potential competition horses or racehorses. If you mix your own feed, base it on a little cereal, sugar beet, dried alfalfa, high quality protein, e.g. soya or proprietary supplemented milk pellets, plus the appropriate dose of a vitamin and mineral supplement and dicalcium phosphate. The foal usually needs additional calcium and salt.

Start by offering small, freshly prepared amounts, e.g. in the 'dip' of a house brick, and build up to using a creep manger or creep area to keep the mare away. Always use a container that the foal can *see* into, just as with the fresh water source that the foal will need from a few weeks old.

It has been noted that one of the most important aspects in avoiding problems in the joints and limbs in growing equines is to maintain an *even* growth rate, so you should check your foal's weight, height and cannon bone length regularly. Keep a simple graph if you like. Be very vigilant for sudden changes, e.g. at weaning, if the mare or foal is ill, when there is a flush of grass growth, when there is a new batch of feed or at times of stress (a new horse in the yard, a first journey or show, etc.) and make any necessary adjustments. If there is a check in growth rate, the trouble is likely to occur when growth then speeds up later to compensate.

## Feeding Weanlings to Two Year Olds

Pregnant and lactating mares and youngstock should be wormed adequately using an appropriate alternating programme. It is preferable, where possible, that they graze clean pasture, uncontaminated by other adult horses, or at least sensibly managed (droppings collected/harrowing/topping/resting/ use of cattle and sheep, etc.). Cattle and sheep are parasitised by different worms to those that parasitise horses.

It is often useful to sit back and envisage your probable two-year-old rations and your yearling ration, fix on your transitional eighteen-month ration (perhaps taking out milk powder or cutting down on soya and introducing protein and energy sources such as cereals). Look at the whole period as a phasing transition from one diet to the other to check on progress but alter feeding by live weight and condition, not age, taking into account quality of grazing, forage, weather conditions, etc. If you have a number of youngstock of all ages, you can make your yearling ration and two-year-old ration and then mix the two so that, at eighteen months, they will receive approximately half of each. Alternatively, use a cereal balancer, increasing the levels of cereals while keeping the level of 'balancer' stable and thus automatically adjusting the nutrient density of the diet. This is my preferred system. Ask your veterinary surgeon or a qualified nutritionist to confirm that your vitamins and minerals are in balance once you depart from a compound feed or concentrate manufacturer's recommendations.

The importance of fresh air, sunlight, exercise, adequate protein, minerals, amino acids and appropriate digestible energy levels cannot be over-emphasised whatever the breed or desired growth rate.

If problems occur, long periods of box rest can have a disastrous effect on bone density and this is not an acceptable management tool for youngstock. You must take steps to correct the imbalance or deficiency causing the problem and get the youngster outside as soon as possible. If it is unweaned, then sort out the mare's diet and feed her properly next time she is in foal and lactating.

For native ponics, a feed block or a supplement and a little molassed, mixed alfalfa hay chaff may be all that is needed in terms of supplementary feeding *provided* there are no mineral deficiencies inherent on the land where they are kept, or any digestive or malabsorption problems in the mare (e.g. poor teeth in an elderly mare; old worm damage, etc.). A probiotic soon after birth will certainly do no harm, even for native pony foals.

Feed the non-racehorse two year old as for an adult according to size and use, although some late-maturing, heavier types may need the feed adjusted accordingly.

### Nutrient requirements (fresh basis) 1

| | Digestible energy (DE) mJ/kg of feed | mJ/lb of feed | Crude protein (CP) % | Calcium (Ca) % | Phosphorus (P) % | Ca:P ratio |
|---|---|---|---|---|---|---|
| First creep feed | 12.9 | 5.86 | 18–20 | 0.8 | 0.55 | 1.5:1 |
| Foal (3 months) | 12.45 | 5.65 | 18 | 0.8 | 0.55 | 1.5:1 |
| Weanling (6 months) | 11.5 | 5.23 | 16 | 0.6 | 0.45 | 1.3:1 |
| Yearling (12 months) | 11.1 | 5.02 | 14.5 | 0.5 | 0.35 | 1.4:1 |
| Long yearling (18 months) | 10.1 | 4.60 | 12 | 0.4 | 0.3 | 1.3:1 |
| Two year old (initial training) | 11.1 | 5.02 | 9–10 | 0.4 | 0.3 | 1.3:1 |
| Resting mature horse or pony | 8.3 | 3.77 | 7.5–8 | 0.27 | 0.18 | 1.1:1 to 1.5:1 |

*Nutrient requirements (fresh basis) 2*

| | *Daily feed (1) intake kg/100 kg or lb/100 lb bwt* | *Ration proportion (2)* Concentrates % | *Roughage* % |
|---|---|---|---|
| First creep feed | 1/2–3/4 | 100 | 0 |
| Foal (3 months) | 9.2 | 75–80 | 20–25 |
| Weanling (6 months) | 11.0 | 65–70 | 30–35 |
| Yearling (12 months) | 13.2 | 45–55 | 45–55 |
| Long yearling (18 months) | 14.3 | 30–40 | 60–70 |
| Two year old (initial training) | 14.5 | 30–40 | 60–70 |

**Note**

1 Based on a foal destined to reach 500 kg (1,100 lb) mature weight ('average' 15.2 hh male Thoroughbred – range for breed 425–625 kg or 937–1,378 lb)

2 Poor roughage. Choose higher proportion concentrates and vice versa.

3 It is essential that adequate amounts of copper and zinc are included in these rations. There is evidence that these two trace minerals are often deficient in youngstock rations, partly because their levels in UK pasture are low.

## Stallions

The stallion is acknowledged by all and sundry for his pre-eminent role in the breeding process, a factor which is reflected in both his value and in the level of stud fees. Surprisingly, therefore, other than in more practical matters such as superior, though not always suitable, stabling, the poor stallion is largely the most neglected animal on the stud, especially when it comes to considering his specific nutritional requirements, whether on a practical level in the feed room or at the level of scientific research.

Despite the financial value and earnings attributable to the stallion, the expenditure on research specific to the health, longevity, welfare and, more particularly, breeding performance of the stallion is almost negligible.

Altruistic motives aside, the willingness of the breeding industry world-wide, along with the veterinary and nutrition research establishments and the feed industry, to let the matter of stallion performance (service/conception rates) rest on a blind faith in genetics and a feed regime which ranges from one that is most suited to a pregnant broodmare to one more appropriate for a child's pony is somewhat surprising and, to nutritionists, exasperating! It is especially ironic when enormous sums of money are spent on heroic measures to treat infertility in the mare when, in many cases, these infertile mares only need a change in diet.

The common use of proprietary stud cubes or mixes for feeding stallions is all very well but these are, by and large, formulated to suit the average requirements of the average mare and average youngstock at an average stage, from six to 24 months, in the hope that they can strike a happy medium. While this might be convenient for a stud that is unable to use a more comprehensive range of proprietary feeds or to mix its own balanced rations, it is really not at all suited to the specific requirements of the stallion.

The stallion will almost certainly be mature (over 34 months of age) and is obviously not pregnant, lactating or growing (as opposed to 'filling out') to any great extent. He may, on the other hand, be elderly, which could necessitate an increase in the nutrient density of the diet as he becomes less efficient at extracting what he needs from it.

In the breeding season, we know for sure that his digestible energy requirements will increase, depending on his work load, exercise and, to a degree, his temperament and demeanour, although these latter aspects can, to some extent, depend on what he is being fed.

The aim in supplying energy should be to maintain condition and, while he should carry reasonable condition at the start of the season, the practice of starting the season with an obese stallion who can work 'off his back' is not going to help nature to help you. Although the typical stallion is far removed from his feral cousins, being 'fat and sassy' is never conducive to a successful stallion career even for a Thoroughbred! Obesity is likely to cause strain on the stallion's heart and legs and, indeed, on the mares, especially maiden mares.

Every season one hears of a stallion dropping down dead when 'in action' and it seems likely that obesity will increase the danger of this occurring, as may the presence of migrating worm larvae blocking various crucial blood vessels, either to the heart or to the vessels servicing the gut (the latter being a common cause of colic). I am unaware of any statistics on this matter but it would certainly seem to be imprudent to risk the longevity of a valuable sire by allowing him to become obese.

Likewise, the worming policy should be carefully assessed with your vet.

Another more specific problem of obesity is that it is thought that excessive deposits of fatty tissue around the testes may lead to the overheating of these organs and a consequent reduction in viable sperm, which may be reflected in reduced conception rates. That extra few kilograms of inappropriate feed could cost thousands in no-foal-no-fee claims, not to mention damage to the stallion's reputation, so it is worth bearing this factor in mind.

Although one expects a Thoroughbred stallion, for example, to 'fill out' when he comes out of training and to carry a certain amount of extra weight, particularly on his front end, the aim must be to keep him fit but not fat if you wish to maximise his potential. Low conception rates are often blamed squarely on the mare but I suspect that the stallion plays a much bigger role in this problem than we may yet have appreciated.

The other, more specific aspect of stallion nutrition, which has received very little attention, is the influence of nutrition on specific aspects of stallion fertility, including sperm production, sperm viability and motility, semen acidity (pH) and libido.

We do know that the stallion is affected by the same seasonal influences as the broodmare and thus by day length and richer food. He therefore suffers the same disadvantages, especially those imposed by the artificially early breeding season practised in the Thoroughbred industry.

It follows that the use of artificial light, combined with an increased nutrient density in the diet, is likely to be beneficial if commencing mid–late December and January, as is the case with the mare. However, the specific feed regimes would be expected to be along different lines as the stallion will not require the same large increase in protein intake which the mare needs in late gestation and lactation.

Out of season, his requirements will be no more than for any other resting, mature horse or as suitable for ridden or driven work if this is undertaken. The aim should be to maintain bodyweight at the optimum level and to ensure that the basic nutrient requirements are met. The simplest method is to feed good grass or meadow hay plus horse and pony cubes or mix, or, where work is being performed, a competition mix or a home mix of cereals, preferably with chaff (especially if filled legs are a problem). Also feed soaked sugar beet pulp, salt and a good, basic vitamin/mineral supplement, plus a salt lick in the field and stable, *or* a little cereal with a proprietary cereal balancer.

At this stage, he will probably be receiving around 2.5 per cent of his bodyweight as dry feed and of this 25–30 per cent may be concentrates (more if he is working) of no more than 8 per cent crude protein, and the rest will be forage. If you feed fresh (wilted) comfrey on the stud, the stallion will benefit from 1.5–5 kg/day (3 lb 5 oz–11 lb) as this is a rich, natural source of good quality protein, calcium and naturally occurring B vitamins.

For Thoroughbreds, start increasing the amount of concentrates to make up 40–50 per cent of the total feed intake by weight in December. In January you can increase the nutrient density of this, i.e. every kilogram of feed you give will contain more energy, vitamins and minerals. For non-racehorse studs, you start later and take into account the better spring grass which becomes available.

If you use compounds, you can do this by changing from horse and pony cubes or mix to racehorse (not stud) or competition cubes or mix but choose one whose crude protein level does not exceed 12 per cent. A stallion whose sweat is foamy and sticky is almost certainly receiving excess protein, as is one who breaks out in a sweat at night. Filled legs may also indicate too little fibre.

Ideally, this should be fed with chop or chaff, the molassed type if this is more convenient, to keep the fibre level up.

If you prefer to mix your own rations, a simple solution is to use a proprietary cereal balancer which is likely to be a blend of ingredients containing energy, protein, vitamins and minerals, which you feed at a fixed daily rate depending on the bodyweight of your horse, and make up the balance with oats, barley, breadmeal (Bailey's No. 1) and sugar beet pulp as you wish, to maintain bodyweight. Again, preferably feed chaff.

I prefer not to feed bran on the stud as it is so unbalanced from a calcium/phosphorus viewpoint and locks up calcium from the rest of the diet. Bran mashes simply serve to upset the digestive micro-organisms (hence their 'laxative' effect). If you need to use them then your diet is unbalanced and lacking in fibre and not suitable for a valuable, high-performance horse.

In the overall diet, you should aim for no more than 10 per cent crude protein; with a lysine content of 0.4 per cent; a calcium to phosphorus ratio of between 1.1:1 and 2:1; a salt content of 0.5–1 per cent; a good range of vitamins and minerals; and digestible energy levels as necessary to maintain bodyweight.

I feel there is a good case for using a vitamin/mineral supplement, even in the absence of specific research, as a few pence a day is a small price to pay for 'insurance' or the reputation of a valuable stallion. There is some indication that vitamin C (ascorbic acid) and zinc may be beneficial where sperm motility is a problem, although ensuring an adequate supply of fibre should enable the majority of stallions to produce their own adequate levels of vitamin C (which is produced in the liver) with the aid of the digestive micro-organisms. There is no point in fiddling about with high-profile nutrition unless you get the balance of your basic ration right first. There is no 'magic dust' that will cure fundamentally wrong feeding.

From 1–4 tablespoons of soya, rice or corn oil a day will help to maintain coat condition and provide essential fatty acids.

If hyperexcitability is a problem, megadoses of vitamin E or, if necessary, vitamin $B_1$ (thiamine) may help but only give this under expert guidance.

I feel quite strongly that, apart from the psychological benefits, adequate quality exercise is likely to help to stimulate an active and finely tuned metabolism, which will be beneficial to health and longevity and, consequently, it is hoped, to lifetime breeding performance.

Suitable pasture is important but I should point out that a surprisingly high number of Thoroughbred studs I visit have stallion paddocks which are surrounded by poisonous hedges (e.g. laurel or privet), often within reach of the stallion who, although he may only snatch the odd mouthful, may, cumulatively, receive enough toxic material to affect both health and performance. No matter how smart these hedges may look, they are simply not worth the risk. The same applies to poisonous ornamental trees *anywhere* on the stud. Horses occasionally get loose, even in the best-run establishments.

All feedstuffs should be clean and free from obvious moulds and dust. If bought-in cereals are ready-rolled, they should be used within three weeks, sooner in summer. Mouldy feed can contain aflotoxins and other mycotoxins which could lead to fertility problems, apart from allergic reactions to the moulds, such as COPD.

# 9     Feeding Elderly Equines

## Defining Old Age

While a competition horse *may* need to be moved on to a new, slightly less strenuous activity by the time it is thirteen or fourteen, I believe we should not be thinking in terms of 'old' where horses are concerned until they are at least eighteen and I see no reason why any horse should not remain active until at least its mid-twenties, given proper care and attention.

This should be the norm but, unfortunately, both owners and their vets seem all too ready to write off the 'oldies' as soon as they develop a few problems and no real research has ever been done on breed variations' potential for longevity, although, generally, native ponies tend to be the longest-lived horses and donkeys the longest-lived equids over all. Recent work suggests that older horses have increased requirements for both protein and phosphorus.

Just as we are learning that, through attention to diet and exercise, humans can have a healthier, more active old age, so I'm sure that, with planning, we can get much more from our older horses and repay them for their lifelong service to us.

This does not mean sticking them in a field to retire and possibly pine away. It is painful to watch a faithful old retainer gazing after the hunt or after its stable mates as they go off to have fun.

Older horses need *more* care, not less, but you can be sure they will repay it manyfold.

A study of humans around the world who have lived to be more than 100 consistently showed that a life of hard – often extremely hard – physical work, frugal living, a tendency to be thin, eat unprocessed foods and little red meat, were major factors in extreme longevity and an active old age. Sitting around getting fat is not a recipe for longevity in any species!

Many of the older horses one meets are old riding school retainers who have worked long and steadily into their twenties. I have also noticed that one sees a fair number of eighteen to 28 year olds in the non-competitive endurance rides of 40–80 km (25–50 miles) – in fact, a number of eighteen year olds have consistently won or been placed in 160 km (100 mile) competitions at international level.

No one can say when a horse becomes 'elderly'. Perhaps, like humans, they are as young as they feel but, unlike humans, they cannot choose to eat and exercise to prolong their youthful good looks and vitality! Many horses are written off by the time they reach fourteen, yet most of us know of at least one still playing an active role at 25 and even 35 or 40 in the case of donkeys. (The winner of the 1993 Super Solvitax Veterans' Competition was still doing clear round jumping at 42, as was the runner-up, aged 40!)

The experience of the Donkey Sanctuary may provide one important clue as to what keeps a horse healthy – or otherwise – into a ripe old age. In conversation with an official from the Greek Department of Agriculture, Sanctuary staff mentioned that most of the donkeys in their care lived happily into their forties. The official expressed his disbelief, pointing out that a working donkey in Greece would not be expected to live beyond thirteen to fifteen. He had never heard of the phrase 'donkey's years' (meaning a very long time) and thought they were exaggerating.

Elizabeth Svendsen and the veterinary team at the Sanctuary decided to try to find the key to this, in conjunction with the Greek Government and various international human aid agencies (donkeys are a major source of 'horsepower' in poorer rural communities throughout the Third World, so their health, well-being and longevity also benefit their owners. They took over the parasite treatment of all equines on one Greek island, with dramatic results. Following this, their sister charity now organises and often funds such projects throughout the Third World.

The Donkey Sanctuary research suggests that it is not unreasonable to expect that lifetime parasite damage – particularly, I suspect, during foalhood – can have a far-reaching effect on the lifespan and working life of all equines.

When young, they may well cope with quite a high parasite burden but they will not thrive. Then, as the gut walls, blood vessels and even lungs are progressively damaged, there will be an inevitable loss of efficiency in absorption of minerals, including those that delay the effects of ageing and have a role to play, for example, in cancer protection (melanoma, a type of cancer, is the biggest cause of premature death in grey horses), anti-arthritic factors, health of the gums, teeth and hooves, and skin and coat condition – all frequently considered inevitable diseases of old age. These are, in fact, degenerative diseases which may be delayed or accelerated depending on the way a horse is managed and, of course, on its response to illness and injuries.

We manage our domesticated horses in such a way that they cannot help picking up a heavy parasite burden. While they can build up a certain amount of resistance, physical damage to tissues and organs can be cumulative and irreparable.

If we buy a horse that is already badly affected by parasites, we can at least endeavour to arrest its future decline. If damage is extensive, we can manage the horse to accommodate this by making its feed more easily digested and absorbed. We can reduce future exposure by appropriate positive management and enhance natural resistance by, for example, regularly feeding garlic, a natural ingredient to supplement, but not replace, the regular worming programme.

## Common Problems of Ageing

Other common 'last-straw' problems in elderly horses include loss of teeth, chronic digestive upsets, crumbling hooves, skin lesions, degeneration of bones and joints and breeding problems. There is something you can do to minimise the effects of all of these and this does not just mean throwing expensive drugs at the problem to mask the symptoms.

As horses get older, their teeth are increasingly likely to wear unevenly and will require diligent and more frequent attention if pain, abscesses and poor mastication of food are to be avoided. Old horses that lose a lot of weight often need their teeth rasping to enable them to bite off and chew their various feeds properly.

The teeth may fall out, especially in broodmares because the mare has mobilised all her reserves of minerals to feed her foal and something had to give. This could be prevented by feeding appropriately and adequately throughout pregnancy and into lactation, taking into account her age and hard-working life to date.

Even once the teeth have fallen out or been removed, it may well be possible to feed sugar beet and alfalfa-based mashes (not bran) with perhaps Bailey's Meal – all soft, small particles and easy to swallow – or soaked compound cubes, with soaked grass meal and nutritionally improved straw cubes for fibre.

In these situations, you have to weigh up the horse's quality of life and usefulness and whether you want to be bothered. I have a number of clients who have acquired horses with no teeth, or whose teeth have been removed. One was still appearing at local shows and winning rosettes when aged between 28 and 33 years old with no teeth at all – so it can be done! It does not cost any more to give horses soaked feed – unless you put a price on a little forethought.

It is unusual for one owner to have a horse from foalhood through to a great age so overall lifelong management is likely to be mixed and we are usually mostly concerned with patching up and making do with older horses but it is possible to reduce or reverse apparently insoluble problems as long as you recognise the damage, try to establish its cause and eliminate or circumvent it by the way you manage the horse.

As an equine friend ages, you may notice that his or her personality traits become more pronounced; the sweet may get sweeter and the cranky become crankier! However, a gradual decline is not necessarily an inevitable one. If the 'sweetie' is becoming more and more subdued, you should make sure this is not because it is, say, short of B vitamins; if its cranky stable-mate is getting snappier, you should ensure that it is not in pain or perhaps in need of something to settle an uncomfortable digestive system.

Sudden changes in personality should certainly alert us to possible disease problems and new behavioural problems, such as kicking and biting, and even newly developed stable vices, such as crib-biting, wind-sucking or eating dung, may indicate pain or some other age-related problem. Development of a curly coat may indicate hormonal problems and must be looked into urgently.

Of course, in such circumstances you should consult your vet to ensure there are no specific disease problems, including parasites, infections or tumours, or undiagnosed injuries or joint problems – for example, a horse lame in all four legs may well appear sound to the uninitiated. You should also consider whether the horse's diet might be contributing to problems and even causing pain, or whether long-term drug therapy may be having side effects requiring a change in drug or the consideration of herbal or homoeopathic treatments to reduce or eliminate drug requirements.

Physical changes are, of course, much easier to identify and they can range from loss of performance, stiffness, loss of muscle tone and skin tone, to a tendency to run to fat or, conversely, a failure to maintain condition, chronic scouring or constipation, poor hoof condition, sarcoids, melanoma and general stumbling and weakness. All of these conditions can be delayed, modified, alleviated or even, in some cases, cured, by an appropriate diet and inexpensive natural methods used to support the treatment available from your vet.

With appropriate care, it has proved possible to wean horses in their late twenties off long-term painkillers and anti-inflammatories and even to return some bored, pensioned-off 'oldies' to useful and enjoyable work.

Whether you are seeking to prolong an elderly horse's active life in competition, hunting, breeding, leisure activities or the riding school, or to help an old friend to pass its retirement years in ease and comfort, you need to sit down and think about what its specific requirements are.

Unfortunately, all too many vets lose interest in seeking solutions for equine problems after the animal reaches the age of about fifteen and are often very quick to suggest euthanasia after a bout of colic, prolonged scouring or difficult-to-isolate lameness, pointing out the massive cost of drugs and treatment. However, unless the horse is acutely ill and in severe pain, it is well worth considering some of the non-pharmaceutical means of keeping it in reasonable health.

## The Ageing Process

As the horse gets older, it will be faced with the results of a cumulative array of old injuries and stresses, the after-effects of former infections and damage caused through the side effects of treatment for various problems, as well as parasite damage to the walls and lining of the gut, blood vessels and lungs. The horse may have been left with severely disturbed gut micro-organisms (dysbiosis), variously acquired allergies and sensitivities, including COPD (heaves or broken wind), and a tendency to management-related chronic diseases such as laminitis, navicular disease and arthritis.

Because of all this wear and tear, combined with less-efficient mastication as the horse gets (literally) longer in the tooth, it becomes less able to extract, absorb and utilise different nutrients in the feed and may also require specific nutrients to counteract or support the effects of long-term drug therapy. Every horse will be individual in the way this affects it and its ability to utilise different nutrients will vary in tune with its life history.

You need to identify where your horse's particular deterioration may be or, if you are planning an active old age for a younger horse, think how its current condition and any illnesses and injuries could affect it in the future and plan to avoid such problems now. No problem is due solely to old age.

If the horse has digestive upsets, including colic, or laminitis or has to have a course of antibiotics which will kill 'good' bugs as well as bad ones, take steps to get the gut environment back in harmony as quickly as possible.

The last thing the horse needs is to have the 'nutritional carpet' whipped out from under its feet by giving it indigestible bran mashes which actually lock up nutrients it may particularly need at such times. Bran mashes should be an absolute last resort and should always be adequately supplemented (after cooling) with vitamins and minerals.

If you need to make a nutritious mash, try using sugar beet and alfalfa meal soaked together. This is rich in minerals, vitamins and digestible fibre and will actually aid convalescence.

You can also 'dilute' the feed with chaff or molassed chaff. If the horse needs a digestible, non-heating energy source, small amounts of Bailey's No. 1 Bread Meal or extruded cereals can be very useful.

If the horse is laminitis-prone or tends to run to fat, a starvation diet is likely to make matters worse, or at least perpetuate the situation. As well as cutting the carbohydrate levels, starvation diets reduce the horse's vitamin, mineral and amino acid intake and may further unbalance its hormone levels, reduce its ability to absorb other nutrients and hasten its decline.

Small, nutritious, balanced feeds with good quality micro-nutrient supplementation, good access to clean water and a suitable fibre source are the best way to maintain health, reduce stiffness and avoid filled legs and other problems.

If you have a 'gets fat on fresh air' type, especially a native pony, check with your vet whether it might benefit from the use of thyroxine, the thyroid hormone, to speed up the metabolism, or homoeopathic thyroxine or TSH (thyroid stimulating hormone). Remember that you must supply the nutrients the horse needs to support this and that it is not effective in every case. The horse should also be checked for Cushing's disease, especially if it develops curly hair.

## Essential Exercise

Plenty of suitable exercise is also important. If the horse is retired to a field, company, interest and a change of scene may also help.

Gently pulling things can be a very useful exercise, especially for older broodmares, as it strengthens the 'sling system' – the sheets of muscles which support the abdomen. These tend to weaken and slacken as muscle tone is lost with age and repeated foaling, especially where poor nutrition, exercise quality and, to an extent, conformation are a factor, leading to a deeply sagging back and abdomen which is almost certainly uncomfortable if not painful.

Both broodmares and competitive horses would benefit from exercises designed to tone and strengthen these muscles throughout life. However, it is probably never too late to start and pulling a set of harrows or a small cart should not be too onerous on well-managed pasture as long as you do not overdo it with an underfit horses.

See also Poor Doers (page 248) and Skin and Hoof Care (page 249).

# 10  Donkeys and Other Equids

## Donkeys and Mules

Donkeys are not simply small horses with boxy feet and long ears and when it comes to their feed and management a number of specific considerations need to be taken into account.

Mules tend to follow their donkey heritage in terms of feed utilisation efficiency, although there are no hard and fast rules. Management should always be carefully tailored to the individual.

The donkey is thought to be a more efficient water conserver than the horse and can, therefore, exist, but not necessarily *flourish*, on a more restricted water supply. On average, adult UK-sized donkeys will probably have a daily requirement of between 18–26 litres (4–8 gal) of water per day, depending on ambient temperature and humidity, work-load or stage of lactation and how lush any grazing is. As with horses, lactating donkeys will generally have a higher water requirement for milk production and donkey foals should have access to clean water in a receptacle they can see into from a few days of age.

Unfortunately, in more prosperous and temperate countries, where the majority of donkeys are kept as pets or for leisure use, breeding and showing, the majority of the donkey population is either overweight or even seriously obese. It is interesting that the Donkey Sanctuary at Sidmouth in Devon, who, at any one time, have something in the order of 2,000–3,000 donkeys in their care, comment that for every one admitted which is seriously underweight, they receive twenty animals which are seriously overweight, even though they are admitted because they are being maltreated.

A useful rule of thumb is to say that the donkey's feed requirements are likely to be in the order of three-quarters (75 per cent) of those published for horses on a bodyweight basis, in view of the donkey's apparently greater efficiency of food utilisation. If you have a new donkey and this feed level is used as a guide, however, a severely underweight donkey will have to be *gradually* introduced to a higher plane of nutrition (possibly with the addition of supportive vitamins/minerals/hormonal therapy) but the 75 per cent level is not an unrealistic level to aim for. In fact, too rapid an introduction of additional feed may overload the system, especially the micro-organisms in the gut and precipitate an attack of laminitis. A new donkey which you think is 'about right', can be observed for any loss or gain of condition at this rate and the feed levels can then be adjusted accordingly.

The severely overweight donkey will benefit from a carefully reduced feeding rate. In this latter context, I understand that it is the experience of the Donkey Sanctuary that the optimum level of weight loss is about 1 kg per month ($2\frac{1}{4}$ lb). Faster weight loss than this may precipitate such metabolic disorders as hyperlipaemia and hyperlipoproteinaemia which can be very serious indeed. Using starvation diets as a means of managing (or mismanaging) laminitis attacks can also precipitate these disorders (see page 122).

Unfortunately, there is, as yet, no simple method of bodyweight estimation available for donkeys. Bodyweight tapes intended specifically for horses appear to be wildly inaccurate when used on donkeys. So far, there seems to be no suitable formula based on body measurements for calculating weight. The best answer is a regular trip to the weighbridge (remembering to subtract the weight of tack and handlers!) or, provided the donkey is amenable and unlikely to struggle and injure itself, a cattle-crush-type farm weighbridge can be used.

As a guide to body condition, the following body parameters for condition scoring donkeys may be helpful.

### Condition scoring for donkeys

| | | |
|---|---|---|
| Grade 1 | very poor | Donkey in danger of permanent damage to health, emaciated, ribs, spine and tuber coxae very prominent. Coat dull. |
| Grade 2 | below average | Donkey at risk. Spine prominent, coat dull. |
| Grade 3 | average/good | Optimum body condition for health, spinous processes |

|  |  | palpable but not prominent. Firm muscle cover. Coat and skin supple, shiny and in good condition. |
| Grade 4 | overfat | Donkey at risk – spinous processes not easily palpated. Coat shiny, skin intact. |
| Grade 5 | obese | Donkey in danger of permanent damage to health. Body well rounded with generous fat cover. Spinous processes not palpable. Coat shiny, skin intact. |

Grade 3 is the one to aim for. In the UK the average 10.2–11.0 hh donkey should weigh between 165 and 170 kg (364–375 lb) with a maximum range of 165–185 kg (364–408 lb). Unfortunately, most show donkeys tend to be about, or over, 185 kg (408 lb) and at considerable risk of certain metabolic disorders including hyperlipaemia and laminitis (founder or 'fever of the feet'). It is very difficult for anybody who cares about both horses and donkeys to see what attractions obesity could have in the showring to excuse this situation. At 190 kg (419 lb) a donkey of 11.0 hh is seriously obese and at *great* risk of hyperlipaemia which can be fatal.

To assess the specific feed requirements, I would say that the total feed dry matter intake should be 1.75–2.25 per cent of bodyweight. Thus a 170-kg (375 lb) donkey will require some 3–3.8 kg (6–8 $\frac{1}{2}$ lb) of *total* feed per day. Jennies in the last stage of pregnancy and the first three months of lactation should follow the upper end of this regime.

It is unlikely that more than 25 per cent of this will be required as concentrates unless the forage is all feeding straw, so this gives a concentrate allowance of 750–900 g (1 $\frac{2}{3}$–2 lb). For a yarded or stabled animal, these figures give a rough guide to the amount of forage to allow (i.e. three times this weight). For donkeys at grass, the requirement is hard to assess but I would suggest that in winter it would not be much less than the allowance for yarded donkeys because, although the donkey will have access to grazing of some sort, it will be of extremely poor feed value and the donkey will not be protected from the elements nor obtain as much benefit from heat given off by its companions in a yard or stable.

Concentrates should be 'non-heating' and may consist of very basic horse and pony cubes or perhaps some rolled barley with sugar beet and chaff, plus clean hay of medium nutritional value and clean feed-grade oat or barley straw ad lib. Trace-mineralised salt licks should also be provided and, if necessary, a very basic vitamin/mineral supplement, perhaps a herbal supplement or a combination of seaweed, cod liver oil and, if necessary, brewer's yeast. Breeding jennies may also benefit from vitamin E or wheatgerm. Breeding stallions should not be neglected when the supplements are given out as micro-nutrient deficiencies can have a significant effect on fertility. Chaff or molassed chaff is generally preferable to bran and for donkeys with COPD moist, packed forages, mixed half and half with barley or oat straw which has been soaked for four hours, or molassed straw chaff, may be fed.

Donkeys appear to exhibit a need for more long-fibre roughage (which includes chaff) than horses or ponies, or, to put it another way, they seem to be more readily susceptible to a shortage of long fibre, having evolved to eat and browse the very roughest pasture and scrubland and, of course, thistles! This is why it is useful to give a basic hay ration in winter, plus added feed straw to top up the roughage levels. It may also be useful to offer straw to donkeys grazing on lush grass to help to bring the fibre levels up and reduce scouring and other problems. In terms of feeding value, 3 kg (6 lb 10 oz) of straw are roughly equivalent to 1 kg (2 lb 4 oz) of hay.

Interestingly, the Donkey Sanctuary have found that donkeys with hoof problems appear to do better on a hay plus barley straw ration rather than on hay plus the vitamin biotin which is often used for these problems in horses. It is my impression that this is because the straw keeps the gut 'fitter' and enhances utilisation of the rest of the nutrients in the diet. It may also be true that the straw-digesting gut micro-organisms are proportionately greater manufacturers of microbial biotin, which the donkey can then utilise, or they may be better at competing against antagonistic yeasts which can use up biotin from the diet before it is absorbed through the gut wall to be utilised by the donkey.

With regard to grazing donkeys, particularly overweight animals, it is important not to defeat the purpose of carefully programmed 'slimming' rations in winter by allowing the donkeys to become overfat again in the summer. Donkeys adapt well to a fairly tight regime of rotational grazing using, if necessary, electric fencing and moving them on before sour patches develop. Donkeys tend to crop the grass very short, so care should be taken to avoid overgrazing as this will retard the recovery of the sward. It should be noted that when donkeys are mixed-grazed with sheep, the sheep will also crop the grass very short. Mixed grazing with other species, however, can help to reduce the parasite burden on the donkeys.

It is important that donkeys are treated comprehensively for lung worm infestation *(Dictyocaulus arnfieldi)*. Lung worm can infest both horses and donkeys and while, contrary to popular opinion, horses can cross-infect other horses, lung worms introduced into a group of horses by donkeys can cause major problems. In the UK it is thought that 70 per cent of all donkeys are infested, as against fewer than 5 per cent of horses with obvious infestations. The majority of donkeys show few or no clinical signs, however, while infected horses have severe respiratory problems which are hard to eradicate. Most standard proprietary anthelmintics have little or no effect on lung worm and a comprehensive programme of specialised treatment, combining isolation, treatment of incoming animals, strict control of the muck heap for infected animals and cleaning of pasture, which may take two or three years, is essential. The Donkey Sanctuary are able to offer detailed advice to both horse and donkey owners if they feel they have problems in this area. The Donkey Sanctuary, Slade House Farm, Salcombe Regis, Sidmouth, Devon, EX10 0NU. Tel: 01395 578222.

The poor old donkey is a very forgiving and put-upon creature which has enabled civilisation to exist and develop over the millennia. Sadly, people take advantage of this and continue to starve and misuse these long-suffering creatures, often due to ignorance and poverty, or else they go to the other extreme and treat them as pampered pets, again through ignorance, thus leading to early, inherent health problems. If, instead of spending time on going to buy extra feed and treats for their donkeys, donkey owners would take the time to work out what they actually require to eat, donkeys would be happier and healthier, with much more satisfactory lives.

Other equids, such as Przewalski's wild horses, zebra, etc. may be encountered in zoos and an increasing number of wildlife parks. The main consideration for these animals is that they are likely to be taken from an environment in which they evolved over thousands of generations. Even if they are actually bred in captivity, as far as possible their feeding should emulate the diet that they would naturally receive, taking into account the different climatic effects which they may encounter in their new environment and the fact that they are no longer free to roam and seek out little patches of mineralised earth or herbs which they may need to correct any imbalances and deficiencies in their diet.

The level of nutrients they require is more likely to be in line with that of the donkey rather than the horse or pony and it is important to remember that, even in large wildlife parks, they will still be receiving less exercise than they would in the wild.

They may also be susceptible to vitamin D deficiencies if they have come from hot sunny countries to temperate climes with a lot of cloud cover. Attempts should be made to find out the prevalent nutrient status of their 'home' territories, although it should also be noted that deficiencies certainly occur in the wild, for example selenium deficiency is well documented in the wild zebra. A diet made up of mixed forages, perhaps supplemented with a herbal mixture, and with adequate supplies of trace-mineralised salt licks, is probably as near as one can get to the conditions these animals would expect to encounter in the wild.

Where a breeding programme is underway, it is particularly important to ensure that the sires and dams have adequate levels of vitamins and minerals, especially if they are expected to produce offspring more frequently than they might in the wild.

# 11 Nutritional Effects on Behaviour and Temperament

Many children, teenagers and quite a few adults derive a certain satisfaction from riding a horse which is constantly cavorting about and is ostensibly 'a bit of a handful'. To the uninitiated, it adds a dash of excitement and seems to demonstrate skill in horsemanship, although, of course, it frequently implies quite the opposite.

Wild behaviour on the part of the horse can be damaging to both horse and rider and in public places, such as on the roads and at shows, can also prove highly dangerous. This is only one aspect of the cost of bad behaviour in horses.

After extreme or repeated exhibitions of bad behaviour, horses are often refused access to various riding areas. Bad behaviour in public can affect the saleability and value of your horse and, of course, temperament problems and nervousness can have a disastrous effect on a horse and rider's competitive aspirations.

Naturally, a great many behavioural problems relate to poor training or fear caused by unfortunate experiences in the past. The result may be nervousness or napping, pain due to unrecognised illnesses, ill-fitting tack, tooth problems, problems which are due to impaired hearing or eyesight, which might even be caused by dehydration, and, of course, an inexperienced rider or just sheer bad riding. However, a considerable proportion of temperament problems and apparent nervousness are induced by various nutritional imbalances or simply by inappropriate feeding.

## The Effects of Bad Behaviour

It is quite obvious that a horse that is 'jumping out of its skin with its eyes out on stalks' is not a particularly good candidate for the dressage arena. Neither is the horse that is sluggish and uninterested in life.

What is less obvious is that the horse that is running backwards at the start of a cross-country course and then leaves the start pulling like a train is far less likely to do well than the cool, calm, collected customer which gathers itself up like a coiled spring and then sets off in a spirit of controlled enthusiasm.

On some occasions, the pyrotechnics may succeed if the joint ability of the horse and rider is sufficiently greater than that of other competitors but that particular horse may well take longer to recover after a competition, have a shorter overall competitive life and will most certainly be more accident-prone.

It is also likely that a pulling horse will wear the rider out much more quickly. A fatigued rider helps to fatigue the horse. A steamed-up horse is certainly not concentrating and is less likely to get out of tricky situations because it simply does not anticipate them and neither does the rider who is too busy fighting to retain a semblance of control.

If the rider does not keep control, the horse is likely to use up a far greater proportion of its energy reserves in the early part of the course and then be flagging towards the end. Even if some sort of control is maintained, a very significant proportion of the energy available to both horse and rider will be dissipated in the fight to keep that control. The horse may well sweat up more than it need have done so that the onset of dehydration will occur sooner.

Transfer all of this to an endurance ride and, even barring accidents, the horse may be driven to its metabolic limits so that the end result could be even more disastrous.

## The Fibre Factor

The most important factor in diet, whether you are showing in hand twice a year or show jumping at county show level twice a week, is to feed the maximum amount of fibre possible for the work rate involved. Increasing the fibre levels in the diet can have an apparently miraculous effect on a number of problems, including filled legs, and especially on the temperament.

If you increase the fibre levels of a horse that has been on a fibre-deficient diet for any great period of time, it may be a good idea also to feed a five to ten-day course of probiotics, or an equivalent course of Thrive, both to help to correct the disturbances in the gut micro-organisms and to enable the horse to adjust to the new diet smoothly.

When the micro-organisms in the diet are out of balance, which can be due to a number of causes, including antibiotics, illness, stress or a fibre-deficient diet, they may produce toxins which can have an effect on the temperament. These are particularly noticeable in horses that are jumpy and exhibit an exaggerated 'startle reflex'.

Horses on a lower fibre diet are also not receiving as many B vitamins through digestion of fibre by the gut micro-organisms and a number of B vitamins can have a calming effect. Greater amounts of B vitamins are required for the horse to utilise a high grain diet, which can compound the problem further. So start by working with nature and keeping the fibre levels in the diet reasonable and then look at the other ingredients in the diet, including its B-vitamin status. Deficiencies of some B vitamins can lead specifically to nervousness.

## Maintaining Fibre Levels

This, of course, includes giving good-quality forage, whether it be hay or moist, packed forage.

Unless they are on a special diet for health reasons, I prefer to see horses receiving not less than 25 per cent (and preferably 30 per cent) by weight of their diet as forage as an *absolute minimum*. In fact, 40 per cent would be desirable as a minimum level, provided the forage is of reasonable nutritional quality. Part of this can be given as chaff or chop with the concentrate feed; in fact, I think this is a good practice.

Molassed chaff is very useful, particularly for horses with wind problems who are on haylage-type forage which tends, with some exceptions, to be rather low in fibre and, in many cases, rather high in protein.

Soaked sugar beet provides a good source of highly digestible fibre and alfalfa (lucerne) chaff or alfalfa/hay/straw mixes are useful too, particularly if your hay is not of a particularly high nutritional value or your horse does not have a good appetite. Grass and alfalfa meal or cubes are also a good source of fibre but you should be careful that you do not end up feeding too much protein in the overall diet.

NIS (nutritionally improved straw) cubes may be used, although you are more likely to find them as a constituent of a compound feed.

## Pollutants and Xenobiotics

It should be noted that quite high levels of nitrate fertilisers are used in the production of grassmeal and cubes, as opposed to alfalfa (lucerne) which, with the aid of soil micro-organisms, produces its own nitrogen. It would increasingly appear that some horses are particularly susceptible to high levels of nitrates and one of the manifestations of this can be behavioural problems. In some areas of the UK there are very high levels of nitrates in the ground water and this should be taken into account when dealing with both behavioural and certain physical problems that are often difficult to pin down.

Other toxic substances, including poisonous weeds, pesticides, high levels of industrial pollutants and the pollution of pastures adjacent to main roads, can also manifest themselves as behavioural problems. It is particularly important to try to remove these materials or to remove the horse from access to them and to ensure that its micro-nutrient nutrition errs on the generous side to enable it to stabilise and detoxify these xenobiotics as effectively as possible. One has to wonder how many sluggish or irritable children's ponies kept in urban 'horse slums' are being affected in this way.

## Digestible Energy

Check that the digestible energy content of your horse's diet is appropriate to the amount of work it is doing.

Deficiencies can cause sluggishness, stumbling and even bad temper and biting if the horse is tired or uncomfortable. An excess of digestible energy, apart from leading to a potential weight gain, can cause severe character and personality changes. This is particularly true of low-fibre diets and where there is some sort of food intolerance.

I once watched an 11 hh pony gallop headlong out of a Pony Club rally field straight across a main road. Apparently, the pony had been behaving badly for about a week and it transpired that the owners had changed from one brand of proprietary coarse mix to a cheaper one made by a local mill that was used to producing cattle feed. The new mix consisted of horse and pony nuts with a few flaked peas and 90 per cent oats because 'horses like oats'! The pony was being fed at the same rate as when on its previous 'non-heating' coarse mix. Luckily no one was killed on that occasion but it does demonstrate that excessive digestible energy intake can have a dangerous effect.

## 'Heating' Feeds

When it comes to 'heating' and 'non-heating' feeds, different people mean different things. Some use the term 'heating' to describe a feed which may be considered to help to keep the horse warm in cold weather when substituted on a weight-for-weight basis for another food.

Digestible energy is a sophisticated means of measuring the usable 'calorie content' of various feedstuffs. In the UK the units used are kilojoules or megajoules. On a weight-for-weight basis, some feedstuffs provide more digestible energy than others. For example, one kilogram of reasonable quality oats may have a digestible energy of 11.0 mJ per kilogram, whereas a kilogram of flaked maize (corn) may have a value of 14.0 mJ per kilogram. Therefore, if in cold weather you substituted a kilogram of oats for a kilogram of maize, the horse will receive more energy for the same weight of 'hard feed' and will keep warmer.

If you leave the horse on this diet when the weather warms up again, provided you do not change the amount of work you are doing, the chances are that it will put on weight or may start tying-up. It may also become nervous and temperamental due to the excess digestible energy it is now receiving. This is one use of the term 'heating' feed, although it would be less confusing to describe it simply as higher digestible energy.

I tend to use the term 'heating' to refer to the phenomenon of ponies that appear to 'hot up' on oats. It is quite likely that you have heard or read that this phenomenon is caused simply by feeding too much digestible energy. If you take the same animal and feed it a different diet with exactly the same amount of energy (called an iso-energetic diet) and it does not 'hot up', which is often the case, then it becomes quite obvious that an excess of digestible energy is not the problem. It is something in the feed itself that is having the 'heating' effect.

Unfortunately, many animal nutritionists frequently assert that there is no such thing as 'hotting up' on oats *per se*. I can only conclude that they have never tried putting affected ponies on to an iso-energetic diet with different ingredients.

If you are feeding an appropriate digestible energy level for the amount of work your horse or pony is doing and it is still 'hotting up' and wasting time and energy, then it obviously makes sense to change the diet. There is more and more evidence, both in equines and other species, including humans, that this effect on temperament is due to food intolerance. This is sometimes described as an allergy which affects the sympathetic and para-sympathetic nervous system via a complex and yet to be fully defined process involving the immune system, hormonal system and hundreds of enzyme processes.

There are certainly factors in oats, such as naturally occurring phenolic compounds, which have quite powerful effects on neurological reactions and this may very well explain the 'hotting up' phenomenon. The fact that many ponies who cannot tolerate 'raw' oats are fine when given extruded (gelatinised) oats further supports the theory of food intolerance. Cooking, which is effectively what extrusion involves, can alter the chemical in the oats which may be causing the problem.

Oats are not the only culprits but are, by far, the commonest, particularly in ponies. Even extremely hard-working ponies, such as those used for carriage driving, can be susceptible. These ponies do have a high digestible energy requirement, however, so a suitable alternative feed source must be found.

## Replacing Oats

If your horse or pony exhibits problems when fed oats, the first thing to do is to cut them out.

If you are using a coarse mix containing oats, you could try changing to cubes as any oats they contain will have been partially cooked during the cubing process. However, very sensitive animals may still be affected.

If you are mixing your own rations, you could use extruded oats. Although they are a useful feedstuff, however, oats are certainly not 'God's gift to horses' and there is no reason at all why you should not use other energy sources.

If you do use a substitute for oats, remember that you will also be altering the fibre and/or vitamin/mineral proportion in the diet, so you should ensure that the whole diet is in balance. Bailey's No. 1 (breadmeal) is a popular choice. Although it has a non-heating energy content it is suitable for both children's ponies and horses working at the very highest performance levels.

## Cereal Intolerances

Occasionally, one comes across a horse or pony which simply cannot tolerate cereals of any kind, although this usually manifests itself in other ways apart from temperament, such as digestive problems, multifocal lameness, arthritis (particularly in younger animals) and various digestive upsets.

You can still produce a high-performance diet for this animal. For a 500-kg (1,100 lb) horse, you can use up to 4 kg (9 lb) per day (absolute maximum) of sugar beet and high levels of feed-grade oil or fat pre-mixes, supplemented with appropriate vitamin E and choline levels, alfalfa nuts or meal, or even with grass nuts or meal (the meal is generally more palatable but dusty), although I am increasingly uncomfortable about the high levels of nitrates used to grow the grass that is used.

You should also use the best quality forage you can obtain so that the maximum nutritional value can be obtained from it. Ingredients such as palm kernel meal and other non-cereals have proved useful with difficult cases.

Allergy treatments using dilute vaccine prepared by the Miller method are also being tested with some early success and may prove necessary in extreme cases where cereal *and* grass intolerance occurs (grasses and cereals are, in fact, related).

## Electrical Sensitivity

There is increasing evidence that some horses are particularly sensitive to electro-magnetic fields and this often starts with very high exposure levels, for example being stabled under, or very near, electric pylons and particularly near electrical transformers – the green boxes that one sees by the roadside or the smaller transformers which are placed halfway up poles.

Horses may become dopey or agitated and may develop food intolerances, which can, at times, be severe. They may then start reacting to other electrical sources, including those used for physiotherapy treatments, and fluorescent lights. This can prove a major problem when, say, competing indoors under fluorescent lighting, when horses have been known to fall over 'inexplicably', causing injury to horse and rider.

The horse may also become light- or dark-sensitive and while specialised vitamin supplementation can help with this problem, the most important step is to identify the original cause.

I would not wish to stable horses within 460 m (500 yd) of electricity pylons. If they are grass-kept and there are pylons in, or adjacent to, the field, it is important that they can get well away from them for at least part of the day and are not restricted to a tiny paddock which gives them no choice. Unfortunately, these electro-magnetic fields can be addictive in some circumstances and some horses will be drawn to them, which can lead to a lifetime of problems.

Sensitised horses may have a tendency to leap about inexplicably on rides and, when they have looked into it, a number of owners, including one city police force, have found that they are crossing over underground mains supplies when the horse does this. You may come to suspect this if the horse always reacts in a peculiar way in a certain spot or, say, to traffic lights, especially temporary ones near roadworks.

This branch of science is, as yet, poorly accepted in the UK, although considerable amounts of research have been done on the subject in relation to humans and, in many areas in the Western world, this problem is well accepted. It is important that horse owners should be aware of it, however, as I suspect that horses have a tendency to be more sensitive than humans who develop a certain level of 'immunity' due to their continuous exposure to electro-magnetic fields, which may not apply to the pastured or stabled horse.

There are well-known cases of racehorses that have been suspected of being stopped or distracted by powerful and very specific electro-magnetic fields and at least one university in the UK has researched this in considerable depth.

Ultimately, life itself depends on subtle electro-magnetic fields which both hold our bodies together and also enable them to function at a sub-molecular level, and it is foolhardy indeed to dismiss the possibility of electrical sensitivity.

If you are looking at stabling or pastures for your horse, you should note the presence of pylons, underground electrical mains and transformers, military early-warning stations, radar associated with military and civil aviation installations and TV masts. You should ensure that stable lighting is earthed properly to a 1.8–2.4 m (6–8 ft) copper rod in the ground.

## Feed-related Behavioural Problems Checklist

Assuming that you are reasonably happy that your training, schooling and riding are not specifically causing the problem and that you are certain that your tack is correctly fitted and there are no sharp edges on your bit, there are various factors that you should check out.

- If the horse tends to toss its head repeatedly or shake it from side to side, you should certainly check its teeth, particularly if it is quidding (dropping food out of its mouth while it eats).

  All horses and ponies should have their teeth checked at least once a year, and donkeys over the age of seven every two years. I also believe that the teeth of competitive horses should be routinely checked every six months, initially when their fitness programme starts if they have been roughed off and then routinely on a three- to six-monthly basis, plus, of course, if any problems are noted.

  If you want your vet to check the teeth on a routine visit, you should tell him or her when you make the appointment, as not every vet carries a dental gag at all times. Remember also that sometimes a second treatment is required soon after the first, particularly if whoever rasps the teeth is inexperienced. In any case, some problems do not reveal themselves immediately, so do not assume that just because the teeth have been done once that eliminates them as a possible cause of problems.

  If checking the teeth does not yield an answer, you may need to discuss the possibility of sinus problems with your vet.

  If you are using anything other than a stainless steel bit, you should also check that your horse is not allergic to the material it is made from, including rubber, vulcanite, plastic and especially nickel, which is a common source of allergic reaction and may cause blistering or a burning sensation on the horse's lips and tongue. Allergies and sensitivities to pollens, moulds and insect bites can also trigger head tossing and should be especially suspect if combined with foot stamping.

- If the horse is easily startled or tends to shy, particularly to one side, you should consider the possibility that it may have a problem with hearing or eyesight and take steps to investigate this.

- If the horse tends to buck, rear or stumble, you should, of course, check for specific problems in the spine, joints and feet.

- You should suspect nutritional problems in the case of multi-focal lameness or lameness which appears to shift from one leg to another; behaviour which is highly variable or characterised by muscle stiffness or tremor, which may either loosen up once exercise commences or, conversely, get worse as you go on; or if the horse tends to get filled legs, or break out in a cold sweat at night.

If you add to these factors such things as constipation or scouring, a craving to lick soil or eat dung and poor coat and hoof condition, then you can be pretty sure that the diet being given is inappropriate for your particular horse.

## Supplementation

If you have considered all of the above and still have an equine homicidal maniac or an inattentive sleep-walker on your hands, there are a number of other actions you can try.

- Feed a probiotic for five days before and after competitions. Alternatively, feed Thrive, a sodium montmerrilonite clay which can absorb toxins and acts as a mineral 'fibre'. However, I would not use this for indefinite periods and would certainly consider its long-term use only as a last resort.
- You could also try a regime of high-dose vitamin E in addition to any other supplementation; I have found that giving 2,000 iu (international units) per day, increasing this to between 5,000 and 7,000 iu for five to seven days before a competition and then tailing off afterwards can be useful.
- You should also check that the horse is receiving adequate B vitamins, particularly vitamin $B_1$ (thiamine) which, again, can have a calming effect. However, I am not in the business of recommending 'magic dust' and would only resort to this if all else had failed. I would certainly make concerted efforts to get the overall diet right first.
- Other B vitamins, including $B_6$ (pyridoxine) should also be checked.
- At the other end of the vitamin spectrum, if you have a competition horse that is becoming sluggish and you are feeding so-called blood tonics which are high in vitamin $B_{12}$ and iron, it may very well be the case that you are overdosing with iron. It cannot be said too often that you certainly *can* have too much of a good thing and while I would almost always give some sort of supplementation to a high-performance horse, particularly when it is on a high carbohydrate (i.e. grain) diet, it is important that this is done in a considered fashion and that the products used are in balance with the rest of the diet.

If you are feeding compounds, it may well be that they are already very adequately supplemented – or maybe not! Check!

- Apart from vitamins, you should also ensure that mineral levels, of both trace elements and macro-minerals, including calcium, phosphorus, magnesium, sodium (from salt) and potassium, are available in adequate quantities. If they are not, the horse may not be 'firing on all cylinders', either mentally or physically.

- If you have tried all of the above suggestions and the horse is still causing problems, a number of herbal products are available which can be highly effective. Along with vitamin and mineral supplements, they can also have a beneficial effect on coat condition, which is particularly important if you are showing.

  If you are competing in affiliated competitions or qualifiers of any sort, however, you should be absolutely certain that the herbal mixture chosen is prepared by a company that has a full understanding of the prohibited substances rules and regulations. A number of individual herbs contain quite powerful substances which would most certainly show up in blood tests, particularly in a fit horse which tends to produce more acidic urine.

  A number of paste-type 'calming' mixtures are also available but, again, I have reservations about the ingredients contained in some of them, despite assurances that they have been used in racing. This is never a guarantee that problems will not arise. One or two of the vitamin-based paste products are acceptable, however, although I would only ever use something like this as an absolute last resort.

- For horses with an intractable problem, it is always worth consulting a good homoeopathic vet to see whether constitutional treatment and specific treatments for symptoms and behavioural problems may permanently solve the problem, provided you then feed a sensible diet.

- Finally, those of you with mares who are difficult when they come on heat should check their vitamin B levels and ensure that they are getting adequate magnesium. Consider giving them linseed oil. If all else fails, raspberry leaf can be extremely useful.

  Again, it can be useful to contact a homoeopathic vet and certainly to check with your usual vet that there are no problems with cysts or infections. It is likely, in the future, that it will be possible to treat mares with homoeopathic vaccines to treat hormone imbalances which have been found to improve the situation in some cases enormously. This is a well-established treatment for women and there is no reason to believe that it would not benefit mares.

If you are having problems with your horse, it really does not make sense to 'wait until the end of the season' as one so often hears, particularly in the racing world. By then, at best, you and the horse will have had a stressful and difficult season which has probably been unsuccessful and, at worst, something may happen which may end the horse's competitive career due to its bad behaviour.

So sit down, think it out and then sort it out – I am sure you will be glad you did. Remember that it can take three weeks to make the transition from one diet to the next. If you are in the middle of a competition season, you can ease this change by giving a course of probiotics. Although some people see a benefit from the change in the diet within days, be prepared for it to take several weeks and do not keep chopping and changing the diet unnecessarily!

It is sad to find individual horses with bad reputations for being temperamental and vicious when, with a little thought and care in both their handling and their feeding, the larger proportion of them could become changed personalities. Unfortunately the person most often in need of treatment is the owner or handler, not the horse.

# 12 Nutrition–related Health Problems and Feeding Convalescent Horses and Ponies

It is sad to relate that, even years after it was well established that bran mashes are a far less than ideal food for sick and convalescent horses, they are still the method of first resort in most stable yards. They are even recommended by some vets as a 'catch all' diet.

I have said elsewhere that this approach is akin to 'whipping the nutritional carpet out from under the horse's feet' when it needs it most. If there is no alternative to feeding bran mashes, then they must be fed correctly supplemented, but there is a whole range of alternatives for the sick horse, which may both assist with healing and reduce recovery time significantly.

I have already stressed the importance of correct feeding in maintaining health and reducing the likelihood of injury and proneness to infection that can follow inappropriate or unbalanced feeding.

A few guidelines are given here on the role of nutrition in various health problems, but if your horse has a serious problem, it is important that you take the trouble to look into this in greater depth.

Many horses are effectively 'wasted', either by being put down because of the expense of keeping them going on drugs, or by being unable to fulfil their intended role and it is my experience that this is frequently quite unnecessary. The older the horse or pony gets, the more likely this is to happen. Many horses spend years in chronic pain and discomfort or suffering from repeatedly recurring problems which need not happen or can be considerably reduced by judicious feeding. Many are kept on long-term medication which could be reduced or even stopped by altering feeding and general management and perhaps by the introduction of a few basic herbs or even homoeopathic treatments, to which horses respond very well without the damaging physical and temperamental side effects of the long-term use of certain drugs. Drugs can be life-saving and dramatically helpful for acute illness and injury but they should take a secondary role in the management of the chronically affected horse.

The horse or pony's state of health is intimately related to the balance of the gut environment, including acidity (pH) and the health of the symbiotic micro-organisms and the parasitic ones which live there. With many problems, it is a case of looking after the gut micro-organisms and the horse will just about look after itself. This is why a reasoned and well-thought-out approach to any feeding programme (and any adjustments which are to be made to it) is essential.

## Abortion and Infertility

Aspects of nutrition may be implicated in cases of abortion and infertility and have been discussed throughout this book. See also mycotoxicosis.

## Allergies and Food Intolerances

While classical immunoglobulin E (IgE) immune, system-mediated food allergies (the antibody IgE mediates allergic responses) in horses are thought to be relatively rare, food intolerances seem to be increasing and may manifest themselves as temperament problems, constipation or a 'lazy bowel', continual diarrhoea or scouring, usually with a 'normal' or slightly lowered *not* raised temperature, stiffness and a wide range of other multi-focal symptoms. Inhalant allergies are well known (COPD) and many horses also suffer from contact allergies, (e.g. to nickel in bits) which should always be suspected if a horse tends to do a lot of head tossing or be tender in its mouth. Such a horse may also exhibit multi-focal joint problems. Modern washing powders, wood treatment, even leather-care products can also cause contact allergies.

The mechanism of food intolerance is not yet well understood but it is quite clear from experience that, for example, many horses (and especially ponies) seem to be intolerant of oats, possibly due to chemicals called phenolics which they contain. I have even encountered horses which cannot eat any member of the grass family, including hay and all cereals, which can lead to a major problem in feeding until the situation is stabilised.

A new technique is being developed in order to 'neutralise' horses to problem foods but this subject is very much in its infancy in the UK. It is called the Miller provocation-neutralisation technique and there has been considerable success so far in treating COPD-affected horses who may have multiple food, chemical (e.g. to the phenol in creosote), mould and dust mite allergies and intolerances.

If you have a horse or pony with continuing problems which you cannot get to the bottom of, it may well be worth changing over to a different type of feed regime for a time, perhaps from cereals to a totally cereal-free diet using, say, alfalfa (lucerne) nuts and sugar beet, to see if this brings about an improvement. Some animals seem to tolerate cooked cereals, whether they are micronised, extruded or just boiled, better than uncooked ones and quite a few that cannot tolerate other grains get on well with brown rice if you can find a reasonably priced source.

A very few horses react badly to sugar beet and may develop mud-fever-like lesions on the legs and belly, although you should also check that this is not some other reaction, perhaps to wood preservatives in bedding or pesticides on straw.

This is a complex subject and, having made a few initial attempts to eliminate obvious problems, it is advisable to seek expert help. This is because food intolerances can be 'masked' and, in fact, the food causing the most problems can be the one which is least obvious and eaten most.

## Respiratory Allergies

These are not generally caused by food allergens in horses but may very well be due to moulds carried on foodstuffs, which are naturally occurring, or even to certain mould and yeast products which may be added to feeds in some individual cases. If the latter are suspected, particularly if the horse has had long courses of steroids or antibiotics, then it is wise to avoid products which are likely to contain moulds, yeast additives (including brewer's yeast) and various new feed supplements derived from yeast until a great deal more work has been done on this subject. The latter products may be excellent for the majority of horses but there are certainly some individuals who they plainly do not suit and this should be taken into consideration.

As far as food-borne moulds and dust are concerned, the important thing is to obtain the cleanest feedstuffs you can buy and, where possible and if necessary, then clean them further.

Hay and straw can both be soaked for a maximum of four hours before feeding, to swell the mould spores, which prevents them from getting into the alveoli in the lungs. These are tiny air-sacs richly surrounded by blood capillaries where the oxygen from the air is exchanged with carbon dioxide from the blood. Some authorities believe that one and a half hours is an adequate soaking time and this would be a useful period for which to soak hay for *any* horse doing fast work in order to reduce respiratory stress, whether it is a COPD sufferer or not. A maximum period of four hours is certainly plenty of time, while longer soaking may well significantly reduce feed value as more soluble nutrients are washed out of the hay. After an initial period of drainage, it is important to feed the hay as soon as possible because if it dries out again further mould formation may occur. This would, of course, cause more problems than ever.

Other useful forage feeds for COPD-affected horses and, indeed, any which are suffering from acute (as opposed to chronic) respiratory infections, including colds and influenza, include the moist, packaged forages (MPFs), dried grass and alfalfa (lucerne) cubes, molassed or otherwise, soaked chaff, hydroponically grown cereals ('barley-grass'), a proportion of soaked sugar beet feed, silage and fresh-cut ('zero-grazed') grass (not dangerous grass clippings which ferment and cause colic). It is useful to include at least one component of a fairly low feeding value because many of these materials are highly nutritious but not very bulky and can lead to the horse having a craving for long fibre. Apart from the distress and discomfort that this may cause, it can lead to vices such as wind-sucking, crib-biting, rug-tearing and so forth. Molassed chaff can be extremely useful in this context and some owners find NIS straw cubes (such as Viton) useful for this type of horse.

It is also useful to feed the moist forages in a small-mesh net so that they take longer to eat and to thus increase their 'amusement value'!

It is most important that the horse's craving for long fibre is satisfied, not only in relation to possible problems caused by boredom but also for the maintenance of the physical health of the gut and the balance of its micro-organism population.

The rest of the diet may be cubed or of a moist, coarse-mix type which is usually either highly molassed or has some other syrup, such as malt syrup, added. Otherwise, you can mix your own feed provided it is well damped, again with the possible addition of molasses and feed-grade oils.

In addition to this, many owners find that it is useful to feed garlic to such horses. This may, initially, lead to increased coughing because it can loosen 'pockets' of mucus in the lungs which the horse then has to shift but you will usually find that this settles down. However, if increased coughing is accompanied by a rising temperature, you should consult your vet as this may be due to an intercurrent acute infection taking place (unrelated to the garlic). Even if this does occur, in most instances it is a good idea to continue using the garlic.

A good standard of nutrition is important, particularly in relation to vitamins, minerals and essential fatty acids, to help to maintain the integrity of the membranes lining the lungs and the muscles which are exposed to increased workloads because of the difficulty of breathing out in badly affected animals. In extreme cases, this can lead to the development of a heave-line (a muscular build-up along the line of the diaphragm due to the double respiratory effort required to breath out).

It would increasingly appear that materials such as methyl sulphonyl methane (MSM) may have an extremely useful role to play in reducing inflammation in respiratory problems. This may either be fed as pure MSM, or in supplements such as Bio-Respirease on a longer-term basis.

A number of commercial herbal blends are available as well as custom-mixed ones which have been found to be useful for such horses. If you are competing and therefore unable to use drugs or if you are concerned about the chronic use of drug therapy in any case, it is a good idea to contact a homoeopathically trained veterinary practitioner as constitutional symptomatic treatment using this technique is remarkably successful in the horse. The Miller provocation neutralisation technique may also be worth investigating, especially for valuable competition horses. The testing is cheap but usually requires an expensive sojourn in a special clinic.

All horses with respiratory problems should be closely monitored by your vet and their treatment and management agreed in conjunction with him or her.

## Allergic Skin Conditions

These are really beyond the scope of this book but it is important that you are aware that different feeds can exacerbate these conditions and that you should pay particular attention to feeding adequate levels of minerals (especially zinc), B vitamins and essential fatty acids to these horses, as they often exhibit poor absorption or utilisation of these nutrients and may have a higher overall requirement.

In the case of **sweet-itch**, which is an allergy to the bite of a particular type of midge, the horse's predisposition may be nutritionally related (which may, in turn, be genetic). Feeding garlic can be extremely useful as it helps to repel the midges. Again, MSM can be a useful anti-inflammatory. It is a good idea to use only natural fibres against the horse's skin, avoiding synthetic rugs or numnahs, and all fabrics should be washed only in 'ecological', and particularly non-biological, washing powders or plain soap flakes, then rinsed with bicarbonate of soda. Alternatively, wash in borax alone.

There are a number of invaluable herbal creams. Homoeopathic calendula and hypericum (hypercal) tincture, can be both soothing and healing, while the latter has been shown to be extremely useful for horses that are prone to **girth galls**.

You should also attempt to obtain organically grown bedding, or at least try different types of bedding and, as far as possible, feedstuffs. Certainly, you must avoid compounds with synthetic preservatives and flavourings in them for this type of horse.

**Warts** can be successfully treated, permanently and usually quickly, with a course of appropriate homoeopathic treatment.

Some horses seem to have severe allergies to other materials, which may be expressed as skin irritation, foot stamping (which may also be due to the bites of harvest mites if seasonal) and head shaking and such horses could become quite dangerous to ride and handle. These horses should always be checked out for allergies and intolerances, particularly to moulds (in the feed and the atmosphere) and pollens. These can be treated either by the Miller provocation neutralisation method or homoeopathically and will almost always benefit from changes in dietary and stable management. For example, if moulds are a problem, being kept in an outdoor corral, rugged and with some form of shelter, may be infinitely preferable to being stabled. Care must be taken during the height of the pollen season, including tree, grass and flower pollens. Some horses are particularly susceptible to oilseed rape pollen and tree pollen. Steroids may be prescribed by your vet to stabilise the situation but are not a long-term solution.

Any horse who is susceptible to allergies of any kind is best groomed out of doors, with its head upwind so that any dusty materials blow away. It should have the cleanest, simplest feeds possible and you must avoid the use of synthetic materials in all aspects of management, including stable wood preservatives etc. Old-fashioned saddle soap should be used on tack and stainless steel metalwork is usually best. If you *must* use shampoos and so forth, use extremely mild herbal ones. Washing-up liquid of any kind should never be used on *any* horse's skin (a foolish but all too common practice) as it leaches it of oils and can predispose a sensitive skin to further problems. 'Medicated' shampoos often kill beneficial bacteria and can do long-term damage. Some horses are also sensitive to clipper-blade washes and, indeed, to the effects of electricity. I have noticed that some allergic horses seem to have been 'triggered off' when they have been stabled under or near to power lines and other electrical installations such as transformers.

Other causative agents include the prolonged use of antibiotics and steroids which may lead to a 'leaky gut' which allows molecules of food which are incompletely digested to pass into the bloodstream, resulting in food allergies and other problems.

Hereditary predisposition may also be a factor, although it may not manifest itself in future generations as the same type of allergy; for example, one parent may have COPD whereas the offspring may have skin-type allergies including urticaria (nettle rash) or sweet itch. The chances of this being passed on increase significantly if both parents suffer from allergic conditions so it is important to identify this problem in proposed breeding stock.

In some cases of irritable bowel problems it is possible that parasite damage may predispose to this but it is also worth noting that some horses seem to be allergic to, or suffer toxic effects from, a number of wormers. If necessary in these cases, one may have to resort to using garlic and herbal parasite control, perhaps combined with a Chinese herbal blend or a homoeopathic nosodal approach but you *must* get qualified expert advice on this. Pay special attention to pasture parasite management in these cases.

## Anaemia

The term anaemia describes the deficiency of red blood cells (erythrocytes) and/or haemoglobin (the oxygen-carrying pigment) in the blood.

Signs of anaemia might include pale mucous membranes, increased rate and force of heartbeat and fatigue. There are a number of non-nutritional causes, such as external or internal bleeding, blood-loss via external parasites (e.g. lice, ticks, mosquitoes), infection by bacteria (swamp-fever), protozoa, (e.g. biliary fever), poisoning or immunological jaundice (e.g. haemolytic foals).

Anaemia may also result from some form of nutritional deficiency which may reduce the output of red blood cells from bone marrow or the levels of haemoglobin produced, or both. It may be due to a deficiency of iron (Fe), copper (Cu), cobalt (Co) – a constituent of vitamin $B_{12}$, folic acid or possibly biotin.

Several types of anaemia are classified according to the size of the red blood cells and the concentration of haemoglobin in each body cell. Haemoglobin is the iron-containing, red-pigmented molecule, designated Hb, which actually carries oxygen from the lungs to the cells. When it is loaded with oxygen it is called oxyhaemoglobin and is bright red as it travels in the arteries from the lungs to the heart and the heart to the tissues. When it has dumped its load of oxygen (e.g. in the muscles) it is called deoxyhaemoglobin as it travels in the veins from the tissues to the heart and back to the lungs to be replenished with oxygen. This is why arterial blood is bright red and venous blood has a bluish/purple tinge.

If there is anaemia due to a dietary deficiency of iron, cobalt/$B_{12}$, copper, folic acid or biotin, making up the dietary levels should correct the state of anaemia. However, some animals display a response to folic acid even when dietary levels appear to be adequate, so there may be some sort of malabsorption syndrome involved.

For animals which are not anaemic, no amount of iron, copper, cobalt/$B_{12}$, folic acid or biotin will increase the red blood cell (RBC) count, packed cell volume (PCV) or haemoglobin levels above *normal* levels, and excessive use of such products as haematinics and $B_{12}$ shots can actually fatigue the horse and be counterproductive. The way to keep the blood count up is to feed a balanced diet, with no deficiencies or excesses, and to work the horse at the appropriate level for the performance that is expected of it. Traditional racehorse training methods frequently do not achieve this but there are no short cuts to be taken via the hypodermic needle. Iron levels in the diet should be around 40 mg per kilogram for mature horses and 50 mg per kilogram for milk-fed foals who are more prone to anaemia (for the same reason that veal calves are fed solely on milk to give them anaemic or white flesh).

Vitamin $B_6$ and vitamin E deficiency may also be implicated in anaemia, as may lack of zinc (which is involved in copper metabolism) and excess molybdenum (which may interfere with copper metabolism). (This has not been confirmed in the horse, only in cattle but most practical nutritionists believe there *is* such an interaction.)

Keeping up the fibre levels in the diet will ensure adequate production of vitamin $B_{12}$ by the gut micro-organisms in most cases. Fresh grass is rich in folic acid as are green dried forages such as dried alfalfa (lucerne) cubes.

## Bone Problems and Nutritionally Induced Osteopathies

Many sources of malformation, disease and injuries in bones are nutritionally induced, facilitated or implemented. A detailed study of problems in young, growing horses is rather beyond the scope of this book. It is the responsibility of any horse breeder to familiarise themself with potential disease problems and take every possible step to minimise the risk of them occurring. Even apparently minor problems at a young age can have a devastating effect later on and reduce the performance of the horse. For example, in the case of knee chips, the prognosis for any surgery in the adult horse is largely dependent on whether the horse had a problem in foalhood.

There are many symptoms of nutritional bone disorder, also referred to as metabolic bone disorder (MBD): for example, epiphysitis (open-knees and also in the fetlock joints), star fractures of the cannon bones (sore shins), knee chips, rickets, fractured pelvis (e.g. two year olds on fast workouts). More chronic situations, such as ring-bone, side-bone, spavins, navicular disease and much rarer, although often misdiagnosed, pedalosteitis, can all be said to have some possible form of nutritional or nutrition/exercise involvement, if not in their onset, certainly in their treatment and prognosis. Animals fed on cereals are generally more prone to the arthritis-related problems of old age, although there are no specific data available to support this. Cereals are certainly implicated strongly as a causative or exacerbating agent in other species.

Wheat bran should certainly be avoided for any animal with bone disorders because it contains phytates which lock up calcium and it is vital that the overall balance of the diet is corrected. It is also important that a good mixture of cereal and non-cereal feed ingredients is chosen. The vitamin D and mineral and trace element levels of the diet must be carefully checked and this is particularly crucial in youngstock where epiphysitis, contracted tendons (hyperflexion) and other problems may be due to mineral deficiencies and imbalances (and *not*, incidentally, to excessive protein levels).

With respect to spontaneous fractured pelvis during exercise or pulling up, star fractures of the cannon bones (sore shins) and knee chips during exercise, it is quite probable that these horses are predisposed to such accidents because their trace-mineral or trace nutrient levels are inadequate or out of balance.

Navicular disease may well be helped by megadosing with various vitamins as a means of improving blood flow and feeding garlic to make the blood more slippery and cause it to flow better in areas of restricted circulation, although this must be considered an adjunct to veterinary care and not a replacement for it. It is interesting to note that excessive concussion and hammering along on the roads, possibly over several years, can be a predisposing factor.

Spavins, ring-bone and side-bone are arthritis-related complaints which *may* relate to long-term unbalanced nutrition or even food sensitivities. The vitamin and mineral levels of the diet should be checked and you could consider feeding herbs such as comfrey, devil's claw or yucca. Many people have reported good results from specially formulated herbal blends and homoeopathy, both of which can reduce or remove the necessity for prolonged and expensive drug therapy. It is also worth considering keeping cereals to an absolute minimum in the diets of such animals because, while there is no proven link between prolonged feeding of cereals and these conditions in *horses*, work in other species would indicate a potential problem and sheer logic would dictate that the presence of phytates in cereals, which lock up other minerals, may very well be less than helpful. A number of physiotherapy techniques have also been found useful for these conditions.

The same general principles apply to arthritis in other joints.

## Breaking-out Syndrome

Some horses are prone to breaking out in a cold sweat some hours after being stabled after hard exercise. Usually, this is due to the animal having been inadequately warmed down after work, although it can also be caused by iodine deficiency. Excess protein in the diet also appears to be a common cause of the syndrome which usually disappears when protein levels have been corrected.

## Choke

Horses can be subject to choking if the oesophagus (gullet) gets blocked anywhere between the pharynx and the stomach, unlike humans who are more likely to choke if food gets into the trachea (wind-pipe), not a very common experience in horses unless they are inexpertly drenched or stomach-tubed.

In the UK, the commonest cause of choke in the horse is feeding unsoaked sugar beet nuts (unsoaked pulp is far less likely to cause problems but is not recommended as there is still a risk). Other major causes are feeding dry bran, carrots incorrectly sliced (they should be sliced lengthways), whole apples (e.g. when grazing in an orchard) or whole potatoes. Some mould toxins can also cause choking.

Symptoms include the horse coughing, slobbering and apparently vomiting – a discharge draining from both nostrils and the mouth. The horse will generally refuse all feed and water, although if the obstruction is in the lower part of the oesophagus, it may swallow some water but only to bring it back up.

If the obstruction is near the top of the oesophagus, it may be possible to feel it and, through gentle massage of the throat, dislodge it, although it is debatable which is the safest direction to massage it in, especially if the horse has been choking for some time. This technique may be most useful for dislodging pieces of carrot, whereas a major blockage will always require veterinary intervention as it may well prove fatal. The vet may inject Carbacol (carbamylcholine chloride) and muscle relaxants and may try to dislodge the obstruction or wash it or poke it away using a stomach tube. The vet is likely to keep the horse under observation for a week or more. During this time the horse may be fed on nourishing mashes (such as *soaked* sugar beet pulp/dried grass/alfalfa) as it will probably have a sore throat!

Of course, prevention is better than cure. *Never* feed whole apples, potatoes, pears, round slices of carrot, unsoaked sugar beet pulp/nuts, dry bran, etc. and keep the ration 'open' with chaff. Discourage the horse from bolting its feed; for example, by using flat stones in the manager or spreading the feed out along the manger. Ensure that water is available at all times, especially prior to feeding cubes.

## Chronic Constipation and 'Lazy Bowel'
(See also Allergies.)

In foals, faeces (meconium) should be removed if not passed within 24 hours of birth or colic may result.

## Colic

The term colic refers to pain in the abdomen or, more specifically, in the digestive system and associated organs and ducts. Broadly speaking, there are three main sources or origins of colic,

1  **Biliary**, which is rare in horses and is caused by a growth, or cyst, or parasites blocking the bile duct.
2  **Renal**, which is also rare in horses and is caused by blockages in the ureter (duct carrying urine from the kidney to the bladder), for example by calculi (kidney stones) which can be due to dietary imbalances.
3  **Alimentary** – it is a testament to the poor standards of management prevailing that this is an extremely common phenomenon in horses. The pain can occur for a wide variety of reasons.

Changes in feed and specific feedstuffs are frequently indicated and can lead to upsets due to the unbalancing of the intestinal micro-organisms or the gut acidity (pH) but by far the most common cause is the effect of a parasite burden (see below) or previous damage caused by parasites.

This colic may also occur due to dehydration, particularly after long journeys or competitions, or in grass-kept ponies in winter if the ice is not broken on their water troughs sufficiently frequently. The cause is often not identified because the horse may not have colic until a day or two after such stresses.

The different types of alimentary colic may be broadly defined as follows.

• **Impacted colic** – A stoppage, usually at the point where the small intestine enters the caecum, at the diaphragmatic flexure (bend) in the caecum or in the colon (hence the word colic), although it may also occur in the stomach or small intestine. A mass of dry food may form at these points and this tends to become drier and drier as fluid is withdrawn from the large intestine as a result of shock.

It may also be a direct result of inadequate water intake, particularly in winter if water sources are not kept ice-free, after trailer or box journeys, and after insufficient re-hydration following competitive work.

Horses which have the annoying habit, often due to management or dietary problems, of consuming all kinds of rubbish such as wood shavings, straw bedding, wood bark, rugs, bandages (a horse belonging to a friend of mine ate a lunge whip!), rope and the cord from rubberised fences, are particularly prone to blockages! With this type of horse, it is essential that you try to work out why it is doing this, for example boredom, lack of fibre in the diet, lack of minerals, nervousness/stress, a gut micro-organism imbalance which may be corrected by probiotics, or sheer plain b-mindedness!

It may take years before such depraved appetites manifest themselves as colic. However, it is essential that you do what you can to break these habits by the temporary use of muzzles, removal of the offending 'snacks' and, where fencing is chewed, either change the fencing or use a strand of reflective strip-type electric fencing inside the paddock and around trees. (The permanent use of muzzles without finding the cause of the behaviour is cruel and will only lead to an alternative form of aberrant behaviour and even more stresses.)

Other blockages may be due to foreign bodies (such as a wood chip) which are accidentally, or intentionally, ingested. As plant material accumulates around them, they grow into a lump called a phytobezoar which may eventually cause a blockage. These are most common where wood chewing is a problem and animals at risk include COPD-affected horses on complete cube diets. The impaction usually occurs when the phytobezoar passes from the stomach into the small intestine.

A similar problem can occur when enteroliths are formed. These are 'stones' in the intestines, which usually have a core (for example a nail or some other hard material at the centre) surrounded by a deposition of minerals, such as magnesium ammonium phosphate, in layers to form a regular or irregular ball. These can be passed with the dung while they are small but if they continue to grow (stones up to 8–10 kg or $17\frac{1}{2}$–22 lb have been reported!), they can cause severe impacted colic, particularly when they pass from the large to the small colon in the hind gut. Up to 100 enteroliths have been reported in one horse and large ones may lead to death due to a ruptured colon.

Apart from the ingestion of the foreign body at the centre of the enterolith, it seems likely that the mineral nutrition of the horse in question may well be implicated and the mineral levels in both the diet and drinking water should be carefully monitored. It has also been suggested that excess levels of magnesium and phosphorus in the diet, especially in a diet containing significant quantities of wheat bran, may well be involved, as may an abnormally high iron intake. It has been suggested that some breeds, particularly Arabs and part-Arabs, are especially prone to this problem.

- **Sand colic**, which is, in fact, a form of impacted colic, can occur when horses drink from a natural water source with a sandy bottom, graze on sandy soil or are fed on the ground in a sand manège. The sand collects in the large intestine, particularly the colon. An astonishing 27 kg ($59\frac{1}{2}$ lb) of sand were reportedly found in the colon of one (fatal) case.

- **Spasmodic colic** – This is characterised by excessive activity of the gut, causing a spasm. Symptoms may include diarrhoea. It may be caused by poisoning, hormonal imbalance, trace mineral imbalance (particularly magnesium and potassium), as a secondary disorder from some other problem or by a severe imbalance of gut micro-organisms which may produce toxins that induce spasm.

- **Twisted gut (volvulus)** – The small intestine becomes acutely obstructed due to a section of it becoming twisted or herniated, or else one of the large gut organs, such as the caecum, rotates on the membrane which suspends it. This is often attributed to the horse rolling due to gut pain but it seems more likely that the horse rolls because the gut is *already* twisted. It is often fatal but surgical intervention may be successful if it is performed soon enough. This is one reason why it is absolutely vital that the vet is called as soon as you suspect any type of colic rather than waiting to see how it develops.

- **Tympanitic colic** is due to gas accumulation from fermenting food, usually in the stomach, caecum or colon. It may accompany impacted colic. It is caused by an upset to the microbial population, possibly due to a sudden change in feeding, to over-feeding or to the prolonged use of antibiotics or steroids. In severe cases, parts of the gut may rupture, although death is likely to occur before this due to shock.

- **Verminous colic** – by far the commonest cause – due to impaction because of the sheer weight of parasites in the gut, bot larvae in the stomach (particularly in foals) or blood clots or immature parasites in the mesenteric arteries supplying the small and large intestine, so that the blood supplies to that part of the gut are cut off. The thrombus (clot) generally occurs because the blood vessel is damaged by migrating red-worm larvae (see below). The wall of the artery may collapse (an aneurysm) which sets up inflammation of the artery (arteritis) causing the blood to clot and adhere to the lining of the artery. It may break up and be carried in pieces (embolism) through the blood stream until they lodge in a blood vessel, thereby blocking the blood flow to that part of the gut, leading to chronic necrosis (death of cells or groups of cells), or acute peritonitis (inflammation of the peritoneum, the smooth membrane lining the abdomen and its contents [outside the gut walls] enabling one part of the gut to slide over another) – possibly causing adhesions (parts of the intestine sticking together or to the gut wall).

  Peritonitis may also occur due to infection by bacteria, migrating red-worm larvae or foreign bodies penetrating the gut wall. It is characterised by grunting, looking round at the flanks, an initially raised white blood cell (leucocyte) count, fever and reluctance to move.

## Treatment of Colic

The first step is to identify which type of colic is occurring. This is a job for the veterinary practitioner, and it is prudent to call the vet *whenever* colic is suspected. *Do not* use proprietary drenches. They may be contra-indicated for the type of colic and so may make things worse and there is always the danger of the fluid going down the windpipe and choking the horse.

While waiting for the vet, try to prevent the horse from rolling by gently walking it but be quite clear that walking the horse for hours without treatment is cruel and will simply tire it out and lessen its chances of recovery. If you keep homoeopathic aconite or Dr Bach's Rescue Remedy in your stable medicine cabinet, these can usefully be given at half-hourly intervals to reduce the effects of shock while you are waiting for the vet. While these will not affect anything the vet is doing, you must tell him or her that you have used them.

You should also carefully note any changes in the horse's demeanour and behaviour, plus their timing and duration, in order to help the vet to monitor the progress of the horse's condition.

The signs of colic are progressive and are all indicative of pain. The first priority of the vet is to control this pain. Once you have seen a horse with colic, you will never forget it. The attack may start mildly with indigestion and refusal to eat, the horse looking round at its belly and being restless. It may even yawn, a common equine response to discomfort, progressing to pawing and bed scraping, kicking at the belly, box walking, griping, repeatedly getting up and down, violent rolling, lying on its back with patchy sweat showing along the flanks and a generally anxious demeanour. The heart rate and respiration rate will almost certainly be elevated and the horse may be visibly panting. If the horse is wearing rugs, they should be adjusted to ensure that it is comfortable and is not tightly surcingled. If the horse is clearly becoming distressed you should be prepared to add or subtract a number of rugs as and when necessary. Check the flanks for sweating under the rugs but do not allow the horse to become chilled. The horse may find it comforting to have its ears rubbed to restore circulation and to keep them warm.

If the pain is severe, the horse's temperature may rise and gut sounds (borborygmi) may be reduced or absent (impacted colic) or increased (spasmodic colic).

Treatment *must* be preceded by diagnosis from the vet and will include pain control in all cases. The pain will be caused through gut distension by (a) gas or food, causing a stretched peritoneum (in which there are many pain receptor cells); (b) peritonitis; (c) spasm of the muscle in the gut wall.

In impacted colic, the horse may show signs of having a full bladder and will straddle in a urinating position. The vet may give liquid paraffin and purgative drugs by stomach pump. If this treatment has been used, it is particularly important to consider giving such horses probiotics to aid them on the road to recovery once they are over the actual bout of colic.

In tympanitic colic the horse may appear to crouch or straddle its limbs and may be treated with anti-spasmodic drugs (such as Buscopan) given by injection or stomach tube, or homoeopathic equivalents.

Most colicky horses recover, although they may be subject to repeated attacks if the poor management which led to the problem in the first place is not corrected. However, the prognosis is bad if pain fails to respond to treatment, the pulse is fast and weak, if the haematocrit (packed cell volume or PCV) rises above 50 per cent and the mucous membranes of the mouth and eyes turn red or purple.

It has been estimated that at least 95 per cent of colic cases are a direct or indirect result of poor or unbalanced horse management, particularly including poor parasite management, and are, therefore, entirely preventable.

Once the vet has stabilised the situation, advice should be urgently sought on how best to avoid it happening again. Most horses that have been affected by colic are likely to benefit from a good quality probiotic as soon as possible, if necessary given in the form of a wormer-type paste if they have severe loss of appetite. Once they are recovering, attention to parasite control, possibly increased vitamin and mineral intake for a short time and an appetising diet, with appropriate quantities of fibre, are vital.

## Coprophagy (Eating Faeces)

It is quite natural for a young foal to ingest some of its mother's droppings as a means of obtaining the initial establishment of its own gut micro-organism population, which is another reason why it is a good idea to give the broodmare a course of probiotics to establish a healthy gut population for her to pass on to her offspring. The foal is born with no gut micro-organisms of its own. This is a normal and acceptable process for the unweaned foal but care should be taken that it does not become indicative of a depraved appetite.

Coprophagy in the adult horse *is* indicative of a depraved appetite. This condition is not uncommon and, once established, it may become a habit.

There are a number of possible causes, such as protein, mineral, vitamin (especially $B_1$) or fibre deficiency, unbalanced gut micro-organisms, stress and so forth. The horse is likely to be unthrifty, both because of nutritional deficiencies and due to continuously reinfecting itself with round worms.

Check the diet, treat any incidence of worm infestation and, again, consider giving a course of probiotics.

## Diarrhoea – Scouring, Including Foal Scours

In foals, scouring may occur during the first 48 hours of life due to the foal's inability to cope with the very rich 'first milk' or colostrum. This may, in fact, be affected by any inappropriateness of the mare's diet or possibly by her exposure to xenobiotic (foreign) chemicals or drugs which can be transferred into the milk.

Frequently, preventing the foal from drinking the mare's milk and bottle-feeding it or stomach tubing it instead with milk from another mare, or giving mare's milk replacer or even goat's milk by bottle (*not* cow's milk) may appear to effect a cure. If this is done, the foal should be given supportive vitamin and immunoglobulin injections to replace those it is not receiving from the colostrum.

However, it is preferable to try giving the foal a paste-type probiotic as soon as possible after the birth, following the recommended regime for the chosen brand for at least the first few days of life, so that the foal will receive the major benefits only colostrum itself can confer.

Scouring (with a raised temperature) may also occur a few days after foaling, probably due to an infection in the gut, especially when accompanied by an elevated temperature. Again, this will frequently respond to the use of probiotics at this time, although it is preferable to start as soon after birth as possible as a preventive. The vet may give antibiotics and kaolin or, better still, bentonite, to try to stabilise the situation, although the prognosis is not always good particularly where probiotics and electrolytes have not been employed. If the foal does recover, again it is important that probiotics are given as an aid to recovery and normalising of the gut environment.

In cases of non-infectious scouring, I have found it useful to try feeding both mare and foal a probiotic supplement (the mare for at least ten days in the feed; the foal as recommended). If it is suspected that the milk is too rich, you could adjust the mare's feed, put her on less lush pasture (beware of putting fibre levels up and an excessive increase of butter fat in the milk), hand-milk her and 'water' down the milk with filtered, boiled water before feeding to the foal, or wean the foal early (say at three months) on to hard feed, or even younger on to creep feed and a proprietary mare's milk replacer.

In adults scouring may be indicative of a number of disorders – principally enteritis (inflammation of the bowel or intestinal lining, caused by bacterial upsets, diet, particularly mouldy feed containing mycotoxins/aflotoxins), chemical poisoning (e.g. chewing lead paint), or vegetable poisons (poisonous plants or phytotoxins).

It is essential that you send for the vet at once; do-it-yourself treatments may not work and could mean that the vet arrives too late to help. *Never* give purgatives. If the vet is not immediately available, kaolin or bentonite (e.g. Thrive) dissolved in water may help to stabilise the situation as these form a 'protective cover' over the gut surface. The vet may then give antibiotics, antispasmodics, sedatives/pain killers and fluid and electrolyte therapy. *Do not* feed these horses a bran mash.

It is, however, a good idea to give a good quality probiotic as soon as possible (using a paste-type formulation if the horse is still off its feed).

When feeding recommences, and with veterinary approval, a nourishing mash, containing principally sugar beet pulp, 25–100 g (1–4 oz) salt, breadmeal or ricemeal, or perhaps some cooked micronised cereal or dried alfalfa (lucerne) which, like sugar beet, all contain highly digestible fibre, may well be appropriate. However, molasses and sugar beet are contraindicated if prolonged antibiotics have been given. Under such circumstances yeast overgrowth may well be a problem, especially if you have not given a probiotic course to follow the antibiotics and restabilise the gut environment.

Keep your horse clean and on a clean bed, if necessary tying up the tail, and put Vaseline or homoeopathic calendula cream on the hindquarters to reduce soreness during the acute stage. Ensure that the horse has free access to clean, fresh drinking water. Do not expect an acutely sick horse to rely on an automatic waterer. Offer electrolytes in water *alongside* plain water, but only under veterinary advice even if the horse was given electrolytes by stomach tube or IV drip in the early stages.

For horses that continually scour mildly, for example when at grass, try reducing the quality of the grass offered or feed some oat straw at the same time to raise the fibre levels. Again consider bentonite (e.g. Thrive) or probiotics. I have known horses who have been scouring for two or more years on and off, with no hair left on their hindquarters, for whom the vet and owner have 'tried everything', which have responded to a five- to ten-day course of probiotics and have not scoured again even twelve months later. I offer this observation as an indication that it is *always* worth trying a different approach for chronic illness.

## Dry Coat

The inability to sweat may be due to vitamin E deficiency and trace element imbalances.

## Exercise–induced Pulmonary Haemorrhage (EIPH)

### *Epistaxis*

This term describes the symptom of bleeding from the lungs after exertion, especially racing. It is suggested that up to 70 per cent of racing Thoroughbreds bleed from the lungs, although only about 30 per cent of those cases manifest as nose bleeds. Such horses are often referred to as 'bleeders'.

Both diuretic drugs (such as Lasix, Furosemide and Clenbuturol) and vitamins (particularly vitamin K and the bio-flavinoids) are often prescribed to try to prevent bleeding. However, there is no evidence that bleeders suffer from pulmonary oedema (excessive fluid in the lungs) and as dehydration using diuretic drugs is likely to *reduce* performance by reducing blood perfusion of the muscles, it is more likely to be detrimental than beneficial to use such drug therapy.

There is also no evidence that bleeders suffer from a blood-clotting defect, so additional vitamin K is unlikely to be of benefit provided normal dietary requirements are met. The evidence in favour of bioflavinoids is even scantier, although, very occasionally, they may provide the answer to an individual problem. It is important that the trace mineral and vitamin levels in the diets of all horses, including bleeders, are adequate in order to maintain good health. If you have a bleeder, you should certainly be looking closely at its diet.

There have been no conclusive results from using vitamins and I have found that using garlic, methyl sulphonyl methane (MSM) and specific homoeopathic remedies is more efficacious for this problem.

It is interesting to note that very little incidence of EIPH has been reported in horses trained using true sports science techniques and kept out, or in low-dust/mould, low-ammonia-level stables. As even the traditional methods of training endurance and cross-country horses are closer to these techniques than those used for racehorses, including the use of a build up of long, slow distance work, interval training and sprint workouts, hillwork and a proper tapering period prior to competition, it is possible that some bleeders are quite simply unfit in *all* their tissues, including the lungs, for the work they are being asked to perform, which is why we see a much higher incidence of bleeders among racehorses than among other horses in hard, fast work.

Warming up adequately before a race or competition may also be an important factor.

It is possible, therefore, that EIPH is, in part at least, a result of inadequate cardiovascular conditioning in preparation for hard work.

Clearly, it also makes sense to ensure that the horse is not subjected to a subclinical respiratory challenge from dust and moulds in the environment, and feeding, stabling and bedding should be adjusted accordingly. Although it seems increasingly certain that EIPH is not a type of COPD and is not specifically feed-related, there could possibly be some sort of food intolerance component. If the problem is due to bronchial blockages, then the drug most suitable would be Clenbuterol and *not* Furosemide but, in fact, neither of these drugs is permitted for use with racing or competing horses in the UK.

It is also possible that the bleeding may be caused by physical air pressure changes which may occur when there are pockets of mucus in some alveoli and not others. This may set up a pressure gradient sufficient to burst the blood capillaries with which the alveolar walls are enriched. Again, a clean environment, dust-free feeds and bedding and plenty of fresh air, along with a balanced diet, may go a long way to assist with this problem. If the problem still remains, I would strongly recommend that you contact a homoeopathically trained veterinary practitioner.

## Filled Legs and Lymphangitis

The term 'filled legs' refers to an oedema (abnormal accumulation of fluid) in spaces below the skin, causing soft swellings that usually leave a dent after sustained pressure. The condition may be caused by blood vessels allowing water and protein to pass more freely, possibly due to toxins (in feed or otherwise), allergies (e.g. grass humour) or infection, or to an abnormal decrease in protein in the blood, encountered in horses suffering from severe undernutrition or wasting diseases, lack of various minerals, or to too much feed being given compared to work done. Too much protein in particular is often suggested as a cause, although I see no specific evidence to support this being the primary cause. More frequently, *too little fibre* would certainly seem to be indicated. Many horses that are prone to this problem respond well to having the fibre levels in their diet increased.

You should check and rule out the possibility of toxicity in water and feeds and also from chemicals such as creosote (phenol) which may have been used to treat the stable and which the horse may be inhaling continuously. Formaldehyde, used to tan leather, causes some horses problems. If toxicities in the feed are suspected they should, of course, be eliminated. The horse should be removed from the vicinity of environmental toxins until they have ceased to give off gas. If the causative agent is known, it is sometimes possible to antidote it with an equivalent homoeopathic remedy and to formulate specific vitamins and minerals under expert guidance to facilitate rapid detoxification.

However, in general, the important thing is to keep the fibre levels within the diet up and to keep the feed in line with work done. It may be found useful to use stable bandages on individuals that are especially prone to filled legs when they are standing in (e.g. some heavy hunter types) and to turn them out as much as possible, to avoid fast work on hard ground and always to warm up and warm down carefully before and after exercise. Hand or machine massage can help the circulation. Highly absorbable glyceryl ascorbate (a vitamin C cream) has proved useful but it is necessary to clip the legs as this is a pure but very sticky cream. Methyl sulphonyl methane (MSM) in the feed can be helpful in some cases.

If possible, animals which are particularly prone, and which do not respond to changes in dietary and other management, are best kept out or perhaps yarded in corrals where they can move about more freely. If this latter course is taken, they should have access to a bedded area so that they can lie down if they wish.

Oedema should not be confused with **lymphangitis**, sometimes called Monday morning leg or weed which is characterised by hot, painful swellings beneath the skin, due to inflamed lymphatics. This can be due to infection or, again, *possibly* to excess feed (e.g. horses fed full rations on a rest day). The horse will run a temperature and have an elevated pulse rate. Frequently only one leg is affected, usually, but not always, a hind. Once the swelling appears, temperature and pulse may return to normal.

The vet may give antibiotics to prevent secondary infection, and the rations should be cut back, concentrates being decreased and forage increased. Massage of the lymph glands three or four times a day, and gentle walking exercise once the horse is able, will both be beneficial. Repeated attacks of lymphangitis may be followed by grease in animals of draught-horse descent. The leg swells up and exudes a foul-smelling, greasy discharge. *Do not* use ointments. Keep the area clean and always feed according to work done.

Both of these conditions may respond well to complementary therapies, in conjunction with veterinary advice, including acupuncture.

## Grass Sickness

Grass sickness is a usually fatal, major disturbance of the alimentary canal. It was first reported in Scotland in 1911 and although it is most common in Scotland, it also manifests itself in southern England (increasingly), northern France, Ireland and possibly the USA.

The cause has not been established, although a virus has long been suspected. It almost exclusively affects grass-kept horses, sometimes a group, sometimes an individual. Whether or not it is caused by a virus or is, perhaps, a toxicosis from specific moulds which grow under unique conditions, or a combination of these and other factors, the prognosis is not good.

There are four main types of grass sickness:

1 **Para-acute** – symptomised by depression, fast pulse, absence of gut movement, 'vomiting' of green evil-smelling fluid through the nostrils, profuse sweating and usually pain. Most horses die within 24 hours.
2 **Acute** – symptoms as above, plus muscle tremor and jaundice. Hard faeces can be felt in the colon by rectal examination. Death is likely to occur within 24–48 hours.
3 **Sub-acute** – symptoms as for **1** and **2** although jaundice is likely to be more acute and the horse may stagger. Muscle tremors are particularly notable between the hip and stifle and near the elbow. The appetite is variable (haematocrit rises progressively from 40 per cent to 60 or 70 per cent). Death may occur between ten and 21 days.
4 **Chronic** – symptoms include firm faeces turning to diarrhoea. Death may occur from exhaustion after about 21 days. Cases in

this latter group sometimes live if nourished by stomach tube, but are unlikely to be capable of hard work again.

It is important that the horse is isolated as the mode of spread of the disease is unknown. The animal may be given intravenous electrolyte therapy. Some fluid may be siphoned from the stomach to ease the pressure. In groups **1**, **2** and **3**, once diagnosis has been confirmed it is almost always the kindest thing to euthanase the animal as quickly as possible. For animals in group **4** this is probably also true, unless some role can be envisaged for a horse that will almost certainly be an invalid should it survive.

Whatever the cause may be, the effect seems to be damage to the nervous system supplying the gut and symptoms relate to the consequent cessation of gut movements. Whether this damage to the nerves is a primary effect or a secondary one has not yet been elucidated.

The use of probiotics, intravenous and intramuscular nutrients and highly absorbable supplements, plus unusual appetisers and homoeopathy may have a considerable bearing on the prognosis for group **4** animals.

## Hyperlipaemia

Like laminitis, this is a metabolic disorder often associated with fat little ponies. One British university veterinary school points out that by far the greatest proportion of cases comes from top-class Welsh Pony and Welsh Mountain Pony studs. The common denominator is that, for some reason beyond my comprehension, many show people like their animals to be in gross condition and fatten them up so that they can wobble around the ring as obesity incarnate. The horse, and pony for that matter, has evolved as an athlete. Grossness is not natural and should be classified as a disability, not a desirable attribute. Unfortunately, until showing judges eliminate these disabled horses in much the same way as a dressage judge will eliminate a lame horse, there is little hope that matters will improve for these unfortunate animals.

The pony's metabolic system is pushed to the limit in metabolising all of a typical show animal's extra food. To add insult to injury, the food is probably not needed to keep the animal warm because it is wrapped up in rugs in a closed stable, thus possibly depleted in vitamin D because it is not exposed to sunlight, which may upset calcium metabolism and further affect the metabolic and hormonal balance. The net result is that the metabolic system suddenly, effectively says 'no more'. The pony goes off its food (i.e. becomes anorexic) and suddenly the rich energy source dries up.

The body fats are then mobilised to provide energy but sometimes this mechanism overcompensates and mobilises more fat than can be utilised by the pony. This excess fat accumulates in the blood, i.e. a state of hyperlipaemia (hyper = high; lip = lipid or fat; aemia = in the blood) exists and the lipid levels may increase from a normal of 100–500 mg per 100 ml of blood to 1,800 mg per 100 ml or more.

It is absolutely vital that these ponies recommence eating and one of the best things for ponies in this state is molasses/chaff/hay/grass mix – molasses for sugar energy and chaff/hay/grass to get the gut going again. Probiotics may also help in this respect and B vitamins and zinc may help to stimulate appetite. Feeds should be small and enticing. If molasses is not enough, feed fruit juice (any sort the pony likes), apples, carrots, etc. and offer a choice of feeds if possible.

Again, homoeopathy has proved helpful for this disorder.

Occasionally, an animal has to be fed through a tube inserted into the oesophagus via an opening cut in the neck. It is sad to relate that many show ponies who have been cured are sent home having lost about half the weight they need to lose and with instructions to get their weight down further but the breeder's response has usually been to feed them right back to where they started because the poor little dears are wasting away. This is eventually followed by a return trip to the clinic or a happy release on the meat waggon.

Hyperlipaemia can also occur in other horses who are suddenly anorexic or deprived of food (e.g. an animal bought at market after a long journey, or being touted from market to market with minimal feed and water on offer – illegal but, sadly, not uncommon). This can occur even if the horse is not overweight, particularly in post-operative cases where, again, it is crucial to get some food into them, by tubing if necessary. This is particularly likely to happen if fluid therapy has not been employed post-operatively. It may also occur in overweight pony mares in late gestation and peak lactation.

## Hyperlipoproteinaemia

This sometimes accompanies hyperlipaemia in similar but more extreme circumstances.

Both of these disorders may be precipitated if laminitic ponies are managed, or should I say 'mis-managed', by starvation methods.

## Intestinal Parasites

There are a number of ways in which intestinal parasites, in their various growth stages, can affect the nutrition and nutritional status of an animal.

- They may cause primary damage to the gut wall, reducing absorption of nutrients.
- They may cause secondary damage to the gut wall, e.g. by stopping or restricting blood supplies to a part of the gut, leading to necrosis (death of tissues) and, therefore, less efficient feed utilisation and possibly colic.
- They may actually cause a blockage at some point in the gut (e.g. a heavy bot burden in the stomach of a foal), again leading to colic.
- They use nutrients which could otherwise be used by the horse.
- They may cause blood loss, either externally by blood-sucking (e.g. lice, ticks, mosquitoes) or internally (e.g. red worms), leading to anaemia which can be sufficiently serious to cause death and will at least lead to unnecessary fatigue.

Virtually all equines have some sort of parasite burden, whether or not any form of parasite control is practised. The degree to which this affects the horse's health, longevity and performance is very much in the hands of the horse owner.

An understanding of the life cycles of many internal parasites is an aid to understanding the approach to their control but is beyond the scope of this book.

There are two aspects of parasite control: one is pasture management and the other is chemical control in the horse with anthelmintics (wormers) and herbal vermifuges whether or not the horse is stabled. Responsible horse owners and keepers should familiarise themselves with practical treatment and pasture management and should work closely in conjunction with their veterinary practitioner on this subject. For more detailed information see *Veterinary Notes for Horse Owners*, M. Horace Hayes, Century Hutchinson, 1987 and *Pasture Management for Horses and Ponies*, by this author, Blackwell

Scientific 1987. See also the section on page 230 on starvation for notes on parasite control in severely debilitated horses.

## Lacrimination (Running Eyes)

Often associated with vitamin deficiencies and imbalances.

## Laminitis

Laminitis is frequently misunderstood, both by owners and by all too many practising vets. In its commonest form, it is a classic example of what can go wrong if the micro-organisms which live in the digestive tract are upset.

These micro-organisms form a very mixed population and some, if they multiply too rapidly, are 'fed' incorrectly or have their environment dramatically changed (e.g. its acidity), may fight back by producing unsuitable chemicals (exotoxins) or may die off and release large amounts of chemicals (endotoxins) as they break down, which the horse is ill-prepared for. One of the results of this can be laminitis.

Although there are several causative circumstances which can lead to laminitis, here we are concerned with feed-related occurrences. Most horse owners, and some ill-informed vets, still insist that it is due to 'too much protein', probably because of its occurrence in ponies on rich spring grass which has a high protein content. However, spring grass also has a very high soluble carbohydrate content and a sudden influx of carbohydrates, from whatever source (including breaking into grain bins in the feed store as well as being turned out on to lush green pasture, particularly in certain weather conditions), has the effect of unbalancing the gut micro-organisms. This leads to the production of large amounts of toxins or excessive levels of chemicals which are out of balance, including lactic acid. For reasons which nobody has yet been able to pin down, this manifests itself by causing inflammation of the fleshy laminae of the feet, leading to heat and considerable pain because the fleshy laminae are confined by the horn laminae and there is nowhere for the swelling to go, so that the pressure becomes immense.

The other factor about lush spring grass which may be significant is that while it is growing rapidly it causes a shortage of trace minerals in the pasture, which may further predispose certain types of horses and ponies to laminitis attacks.

Laminitis may be acute, i.e. a one-off occurrence which may not recur, particularly if it is dealt with rapidly and appropriately; or it may become a chronic problem, classically in small, 'get-fat-on-fresh-air' ponies, particularly those with boxy feet, who are especially prone to recurrent attacks.

Recent experience has suggested that some 'get-fat-on-fresh-air' ponies may suffer from a hormonal imbalance due, in part, to hypothyroidism (an underactive thyroid) and, consequently, insulin insufficiency which would make it difficult for them to deal with a sudden influx of soluble carbohydrate. This might explain why one pony in a field succumbs while its pasture-mate chomps away happily with impunity. The effects of giving the hormone thyroxine or insulin to this type of pony look promising but the difficulty will undoubtedly be to identify appropriate animals for treatment. However, a few hormone tablets are no substitute whatsoever for proper management of these ponies and imbalances can often be corrected, permanently, using constitutional homoeopathy.

The so-called 'starvation' technique is not proper management. Although it will restrict carbohydrate intake, it will also restrict intake of other essential nutrients including minerals (e.g. iodine, essential for thyroid function), vitamins and protein, including certain amino acids essential for healthy hoof formation. By starving the pony, you may contain a particular attack but will probably prevent it from being possible for the pony to become laminitis-free as it will always be prone to attacks and other problems due to malnutrition. If it is *very* fat, you may also precipitate an attack of hyperlipaemia, a potentially fatal wasting disease precipitated by sudden rapid weight loss.

Another deficiency and consequent imbalance which may be implicated in chronic laminitis is calcium deficiency which, again, is likely to occur on starvation diets. Combining starvation with bran mashes – a common management, or mis-management, technique – causes calcium and phosphorus imbalances which may help to turn an acute case into a chronic and recurring one.

Avoiding laminitis in the normal horse or pony is a matter of balancing work with correct and adequate levels of nutrients and, above all, avoiding upsetting the harmony of the digestive micro-organisms – if you look after the 'bugs', the pony will look after itself! This means no sudden change in the diet, feeding little and often (including managed access to pasture) and, of course, feeding appropriate feedstuffs. If you cannot do this, then you must accept that you do not have the appropriate facilities to keep the pony and must find it a more suitable home.

## Mildly Laminitis-prone Horses and Ponies

In the case of the mildly laminitis-prone horse or pony, you must be prepared to call in your vet if there is any 'iffiness' and to nursemaid the digestive micro-organisms.

- Keep an eye on the pasture. If the grass is growing rapidly, particularly if there has been mild, wet weather following plenty of sunshine, which encourages sappy growth, restrict access to it. Rather than, say, turning out for four hours once a day, try to make it two hours twice a day, or whatever seems suitable, to break it up so that you are still feeding little and often. Putting hay or straw out in the field will prevent scouring and will keep the fibre content of the diet up; if this is not consumed because the grass is too tasty, try molassed chaff instead.
- For the more susceptible animal, consider feeding a good quality, carefully stored, probiotic for a few days, or another gut stabiliser like smectite earth (bentonite), which is a clay related to kaolin, and is found in the additive Thrive. Ensure that a trace-mineralised and iodised salt lick is available at all times and that levels of other nutrients are appropriate for the horse or pony's body-weight, age and work rate. This means you will be feeding *extra* supplements when you restrict grass intake.

  A useful means of doing this is to give feed-blocks (range-blocks) but do be sure that plenty of long fibre, such as hay, is also available because if the horses are too hungry they will gorge on the blocks. Another convenient supplement for ponies which are not otherwise receiving feed are horse biscuits such as the Salvana Briquette which can be fed on their own and which contain a certain amount of vitamins and minerals.

## More Susceptible Animals

If you have a more susceptible pony or one that has already had an attack at some time in its life and you find you have to restrict grazing seriously and use a so-called 'starvation paddock', then you must also take the responsibility for the horse or pony's entire dietary intake and not just leave it at that.

- Ensure that there are no poisonous weeds, trees or hedgerow plants which may be eaten in desperation.
- Make sure that you supply some hay or oat straw that is *low in nutritional* value (*not* of poor physical quality, i.e. not mouldy or dusty).
- Provide an adequate trace nutrient and vitamin and amino acid source.
- It is also important that you feed little and often to keep beneficial digestive micro-organisms ticking over.

## Working Horses and Ponies

For horses or ponies in work, I found some years ago that a particularly safe ration may be made up of soaked sugar beet and breadmeal (such as Bailey's No. 1), plus chaff, in addition to a top quality vitamin and mineral supplement which also contains amino acids. In theory, this diet should not work because much of the carbohydrate in it is fairly available; it may be effective because of the highly available calcium and potassium from the sugar beet.

Depending on how much sugar beet you find you use, you may also need to add additional calcium in the form of limestone flour. In problem cases, you should also consider using one of the more expensive calcium sources – a gluconate, citrate or orotate – which has more available calcium. Diets based on these principles were developed in conjunction with the Royal Veterinary College some years ago, for use in preventing recurrent attacks after foundered patients were discharged.

## Laminitis-prone Ponies in Hard Work

With a laminitis-prone pony in hard work, I start by feeding it only 80–90 per cent of the appropriate level of digestible energy for its bodyweight and work rate and only increase this if I find that the pony is losing weight or lacking the energy to keep up. If this happens, I add a fat premix or oil, such as soya or corn oil, as a non-carbohydrate energy source, supplemented with vitamin E. I have tried this on many laminitis-prone ponies in hard work, such as competition carriage driving, to good effect.

These ponies also benefit from the judicious use of probiotics and Thrive to provide a stable gut environment in times of stress, such as changes in feeding, travelling and competitions. I also use a supplement with the most suitable vitamin/mineral profile, which is also a good source of amino acids. There are several on the market – look out for good levels of lysine and methionine.

Horses and ponies recovering from a laminitis attack, however severe, are bound to have a certain amount of hoof damage and the growth of a new hoof wall will take six to nine months.

Although biotin was heralded as the 'answer' to hoof damage as with any nutrition it is more complicated than that as there are many interactions between different nutrients. I believe that one reason why biotin is beneficial could be that the post-laminitic pony may well have a very high yeast population in the gut, which tends to mop up biotin in the normal diet, preventing the pony from receiving adequate levels. The pony may be receiving what would normally be adequate levels in the diet but very little is getting through the gut wall and into it!

Other nutrients which are particularly important in this context are the amino acids lysine and sulphur-rich methionine, the minerals zinc, selenium and calcium and a number of vitamins including vitamin A. Another nutrient which gives good results, by providing a readily available source of sulphur in a organic form which the horse can easily utilise, is methyl sulphonyl methane (MSM). This is likely to become more important as pastureland in Britain is becoming severely depleted of sulphur, particularly where high levels of fertiliser have been used and, ironically, as levels of sulphur-containing acid rain reduce!

Sulphur is important in the structure of the hoof wall which is made up partly of a protein called keratin (the source of the distinctive smell when a horse is being hot shod is the sulphur bonds breaking in the heat).

Under professional guidance, you can use MSM in its pure form to create the desired effect. As it also acts as an anti-inflammatory, it is hoped that vets will encourage horse owners to feed pure MSM at the onset of an attack to help to reduce heat and inflammation. Some vets have already begun moving towards this concept by using the sulphur compound 'DMSO'. Unfortunately, this has a number of adverse side effects. MSM is the more natural form of DMSO and is far better suited for use in the horse. MSM-containing broad-spectrum supplements are also formulated for home use and contain some of the other nutrients mentioned above to support the beneficial effects of the MSM.

## Monitoring Bodyweight

A simple laminitis prevention measure is monitoring your horse or pony's bodyweight. This is particularly useful with the unclipped pony out at grass, because the transition from the woolly pony who may, in fact, have lost quite a lot of weight over the winter and the potential laminitis case on rapidly growing spring grass can be very quick and may otherwise go unnoticed. Complicated formulae for assessing bodyweight are really not necessary. You can use a formula based on simple heart-girth measurement or a bodyweight tape. If you get into the habit of checking the bodyweight once a week at the same time, this could give an early warning which may save a lot of trouble, expense and pain for your pony.

## Lampas

The term 'lampas' refers to the oedematous swelling of the soft palate in the mouth and may occur if the horse's teeth require attention. It is not considered significant by vets. It used to be treated by lancing and rubbing salt into the wound but this is not done now.

It may be that a diet containing plenty of long fibre will help to massage the affected area.

It has been suggested that lampas may be caused by some form of mineral imbalance and I have come across one yard where all the horses had it but did not have problems with their teeth. There is almost certainly some sort of dietary involvement and it may be indicative of other health problems but these relationships have not yet been discovered.

## Malabsorption Syndrome

This occurs when some, or all, nutrients are poorly absorbed across the gut wall into the blood circulatory system for distribution and further processing by the body or direct utilisation.

Most cases of malabsorption appear to be due to damage to the gut wall, usually but not always by parasites, including worms and yeast overgrowth, but ingestion of poisonous materials, the action of microbial toxins, ulcers, severe dietary imbalance, lack of water and salt, lack of fibre and so forth may also be indicated, as could chronic diarrhoea associated with villous atrophy (established by the use of glucose or xylose tolerance tests) and feed intolerances and allergies.

I suspect that some types of folic-acid-deficiency-induced anaemia, or crumbling hooves which respond to biotin supplementation, may, on paper, appear adequate in the diet but those conditions may relate to some form of malabsorption syndrome. If yeast overgrowth is implicated, these nutrients could be being used by the yeasts themselves before they can be utilised by the horse. The diet may therefore seem to be 'adequate' yet the horse does not get a 'look in' with certain nutrients before the yeasts 'steal' them.

'Poor doers' who are nervous and irritable sometimes turn out to have malabsorption problems, although this might not be the primary cause of their temperament problems.

Obviously, parasite control must be effective and the vet may decide to take a biopsy of the gut-lining. He will also check the horse's teeth, as inadequate chewing may also be a factor.

Keep the feed easily digestible, particularly the fibre (e.g. sugar beet pulp, dried alfalfal/lucerne). Consider using mineral supplements with highly absorbable mineral sources (usually more expensive) and consider using amino acid supplements to supply protein quality with free-form amino acids which are easily absorbable. Unfortunately, sugar beet and molasses are contra-indicated if yeast overgrowth is suspected and until it is under control.

As about 70 per cent of dietary protein is absorbed from the small intestine, it is particularly important to ensure a good supply of high-quality protein for horses with this problem. This may be one instance where stud nuts are of more value to mature, non-breeding animals.


## Malnutrition

The results of nutrition may range from obesity (severely overweight horses), through various dietary imbalances, to starvation.

The various disadvantages of obesity have been discussed elsewhere and imbalances have been discussed throughout this book. Starvation is another matter.

Due to the survival mechanism which keeps the brain and nervous systems supplied with glucose up to the 'last gasp', the horse may be recumbent and unable to rise. As the body is depleted of fat reserves, muscles (first glycogen stores and then protein muscle fibres) are broken down to maintain blood glucose levels. The horse loses muscular strength but will (sadly), be both alert and aware as the brain continues to function normally until almost the very end.

The horse may well exhibit various symptoms, both external and internal, of vitamin and mineral deficiency (lachrymination [see below], bone disorders, nutritional anaemia, staring coat, poor hoof condition, etc.). If the animal is badly managed, it is also likely to have a considerable internal (worms/bots) and external (lice/ticks etc.) parasite burden which all goes to contribute to a state of anaemia and possible malabsorption. Secondary infections of various kinds may also be present, along with constipation or scouring, and the horse may also be dehydrated, particularly as it is severely weakened or if it has been scouring for some time and has gone down and cannot get up again to reach water. Death may be due to these secondary aspects, e.g. pneumonia or the dehydration of a horse debilitated by starvation.

Veterinary intervention is advisable as soon as possible as inexpert management may precipitate further problems. The vet will probably use some sort of intravenous therapy to provide glucose, electrolytes and liquid, plus steroids to get the horse on its feet, and will institute a gradual regime of parasite control.

The horse, mule or donkey should be fed nourishing feeds and this is one instance when the animal will require additional protein to build muscle. It is a good idea to give probiotics at an early stage, as a paste if necessary, to help to re-establish and rebalance the gut micro-organisms and facilitate improved digestion and absorption. Highly digestible feeds, such as breadmeal, sugar beet pulp and dried alfalfa (lucerne) cubes, plus a high quality vitamin/mineral mix including amino acids, adequate calcium and salt should be given to encourage eating and the feed should be balanced carefully once the horse is strong enough to eat. *Do not* feed bran mashes – they are the last thing this type of animal needs.

Feed small, frequent, appetising feeds with succulents added to them, and consider introducing a well-balanced herbal conditioner which, apart from anything else, will provide additional vitamins and minerals that may not be covered in the manufactured supplements but may be crucial for a severely depleted horse.

The use of herbal supplementation should also be considered in conjunction with early homoeopathic constitutional treatment which may also reduce the need for steroids. A horse or pony found in this condition is also likely to benefit from homoeopathic aconite (for shock and trauma) or Dr Bach's Rescue Remedy, which is always useful to have in any stable first aid kit. These should not, of course, be used as an alternative to veterinary treatment but they can, I believe, help the horse to feel more comfortable in itself. It is assumed that you are dealing with some sort of rescue case, although certain health problems, e.g. hyperlipaemia (see page 221) or poisoning can also lead to rapid starvation.

Although irreparable damage may have been done to the gut and other organs if auto-digestion has taken place, it *is* possible to bring many of these animals back to a reasonable state of health, particularly if secondary infections, such as respiratory infections, are dealt with rapidly and effectively. Gentle hacking/driving or a life in retirement as a companion animal may be possible. However, do not try to rush things and keep to an easily digested diet throughout.

I know of a number of animals, which had been serious rescue cases earlier in life, who have reached their forties and have even continued competing quietly and have certainly been ridden at that age.

As the muscle returns, the protein level of the diet may be reduced but do ensure that good quality feedstuffs are used throughout.

Do not try to rush things or you may find the compromised animal getting colic, laminitis and so forth. Look for steady, gentle gain in condition and do not overcompensate and allow the animal to become overweight as this would further tax its beleaguered resources.

Be very careful about dealing with heavy worm burdens as, in its weakened state, the animal may not be able to tolerate the toxins released by the death of huge numbers of worms and parasites all at once. I believe it is a good idea to give an 'ordinary' wormer dose and wait for a reasonable interval while keeping the animal in isolation, giving it time to begin to recover (perhaps a week or longer), before giving it whatever higher dose the vet may suggest and possibly even waiting again before giving an anthelmintic which kills the larval stages as well. Otherwise, massive oedema and shock can occur and a number of horses have died because they were not able to cope with the additional acute stress to the system caused by massive parasite death. It is essential to get the parasites under control but do be guided by the vet and take the 'softly, softly' approach if in any doubt.

## Muscular Problems – Feed/Exercise-induced

Feed/exercise-induced muscular problems and diseases (myopathies) go by many names, many of which describe the symptoms rather than their causes, e.g. azoturia, tying-up syndrome, set-fast, Monday morning disease, paralytic myoglobinuria, exertional rhabdomyolysis and myositis. These include broadly related syndromes or are alternative names for the same syndrome.

Other feed-related myopathies may be very non-specific and be indicated by stiffness before or after exercise, muscle pain and twitching, and, basically, any abnormality in the muscles not caused by injury.

The first group of syndromes are very painful conditions affecting a large group of muscles, especially of the hindquarters and occasionally of the shoulders, which can lead to muscle fibre damage.

The condition is usually brought on by an imbalance of feeding to work, although some individuals appear to be particularly susceptible and any animal that has had an acute attack is likely to be more susceptible in the future.

The symptoms usually appear after a rest day (hence the name Monday morning disease) if the feed has not been cut back during the rest period. Lay-offs due to snow and ice may also precipitate an attack, particularly when strenuous work recommences (especially trotting in deep snow etc.) if feeding has not been cut back accordingly.

The cause of these attacks is thought to be the rapid use of glycogen laid down by the liver and muscles during idleness. This leads to excessive production of lactic acid in muscles as a by-product of its breakdown, which fails to be removed fast enough to prevent destruction of muscle fibres. This is especially common in muscle-bound animals such as heavy draught horses which seem to be very prone to it. Horses which are cardiovascularly fit are *probably* less likely to succumb.

Symptoms include the sudden onset of profuse sweating, stiffness behind, which may be progressive or may first be noticed as severe muscle cramps, hard, painful muscles, especially in the back and hindquarters, restlessness, rapid respiration and pulse, raised temperature, difficulty in urinating and the production of port-wine-coloured urine. It is this latter symptom which gives the name myoglobinuria, as the coloration is not due to blood but to muscle (myo) pigment in the urine as the muscle tissue breaks down.

Often the horse is all right until it has stopped *after* fast work, the classic case being a hunter standing at a covert after a brisk gallop or riding through heavy going. The horse will stop and refuse to move (a shortening of the stride preceding an attack may be noted by an observant rider) and some horses may even sit down in a dog-like position.

You should immediately dismount, throw your coat over your horse's loins to keep it warm and get help. *Do not* attempt to walk it off as this will only increase muscle damage. If possible get help and a vet to where the horse is or get the horse into a horse box (preferably rear-facing) and drive *very* carefully home or to stables or a barn nearby. If you have gone hunting or to a show in a trailer, it is preferable for someone else to take the trailer home and for you to borrow a box. In a two-horse trailer, use the section on the crown-side of the road. Initially, the vet will probably prescribe painkillers, antispasmodic and anti-inflammatory drugs and steroids. In the future it is possible that intra-muscular magnesium injections may be given to reduce the cramps.

You should keep the horse warm without loading it down with heavy rugs. If you have had to transport it, if necessary keep it in the horse box until its situation has eased. Use hot water bottles or a heated pad if available (not *too* hot though) or heated blankets or towels, as this will both help to ease the pain and may improve the circulation to the area. You may also be able to apply homoeopathic ruta cream if you have some by you or rhus tox cream, particularly to a clipped horse. Many stables also keep these homoeopathic remedies in the oral form in the medicine chest, along with aconite for shock and arnica for bruising, and all may prove useful until you can obtain advice on a more specific treatment. However, in the first instance these should be used as an adjunct to and *not* instead of urgent veterinary treatment.

Most horses make an initial recovery in a few hours if rested but some lie down, are unable to get up again and may die. Once the initial attack is over, the horse *must* be rested until muscle damage has ceased. This can be monitored by blood tests which will be all the more useful if your horse's blood profile is routinely monitored so that you know what its individual normal levels are.

The feed must be cut back and kept low in carbohydrates (e.g. feed only forage and use feed-grade oil as an energy source). Bran mashes will *not* help and may delay recovery. Modern physiotherapy techniques, applied by a suitably qualified expert, may be useful to stimulate regeneration of muscle and enhance removal of toxins but should not be applied too soon or without veterinary approval and guidance. The vet will almost certainly check the SGOT (serum glutamic oxaloacetic transaminase), AST (aspartamine transferase) and CK/CPK (creatinine phosphokinase) enzymes in the blood, which give an indication of the extent of muscle damage and can be used as a guidelines as to when the horse can safely be exercised again, beyond gentle walking. It is vital that you go cautiously, particularly if you wish to avoid a proneness to recurrent attacks.

This is especially important for horses which are repeatedly affected, often for no apparent reason (usually, in fact, due to dietary and exercise imbalance). I have seen one horse who had 'tied-up' severely seven times and on a day on which the horse was judged fit to compete in an indoor show jumping competition, based on visual appraisal by the vet, its SGOT/CPK levels were still four times the normal level!

Basic prevention is obviously better than cure, so always keep your feeding in line with exercise. The night before a scheduled rest day, cut back cereals in the diet by 50 per cent. If you feed compounds, these will have to be cut back in their entirety by 50 per cent but, through the rest day, feed the reduced amount of feed in the normal *number* of feeds, as cutting a feed right out is psychologically stressful and upsets the digestive micro-organisms. You can increase the levels of chaff and other fibre sources.

On unscheduled rest days (e.g. snow, illness of horse or rider) try at least to walk the horse out if possible or, weather permitting, turn it out so that it is not standing still in the stable all day. You may find that adding bicarbonate of soda (baking soda) or a proprietary buffer solution to the feed will help for a few days, particularly if you are not sure how long the lay off is likely to be (see page 233). Again, cut the concentrates and adjust the feed as for scheduled rest days as soon as possible. You should immediately cut back the concentrates and increase the forage content of the diet. Massage, ranging from the very gentle if the horse is ill, to good and diligent strapping, will help to maintain the circulation in the large muscles. If the horse is kept in a yard where there is an indoor arena or even an enclosed barn space, even ten to fifteen minutes' loose exercise, either alone or in *safe* groups (perhaps while you muck the stable out), can make all the difference. A straw/muck exercise ring on snow may also be used.

Some horses, particularly those that seem especially prone to this problem, tend to have selenium deficiency and malabsorption problems, and there are certain areas of the UK, particularly on hill country and especially in parts of Cornwall, North Wales, northern Scotland, etc. where selenium is deficient in the soil. Vitamin E, which works with selenium, may also be deficient and it is a good idea, particularly if you live in a known deficient area, to ensure that your horse is obtaining adequate vitamin E and selenium in the diet.

For horses in hard work, it may be that additional vitamin E with a selenium supplement may well be justified, particularly if high levels of oil are being fed, but you should, in any case, ensure that such horses are receiving a broad-spectrum supplement supplying at least 0.1 mg of selenium a day plus at least 1,000 iu of vitamin E per day either added to a home mix or in the compound feed. You should keep the fibre levels in the diet as high as possible and consider obtaining some of the energy component from highly digestible fibres which are more slowly available than carbohydrates in cereals, for example dried alfalfa (lucerne) cubes or chaff and sugar beet feed. If you are still finding it a problem, you can consider using fat or oil as a significant energy source, provided you supply adequate levels of vitamin E.

*Do not* give these horses proprietary kidney powders or condition powders – they may well make matters worse and cannot replace good management.

For horses that are more chronically affected with a milder form of tying-up or set-fast, you must monitor their enzyme levels on a routine basis, once you realise you have a problem, to try to establish their normal levels. It is also vital that you ensure they are receiving adequate levels of sodium, as salt, in the diet. Feed 25–100 g (1–4 oz) of salt a day, plus a trace-mineralised salt lick for insurance. Also feed readily available potassium (sugar beet is a good source) and be particularly vigilant about the other mineral levels in the diet.

While forage is usually a good source of potassium, soaking hay may remove significant quantities of soluble potassium and, in some forages, potassium may not be well utilised. It is a particularly good idea to ensure that this type of horse is offered an electrolyte drink if there is the slightest possibility that one is needed, as electrolytes certainly seem to be implicated in some of these problems. Nobody has ever quantified the amount of electrolytes lost in soaked hay, so, if the animal also suffers from COPD and you are soaking the hay, it is quite possible that this would be sufficient to tip the balance. The old-fashioned hay tea was used as an early form of electrolyte drink for this very reason!

Once you have tried the foregoing, ensured that your overall diet is balanced and that dietary management is in tune with work levels on a day-to-day basis, it may be useful to give horses *other than endurance horses* 50–100 g (2–4 oz) of sodium bicarbonate (baking soda, an alkali) per day, spread through the feeds, or a proprietary buffer mixture which will probably contain sodium bicarbonate, potassium bicarbonate and calcium carbonate. Homoeopathic lactic acid may also help to reduce any possible acidosis (which causes muscle pain and cramps). However, while homoeopathic lactic acid may be useful to reduce pain in acute attacks, it should not be used as a means of keeping this sort of horse going because it may mask minor symptoms and lead to an even worse attack at a later stage.

Endurance horses work mainly aerobically and are more susceptible to alkalosis than acidosis (i.e. lactic acidosis) so *never* feed them bicarbonate of soda. There are properly balanced buffer mixtures suitable for endurance horses but it is important that you check this with the supplier because those that are suitable for flat-race racehorses, for example, are *not* suitable for endurance horses.

'Tying-up' can also occur if Faradism or Faradic stimulation is used to warm up a horse prior to strenuous (particularly anaerobic) exertion. This is *not* what these machines are intended for and it is possible that, by initiating lactic acid production if used excessively, they may, at the very least, hasten the onset of stiffness and fatigue, and, at worst, full-blown azoturia. Warming up is an important part of high-performance exercise but it should start off with sufficient aerobic (slow) exercise and will not help much if cardiovascular condition conditioning has been inadequate and inappropriate.

Many of the milder, non-specific muscle problems will respond to careful supplementation with a high magnesium supplement. Horses have generally not been considered to be as sensitive to magnesium levels in the feed as, for example, high-yielding dairy cows but in some instances it may be that they absorb or utilise magnesium poorly or that they have a higher than expected requirement for magnesium, perhaps because they are stabled near industrial complexes, main roads or other sources of pollution. In these circumstances, the detoxification pathways of the body have to work harder and, as magnesium is involved in over 300 enzyme systems related to detoxification, along with other minerals, particularly selenium and zinc, a horse being fed normal levels may still be compromised. Very little specific work has been done on this but good results have been achieved with horses that have had problems with stiffness, mild tying-up, various multi-focal lamenesses and other non-specific problems. Poor absorption of magnesium seems to be the problem in some cases, so different forms of magnesium may be fed and, again, treatment with homoeopathy, both constitutionally and with differing forms of magnesium, may correct the problem alone or may facilitate absorption and retention of the necessary nutrients *provided* adequate material levels are being fed in the diet.

High magnesium-content salt licks are also available and may be worth trying for this sort of animal. This field is not well researched in horses but clinical trials have given good results and a number of specialist products (e.g. Canzoglycan), which are rich in absorbable magnesium, are becoming increasingly available.

In most cases, provided the rest of the diet is adjusted to ensure nutrient levels are adequate, a course for one to three months will put the situation right. It is important that horses prone to this problem have a good mixed diet which does not overly rely on cereals as energy sources and, again, dried alfalfa (lucerne) and sugar beet have an important role to play. Chromium is also found to reduce lactate acid levels in hard-worked horses and is often given as a supplement in these cases. It is also known that horses with low dietary levels of copper suffer a similar syndrome of pronounced myopathy.

## Mycotoxicosis

Mycotoxicosis (mycotoxin poisoning) in horses is a recognised phenomenon in the United States, particularly in relation to a specific type of fescue, to such an extent that it is called fescue toxicity there. However, it is not the fescue grass which causes the problem but microscopic moulds which grow on the grass.

In all pasture there are moulds, both in the form of spores and in long tendril-like mycelia which proliferate throughout the soil: there are hundreds of varieties, and thousands of organisms per square metre of pasture. Normally, the majority of them are harmless and some are even useful as they help to break down dead plant matter. Unfortunately, under certain circumstances chemical changes can occur which cause the moulds to release highly poisonous substances called mycotoxins. Some varieties, on the other hand, have some degree of toxicity at all times.

In the USA, a very clear-cut link between the fescues, the fungi and ailments in mares and foals has been discovered. Grazing on such pasture can lead to little or no milk production (agalactia) in early-foaled mares, prolonged gestation periods and exceptionally thick placentas which can suffocate unattended newborn foals, and there is also a probable association with abortions and still births. The American researchers believe that the fescue/endophyte toxicosis problem is almost certainly present in the UK. These endophytic fungi have been identified in both *Fesctuca* (fescue) and *Lolium* (rye grass) species in the UK. The fungi in question are probably related to ergot fungi (*Claviceps* spp.).

The spread of the infection seems to take place through the grass seed and a service has been set up in the USA to examine both growing plants and seedheads for infections. This service is also available to UK horse owners but, unfortunately, until advisors and veterinary hospitals are aware of the situation, many of these problems are put down to mysterious circumstances and never properly identified.

Horse breeders should be aware that a diagnostic facility is available at Auburn University College of Agriculture, Alabama, USA.

Other mycotoxins may be at least as important with regard to equine health and a number of fungi produce toxins, known as aflotoxins, in grain and oilseeds, which can prove fatal.

It is possible that grass sickness is in some way exacerbated or even caused by pasture or grain mycotoxins and there appears to be an increasing number of mysterious illnesses, particularly in grass-kept animals, which may be related to this, although the use of organo-phosphate pesticides and their contamination of water courses and feedstuffs has also been implicated. These illnesses often manifest themselves either as a mild form of grass sickness or as a severe muscle myopathy which mimics azoturia or tying-up, but which does not occur in the usual circumstances. For example, grazing breeding and youngstock may apparently be affected with azoturia and shifting multi-focal lameness, severe, usually very noisy (tympanitic) colic, or other rather non-specific symptoms. There is frequently some degree of muscle damage and damage to the liver. The illness is usually mis-diagnosed or unexplained.

It often appears during odd weather conditions, which gives the first clue to the possible link to mycotoxins as this is a well-known phenomenon in the similar foggy morning disease in cattle. It has also been noted that it is quite common for this to occur when major excavations have taken place in the pasture or adjacent to the pasture (for example, the laying of a pipeline or the building of a new road or housing estate nearby). One possible explanation for this is that heavy metals and even unusual moulds deep in the subsoil or bedrock have been stirred up during the digging of foundations. The horse may either be directly affected by these or, as seems more likely, the herbage which the horse is grazing may be affected as it may exhibit luxury uptake of these materials and this may facilitate the change in the fungal growth on the plants. This can affect grasses, clovers and herbs. Then, when appropriate weather conditions arise, these fungi may produce mycotoxins which lead to this syndrome when the horse grazes the area.

The link with excavation seems to be so strong that it would seem sensible to fence off pipelines etc. for some years after they have been laid and to avoid keeping grazing animals downhill from, for example, a new building plot.

While limited research is being done, it is difficult to suggest an appropriate management technique if you have an animal which you suspect is affected. You should certainly note the prevailing weather conditions, the horse should be brought in off the pasture and the vet should do a full biochemical work–up. The horse should be kept on simple rations and consideration should be given to using herbal and homoeopathic conditioners as the liver is usually compromised and will not withstand the side effects of most prolonged drug therapy.

Great care should be taken in bringing these horses back into work. If possible, they should be moved to different grazing.

If this is not possible, you should endeavour to have your pasture checked for herbage species which are prone to mould infections or, if you are running a stud, even have them screened at the Auburn toxicity centre in Alabama. Unfortunately, at this time it is not possible to say whether anything at all will be gained by ploughing up the pasture and starting again, as nobody has really adequately looked into the problem in the UK. However, there is little doubt that you will have to change the management of affected horses completely, should they survive an initial attack. I am currently endeavouring to collate information about this problem with a view to giving sensible management advice in the future and would be most interested to hear from anybody whose horses have been affected by, or indeed have overcome, the problem.

As many horses scour quite badly during a bout, in the early stages, I feel sure that feeding probiotics to help to recolonise the gut with healthy micro-organisms, and perhaps giving a limited course of Thrive to help to detoxify the system rapidly will certainly do no harm in the short term. Large doses of certain vitamins have also been found useful in similar conditions.

The most important thing is that, probably for the rest of the horse's life, you will have to watch it very carefully for symptoms of the start of a recurrent attack and will have to be very aware of weather conditions and the pasture you are using. Most people with recovering horses find it best to avoid turning them out in muggy or foggy weather or at dawn or dusk, if at all, and try to turn them out in the middle of the day when the dew has dried on the grass and the air is clear and fresh. Some find that early signs of recurrent attack are that, perhaps, the horse starts to go a little stiff behind, or that there are a lot of gut sounds. If this happens you should bring the horse in as soon as possible and cease any activity that you are undertaking at the time.

The diet should be simple, home-mixed with no compounds, easily digestible and certainly of very good, plain nutrition. It is probably best not to feed these horses mould-derived supplements, including brewer's yeast, and you should check that other B vitamins and selenium are from a yeast free source, as a sensitivity to yeast may arise after this type of illness. The use of herbal tonics gives noticeably improved results, presumably because of their inherent beneficial effects on liver function.

## Nutritional Factors Affecting the Hoof Condition

It is worth considering that, unless you are dealing with endurance horses or racehorses, which are reshod very frequently, there is little to be gained from attempting to speed up the rate or quantity of hoof growth. There is, however, much to be gained from enhancing the *quality* of hoof material produced and there is no question that correct nutrition plays an important role in this. Hoof horn is made up largely of keratinised protein material, very similar to hair, so, obviously, the diet needs to be adequate in protein. If the horse is deficient in energy, some of the protein in the diet will be used selectively as an energy source, which may be disadvantageous to healthy hoof-horn formation.

Keratin is an insoluble protein which contains sulphur. Its formation is dependent on the presence in the diet of the sulphur-containing amino acids, methionine and/or cystine. Methyl sulphonyl methane (MSM) is an organic source of sulphur. It is well absorbed by the horse and facilitates the maintenance of adequate supplies of sulphur.

The hoof wall contains about 25 per cent water and may become dehydrated especially if the periople (protective natural varnish) layer is damaged (e.g. by excessive cosmetic rasping by the farrier) or the tubules of the horn are blocked at the base by hot shoeing (fusion), hoof oil or Stockholm tar.

Other nutrients which are implicated in the healthy formation of keratin are vitamins A and biotin and the trace elements zinc and selenium. Vitamin-A-deficient horses are particularly prone to flaking periople. In a severely depleted horse, other nutrients may become more significant as they are diverted to more essential life processes when they are in short supply. Adequate levels of calcium are also thought to play a part in healthy hoof formation.

Megadosing the vitamin biotin at a rate of about 15 mg a day for a 450-kg (1,000 lb) horse, for three to nine months (to allow time for the growth of a completely new hoof) has been found useful, particularly for flaking and crumbling hooves, and it has also been used to treat sandcracks and quarter cracks. This treatment seems to improve the integrity of the hoof wall, as do methyl sulphonyl methane supplements. MSM can either be fed alone or in combined supplements which provide high doses of all the nutrients specifically involved in hoof wall production. This type of supplement may be used for a limited period in conjunction with an ordinary broad-spectrum vitamin-mineral supplement until the problem has been corrected. Once the hooves have improved, provided the rest of the diet is adequate, hoof condition will usually be maintained without continued therapeutic doses.

It is worth noting that the Donkey Sanctuary in Devon has found that feeding straw to donkeys gave better results than the use of biotin in improving hoof condition. This was probably the result of the effects of straw on gut fermentation. A number of yeasts use large amounts of biotin and it is possible that some horses with hoof problems have been receiving prolonged courses of antibiotic or steroid therapy which has so altered their gut microbial population that the yeasts have come to predominate. While these animals may be receiving sufficient biotin for a normal horse, the yeasts may 'mop-up' the biotin before it passes through the gut wall to be utilised by the horse. This is just one possible explanation for the high biotin requirements of some horses. In the long term, it is a good idea to ensure that the horse is receiving at least 1 mg per day of biotin.

Many ponies have grass rings or ridges resulting from the better nutrition during spring and autumn grass growth, which again demonstrates the effect of good nutrition, particularly as the grass flush will be rich in protein, vitamin A and probably sulphur.

Massage of the coronets can increase the rate of hoof growth, but not necessarily the quality of the growth formed, by stimulating the circulation in the area, and this is probably the main benefit of applying various stimulating creams and potions. While the application of hoof oils may be useful on the hoof walls if they have been rasped, it should be avoided on the base of the wall and the soles to facilitate moisture absorption.

When presented with a horse with poor-quality hooves, apart from checking the overall diet, the possibility of selenium toxicity should not be discounted, particularly in areas where soil selenium levels are high, or where a number of supplements have been used without checking their compatibility. Selenium toxicity can lead to sloughing-off the entire hoof, along with loss of hair, particularly from the mane and tail and, in extreme cases, is fatal.

## Peritonitis (see Colic)

## Photosensitisation

The definition of photosensitisation is 'induced sensitisation to ultra-violet radiation of those areas of the skin unprotected by melanin' (melanin is a form of pigmentation). It is a surprisingly common but often misdiagnosed problem. It is my impression that it is on the increase, although it may simply be that people are becoming more aware of it.

Typically, the most commonly affected horses are chestnuts with white hair on their legs and faces overlying pink (i.e. unpigmented) skin. Greys and skewbald/piebald and Appaloosa horses may also be affected where the underlying skin is pink, and albinos are likely to be particularly susceptible.

It is my impression that mares are more frequently affected than geldings or stallions, although I have never come across any figures which would specifically bear this out. If this is the case, it may well be that the hormone melatonin may be involved.

There are a number of trigger factors for photosensitivity but I think of this as a 'three-cornered' disease. Two of the corners are constant, i.e. the action of sunlight and the presence of pink (unpigmented) skin. The third corner is the trigger factor or sensitiser, which can be one of several things.

Probably the most common trigger factor that I have encountered is the use of thiabendazole anthelmintics (wormers), particularly when fed in conjunction with 'trifoliate' herbage or hay. The trifoliates are the legumes, particularly clovers, and it is possible that once the animal has become very hypersensitive, other legumes, such as vetches and trefoils, may be implicated. I have not specifically identified the problem in relation to alfalfa (lucerne) which is also a legume but if you are having difficulty in eliminating this problem with a susceptible horse, it is certainly worth checking whether alfalfa is affecting it.

The other most likely trigger factor in pastures is a herb called St John's wort (*Hypericum* spp.) which, like the clovers, contains a naturally occurring substance which can trigger photosensitivity.

Having said this, I have a feeling that moulds and fungi which occur on certain legumes are more likely to be responsible agents than the legumes themselves. Infestation of the feed by certain types of greenfly has also been suggested as a trigger for photosensitivity but, again, I would suspect that this probably works by allowing various moulds to become established via the damage done by the insects and that these moulds contain or produce the photosensitising agents.

As far as I can tell, for an initial attack to occur you need to have the three-cornered scenario but once the horse has had an attack, any one of these things can trigger another and it is quite usual for future attacks to be worse.

What happens to a horse affected by photosensitivity? Basically, only the white areas of the coat are affected – especially the blaze and lower legs – although occasionally there may be secondary infections. The appearance is of blue or red, often swollen, crusty, weeping lesions, swelling and later death (necrosis) of the skin and underlying tissue which peels to expose raw areas. 'Blue-nose' is a common name for the condition in some parts of the world.

The most important diagnostic factor is that this can only occur on pink skin: then you have to check that the other corners of the 'triangle' are, or have been, present preceding or during the attack.

In the initial stages, it is obviously important to relieve distress. If this means using anti-inflammatory creams or drugs and pain killers, then you may have to do this while you sort the problem out. However, this is absolutely not a long-term solution.

I suggest that you:

**1** Bring your horse in to get it out of the sun.

2 Check whether thiabendazole was present in the worming preparations you have used in the last six months and do not use them again once the horse is sensitised (warn new owners if you sell the horse).
3 If you have used a thiabendazole product, check your feed and pasture for alfalfa (lucerne), sainfoin, clover, vetches or trefoil.
4 Eliminate St John's wort from your pasture, hedgerows, ditches and hay.
5 Feed garlic to help to keep flies away from affected tissue.
6 Give methyl sulphonyl methane (MSM) or a supplement which contains this, such as Hoof and Hide, to help to reduce inflammation and treat the skin and underlying tissues.

While riding in the daytime, you could take steps to cover white areas. Once they have healed, the legs can be protected with boots and bandages. You could use a sun screen on highly susceptible animals but this can be expensive. If you do use one, ensure that it is hypo-allergenic and fragrance/lanolin-free. I really do not think that black leading, which is suggested by some vets, would be an awfully good idea, particularly as the tissue of the skin will already be compromised.

While painkillers, steroid injections and creams will have eliminated your horse's initial distress, you might find it helpful to feed extra zinc as a constituent of a good quality supplement, plus increasing the oil content of the diet. You can also apply homoeopathic hypericum cream, which is derived from St John's wort (homoeopathy treats 'like with like', using tiny doses of the 'causative agent' to stimulate the body to heal). You might find it very helpful to contact a homoeopathic vet to discuss the possibility of giving the horse oral homoeopathic treatment, including hypericum tablets, powders or drops of an appropriate strength and possibly sol, ultraviolet and histamine in potentised form, as well as constitutional treatment, as all work very well.

You can obtain hypericum ointment or hyperical tincture from larger chemists, although they will probably have to order it. Do check that they give you a *lanolin-free* formulation. Alternatively, you can obtain it direct from a homoeopathic pharmacist.

## Poisoning

Poisons may be defined as substances which harm the body externally or internally and which disrupt the normal metabolic processes in the body. They may cause only temporary, but also permanent, damage, particularly to the liver, or even death.

When poison is suspected, it is vital that the vet is called as soon as possible. Of course, the horse must be removed from the vicinity of any obvious poisons. An attempt made to establish the cause prior to the vet's arrival (check for lead paint, poisonous plants, access to drugs, e.g. in feed for other livestock, mouldy feed or bedding, slug pellets, dressed farm seed, etc. so that he or she may have some idea of what they are dealing with). If you can identify the poison there are sometimes specific antidotes. In particular, it is sometimes possible to use homoeopathic antidotes to neutralise the after-effects of a wide range of substances.

A comprehensive list of the poisonous plants which may be encountered may be found in my book *Pasture Management for Horses and Ponies*, published by Blackwell Scientific Publications.

The commonest ones in most areas are ragwort (*Senecio* spp.), horse tail (*Equisetum*), bracken (*Pteridium aquilinum*) and many marsh plants. Many trees are poisonous and care should be taken to avoid overhanging boughs which can either be reached by grazing horses, or may be blown down in high winds when they are likely to wilt and become more palatable.

Horses and ponies tend to avoid most growing poisonous plants but may consume them:

- when wilted (e.g. cut in hay, cut down in pasture by galloping hooves, fallen over-hanging branches)
- in desperation when other fodder is sparse
- some individuals can graze in between ragwort seedlings more efficiently than others who swallow everything in their path like lawn mowers!
- certain individuals exhibit a depraved appetite for certain poisonous plants. Nutrient deficiency should be suspected as a primary cause and also as zinc deficiency, for example, can reduce or eliminate the sense of taste so that the bitterness which many poisonous plants exhibit may not be perceived.

Substances may be harmless in some circumstances but highly toxic in others. The majority of plant poisons are some form of toxic alkaloid, glycoside or other phytotoxin. (Many of these are, in fact, sources of useful drugs when used appropriately.)

The other common form of poisoning is due to ingestion of inorganic materials including heavy metals such as lead, arsenic or cadmium, e.g. when human sewage has been used as fertiliser. Inadvertent ingestion of agrochemicals is also likely to cause poisoning. Ask neighbouring farmers to warn you when they are spraying their fields and beware of spray as it will drift. Agricultural and industrial materials may also leach into water supplies and ditches, sometimes from miles away.

Some fertilisers may also cause poisoning – e.g. nitrate poisoning – the effects of which may be immediate but *may* also manifest themselves as unthriftiness or possibly abortions. *Do not* fertilise horse paddocks heavily as if they were for dairy cows. When using agrochemicals or fertilisers, ensure that the horses are kept off the paddock after application for at least the minimum period specified by the manufacturer, taking into account whether there has been a drought which may prevent rain from washing these materials off the herbage and down into the soil. A minimum of three to six weeks may be needed, preferably including periods of fairly heavy rain to break down residues.

The exception, from a safety point of view, is Cornish calcified seaweed which is, in fact, also usable as a feed calcium source. Horses can safely be turned straight back out on to land which has been treated with this, although, ideally, it is best to wait until it has rained so that breakdown commences.

Apart from substances which burn (strong acids and alkalis), most poisons must be ingested to be toxic and are absorbed into the body by being eaten, drunk, inhaled, absorbed through the skin or by injection.

The dramatic symptoms seen are usually due to the body's attempts to detoxify such materials. The tissues are usually damaged or at least inflamed. Some reactions are complicated by the effects of sunlight (see photosensitivity). Symptoms range through diarrhoea, convulsions, twitching, coma, muscular uncoordination, aberrant behaviour such as pressing the head against walls or trees, staggering, dilation of pupils, distressed breathing, sensitisation to sound and movement and blood in the urine. *Always* call the vet.

The most appropriate feeding management is probably along similar lines to that suggested for elderly horses or those recovering from starvation and, once again, the use of probiotics is probably a good idea. Detailed feed programmes are beyond the scope of this book.

## Poor Doers

As they get older, some horses tend to lose condition and this may be due to poor appetite which may, in turn, be due to mineral and B vitamin deficiencies, pain, digestive upsets and so forth, or to malabsorption problems caused by dysbiosis. It could even be due to irritation by flies which prevents grazing.

You should also check for problems with the teeth and, of course, parasites. Feeding garlic can help stiff joints, COPD and keep off flies which can drive an old horse to distraction.

Assuming that you have dealt with these, you then need to try to stimulate the appetite and maximise nutrient uptake and utilisation.

- Make sure feeds are fresh and tasty.
- Try a good quality vitamin/mineral supplement which contains good levels of zinc, amino acids, lysine, methionine and B vitamins, including choline and inositol.
- Use very easy-to-digest feeds, such as Bailey's meal, sugar beet and Dengie dried alfalfa to form the basis of your feeds.
- Alternatively, if you are using compounds, you *may* find a stud mix appropriate, at least until the horse's condition is restored, or perhaps to maintain condition through the winter.

This type of horse will almost always benefit from a course of probiotics and there are also several blends of herbs available, which can prove helpful as appetite stimulants, or more specific herbal mixtures to alleviate arthritis, navicular, laminitis and even sarcoids.

Several companies produce both single herbs and blends which can prove extremely useful and I have found it very effective to use customised blends attuned to the specific problems of individual horses.

## Rickets – Osteomalacia

The vitamin D, calcium and phosphorus status and balance of the broodmare and foal should be maintained to prevent these unnecessary disorders.

## Skin and Hoof Care

Whether your horse tends to be overfat, overthin or just right, as it ages you need to ensure that it is receiving adequate nutrition to maintain skin and coat condition.

There is no reason why the skin should become thin and lose its elasticity, or the winter coat become long and wispy. These are signs of micro-nutrient deficiency or malabsorption and you must try to counteract them by introducing a supplement or upgrading the supplement you use or the compound you feed and perhaps looking at herbal conditioners. Simply putting feed blocks in the field or giving a Salvana Briquette (a vitamin-enriched and mineralised 'horse biscuit') may be all that is needed. However, you do need to do *something*. Do not give up if the first technique or brand you try does not prove suitable for your horse.

An older horse may be less inclined to move about in the field and will be more prone to rain-scald (sores on the back caused by the same bugs that cause mud fever on the legs and belly) if it stands under dripping trees for hours. A rain sheet may help in these circumstances. If the horse's skin is compromised, you should also ensure that its rugs and tack do not chafe. As the horse 'sags' and changes shape, you may need to have the saddle restuffed, twice a year if necessary. Avoid synthetic numnahs and stick to sheepskin or cotton, washed in non-biological powder, preferably of the less-irritant 'ecological' type.

Hoof and coat condition tend to go together and I would almost always give a course of probiotics for five to ten days when embarking on a course of nutrient therapy for poor hooves, especially where biotin seems to be a key factor which is quite often the case where hoof problems follow some time after antibiotic or steroid treatment.

Check the fibre level in the diet and sources of sulphur – it is the sulphur bonds breaking that causes the distinctive smell when hot shoeing. Sulphur sources include amino acid methionine and/or the organic sulphur source MSM (methyl sulphonyl methane) which is also a useful anti-inflammatory for lung and arthritic problems and which may be more easily absorbed by some horses. Also check sources of the other major essential amino acid, lysine, and vitamins A and D, biotin and calcium, as well as trace elements including zinc and minute amounts of selenium, all of which are involved in maintaining the integrity of the hoof wall.

Regular visits from the farrier should not be neglected, even for retired horses. It is cruel and unforgivable to leave an old retainer with painful, cracked and overgrown hooves and it will undoubtedly accelerate or increase the pain associated with degenerative joint diseases. Many horses will be quite happy with at least their hind shoes removed and a regular trim, even if they are doing gentle road work.

One of the techniques I have found specially useful in the treatment of chronic conditions is homoeopathy – the use of minute doses of specific remedies to stimulate the horse's own healing response.

In the case of acute illness, you should always consult your vet. There are an increasing number of homoeopathically trained vets in the UK who specialise in equines as this drug-free approach is especially suited to competition horses. For chronic problems which are especially common in older horses, homoeopathy can give an effective, reasonably priced treatment regime, usually based on drops in the drinking water, without the damaging side-effects associated with most long-term drug use.

The British Association of Homoeopathic Veterinary Surgeons should be able to give you the name of a vet in your region. They can be contacted at Chinham House, Stanford-in-the-Vale, Faringdon, Oxon SN7 8NQ. You may also find it useful to talk to Macmillan Nutrition who, while specialising in dairy cows, produce a number of remedies (nosodes) that are appropriate for horses with laminitis, ringworm and other chronic conditions.

Whether your elderly equine is to have a healthy and comfortable retirement, perhaps as a companion, or compete into its forties, how you feed and manage it can have a significant bearing on its health, ability to sustain exercise and longevity.

## Sweet Itch (Also Called Sweat Itch, Summer Itch in Europe/Queensland Itch in Australia)

This is not caused by inappropriate feeding but it is mentioned here because so many horse owners think it is. Sweet itch is an allergic reaction, possibly complicated by hypersensitivity in summer, to the bites of midges of the *Culicoides* species; in the UK *C. pulicaris*. However, it *is* possible that susceptible ponies and horses have a predisposition because of malabsorption of zinc which almost always plays an important role in skin conditions. It is important that adequate zinc levels are maintained and it is possible that megadosing with zinc can be beneficial in some instances. If zinc mal-absorption is suspected, in severe cases the vet may give zinc intravenously. Alternatively, a highly absorbable form of zinc may be made up into a paste and given orally. Zinc supplements can also be given in feed, but it is best absorbed on an empty stomach which is why paste can be useful.

It is also useful to feed garlic, as this tends to repel insects, including the biting midges.

Sweet itch is a type of dermatitis, usually confined to the mane and tail but which may spread along the back. The skin becomes thick and scaly and may well have small pustules on the surface. The condition is intensely sore and irritating and the hairs of the mane and tail break off, or are rubbed off at the skin surface, giving a rat-tailed appearance. Rubbing may lead to the development of large sores.

Various soothing lotions and ointments have been produced, to be combined with cortisone (which can cause further thinning of the skin if overused) and antihistamine injections. A vaccine is being developed. Once again, I have found that homoeopathic treatment tends to be more effective, particularly in the long term, than repeated steroid use.

Judicious stabling of animals when the midges are most active (i.e. May and September in the UK) at least from around four p.m. until dark and the use of non-organophosphate fly-repellent strips in the stable will help to reduce the problem. Liquid paraffin may also be applied to the coat to make it harder for the midges to crawl to the skin to bite – it is unsightly but then so are sweet-itch sores. Fly repellents tend not to be very long-lasting although the new ones which can be attached to the head collar, hock or tail may well be a more effective deterrent. Diluted tea tree oil (an essential oil) may also prove useful.

The ability to develop this allergy is inherited so it is irresponsible to breed from affected animals.

## Teeth

The health of the teeth is of fundamental importance to the health of the horse and has been discussed at some length on page 3.

## Urine, Thick and Cloudy

This should always be checked by the vet as a matter of urgency.

Apart from various infectious diseases, it can be caused by eating mouldy hay/bedding, eating damp bedding (shortage of fibres/minerals in the diet), excess protein in the diet, the sudden introduction of high-protein feed (for example, a rapid change from grass hay to alfalfa hay), or very high calcium levels in the feed (for example, grass to alfalfa hay again). It is sometimes ascribed to low phosphorus levels but this may be a confusion between the relevance of high calcium to low phosphorus.

Adjust the feeding and *never* give mouldy feedstuffs. Some toxins and moulds can actually prove fatal or lead to spontaneous abortion or miscarriages ('slipping a foal') in broodmares and infertility in mares and stallions.

## Urticaria – Nettle Rash or Blane

This is an allergic condition, resulting in raised lumps, blotches or weals on the skin. It is often attributed to excess protein but, again, is probably only a question of allergy to a specific protein type. It may also be caused by insect stings and takes its name from its similarity to nettle stings. It has been suggested by herbalists that feeding *wilted* nettles or nettle tea to the affected horse may cure it. Certainly, homoeopathic treatment with urticaria (from nettles) and other remedies can be very successful.

## Vitamin/Mineral Deficiencies – Imbalances and Excesses

Vitamin, mineral and other nutrient imbalances and excesses are a complex subject involving many interactions, many of which have not yet been fully evaluated. There is always a danger in isolating nutrients, especially when they are linked to specific disorders. If they are utilised in isolation, almost like drugs, this approach, if not carefully monitored, can often result in other deficiency problems.

It is always important to check the individual horse's specific requirements, particularly in relation to why it has become deficient in a specific nutrient. For this reason, I believe it is beyond the scope of this book to give detailed recommendations for correcting nutritional imbalances because of the likelihood of misuse if this information is put in overly simplistic terms.

However, many of the syndromes mentioned in this chapter, and elsewhere in the book, involve some degree of trace nutrient imbalances, deficiencies or excesses and these are covered more specifically in the appropriate sections.

## Wood Chewing and Other Vices Related to Feeding

Wood chewing, crib-biting, wind-sucking, weaving and tree-barking may all be feed-related in two ways:

1 **Boredom** – For the bored horse, repetitive actions such as weaving may well induce a state of euphoria due to the release of, and subsequent addiction to, natural endorphins (similar to the drug morphine). This state is similar to that exhibited by serious (human) joggers, runners and people addicted to alcohol and various foods. (The term 'chocaholic' is no joke but an indication of a masked allergy due probably to endorphin addiction!) Similar effects have been noted in pigs. When the horse stops weaving, it comes off its 'high' because it no longer produces these endorphins. It then feels depressed and agitated, exhibits signs of stress and starts weaving or whatever other aberrant behaviour it has adopted, again.

The use of hanging bricks and other deterrents only masks the problem and probably increases the stress. Likewise, the use of various 'gunges' to prevent crib-biting, cribbing straps or even surgery to prevent cribbing or wind-sucking, both of which damage the horse's teeth and upset the digestion with swallowed air, is treating the symptoms and not the problem. The primary thing is to find the cause (boredom/stress), remove it and then try to stop the habit. Unfortunately, once the aberrant behaviour has become established, there is now a habit that is extremely hard to break. Naloxone injections to block the effects of the endorphins have been tried successfully in a few cases and homoeopathic alternatives or even acupuncture may offer a solution in some instances.

Try hanging a (punctured) football/swede/mangold/stable toy up in the stable to keep the horse amused. If you are feeding complete diet cubes and the horse suffers from COPD, switch to ordinary cubes and dried grass/alfalfa cubes and molassed chaff and use moist, packed forage or hydroponic cereals fed from a small-mesh net, so that they take longer to eat. The use of extruded concentrates may also increase the time taken in eating.

If the horse is bored, put it in a stable where it can see plenty going on outside and do not shut or bar it in. Make sure everyone says 'Hi' to it at every opportunity. If you have only one horse and work all day, stable it where it can watch the road, get a goat, cat or some chickens or, better still, turn it out, preferably with a companion.

If the horse is highly strung and subject to stress, ensure that it is not being bullied/intimidated by neighbouring horses or even stable staff. Ensure that stable staff are tactful when handling/ feeding it – no crashing about or, conversely, creeping up on it too quietly. Again, if possible, turn it out on its own or with a donkey if it is low in the pecking order. Some say these vices are inherited. It may be that being highly strung is inherited and that a foal from a highly strung mare can pick up bad habits from its dam.

2 **Nutritional** – The other reason for such vices may well be nutritional imbalances/deficiencies. Check salt, mineral, vitamin and fibre levels in the diet. If the horse licks the stall, it may well be a salt or mineral problem. Again, sometimes, a course of probiotics may help, or even vitamin $B_1$ or vitamin E. Allergies and feed intolerances should also be checked.

Make sure animals are not chewing anything toxic (e.g. black walnut bark, creosote, etc.) and ensure that they are not infested with worms or bots. (NB: toxins require extra antioxidant nutrients to help to detoxify them and can create a vicious circle of toxic stress to nutritional imbalance to increased susceptibility to toxins etc.)

## Yeast Overgrowth in the Digestive Tract

This is a very poorly recognised problem in the horse but most veterinary laboratories will admit that they culture abnormal quantities of yeast in samples taken from horses with a number of illnesses and particularly after prolonged antibiotic therapy. Many of these yeasts occur naturally as part of the gut microbial population but when, for any reason, other 'competing' micro-organisms are suppressed due to illness or drug treatments, the proliferation of yeasts may go ahead unchecked.

In bad cases, the yeast can change into a mycelial (fungal) form which can grow *through* the gut wall and is then thought to proliferate through the body. It may also lead to a leaky gut which allows through larger molecules of only partially broken-down feed which would normally be 'filtered' by the gut wall and prevented from entering the body until they had been further broken down in the digestive tract. If they do pass through the wall, the body then recognises these as foreign materials and feed intolerances or allergies may result.

Manifestations so far identified in the horse include various feed intolerances (allergies), especially to yeast and sugar-containing feeds such as molasses, and various painful syndromes (e.g. flinching for no apparent reason due to infestation of the fascia), skin lesions and nervousness or dullness due to the production of aldehydes. These occur especially in horses exposed to high levels of chemicals from nearby industrial areas or from wooden-stable treatments. There may also be mucous membrane infestation, including the urinogenital tract, possible breeding problems, virus-like symptoms which cannot be diagnosed and an increased susceptibility to all kinds of infections due to the overstressed immune system trying to cope with the infestation.

Biotin deficiency may well be due to yeast overgrowth as the yeasts themselves use high levels of biotin and other nutrients and may effectively be 'stealing' them from the horse before it ever gets them! This may well explain why some horses require massive doses of biotin when their diets are not overtly deficient.

Treatment is only just being developed and many veterinarians are as yet unaware of the problem or its significance. Much further scientific investigation is required. Treatment may include the use of probiotics and massive doses of various vitamins and minerals including zinc (from non-yeast sources), feeding high levels of garlic and aloe vera juice, although this is rather expensive in the UK, and ensuring that adequate levels of fibre are available. It is prudent to reduce the feeding of any excess sugars, which usually means that the diet has to be home-mixed to eliminate molasses and other syrups. Sugar beet pulp and foodstuffs from yeast sources, such as brewer's yeast, should also be avoided, certainly until the problem is under control.

The avoidance of non-essential antibiotic and steroid (including cortisone) treatment, at least for a few months until the infestation is under control, is also advisable and fungicides may be fed, injected or applied directly (topically) to the skin.

# Index